AF506003

Rethinking Peace and Conflict Studies

Series Editor: **Oliver P. Richmond**, Professor, School of International Relations, University of St. Andrews

Editorial Board: **Roland Bleiker**, University of Queensland, Australia; **Henry F. Carey**, Georgia State University, USA; **Costas Constantinou**, University of Keele, UK; **AJR Groom**, University of Kent, UK; **Vivienne Jabri**, King's College London, UK; **Edward Newman**, University of Birmingham, UK; **Sorpong Peou**, Sophia University, Japan; **Caroline Kennedy-Pipe**, University of Sheffield, UK; **Professor Michael Pugh**, University of Bradford, UK; **Chandra Sriram**, University of East London, UK; **Ian Taylor**, University of St. Andrews, UK; **Alison Watson**, University of St. Andrews, UK; **R.B.J. Walker**, University of Victoria, Canada; **Andrew Williams**, Univeristy of St. Andrews, UK.

Titles include:

Jason Franks
RETHINKING THE ROOTS OF TERRORISM

Vivienne Jabri
WAR AND THE TRANSFORMATION OF GLOBAL POLITICS

James Ker-Lindsay
EU ACCESSION AND UN PEACEKEEPING IN CYPRUS

Roger MacGinty
NO WAR, NO PEACE
The Rejuvenation of Stalled Peace Processes and Peace Accords

Carol McQueen
HUMANITARIAN INTERVENTION AND SAFETY ZONES
Iraq, Bosnia and Rwanda

Sorpong Peou
INTERNATIONAL DEMOCRACY ASSISTANCE FOR PEACEBUILDING
The Cambodian Experience

Sergei Prozorov
UNDERSTANDING CONFLICT BETWEEN RUSSIA AND THE EU
The Limits of Integration

Oliver P. Richmond
THE TRANSFORMATION OF PEACE

Bahar Rumelili
CONSTRUCTING REGIONAL COMMUNITY AND ORDER IN
EUROPE AND SOUTHEAST ASIA

Rethinking Peace and Conflict Studies
Series Standing Order ISBN 1–4039–9575–3 (hardback) & 1–4039–9576–1 (paperback)

You can receive future titles in this series as they are published by placing a standing order. Please contact your bookseller or, in case of difficulty, write to us at the address below with your name and address, the title of the series and one of the ISBNs quoted above.

Customer Services Department, Macmillan Distribution Ltd, Houndmills, Basingstoke, Hampshire RG21 6XS, England

Constructing Regional Community and Order in Europe and Southeast Asia

Bahar Rumelili
Department of International Relations
Koc University, Turkey

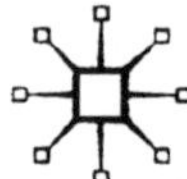

First published in 2007 by
PALGRAVE MACMILLAN
Houndmills, Basingstoke, Hampshire RG21 6XS and
175 Fifth Avenue, New York, N.Y. 10010
Companies and representatives throughout the world.

PALGRAVE MACMILLAN is the global academic imprint of the Palgrave Macmillan division of St. Martin's Press, LLC and of Palgrave Macmillan Ltd. Macmillan® is a registered trademark in the United States, United Kingdom and other countries. Palgrave is a registered trademark in the European Union and other countries.

ISBN-13: 978–0–230–00702–4 hardback
ISBN-10: 0–230–00702–3 hardback

This book is printed on paper suitable for recycling and made from fully managed and sustained forest sources. Logging, pulping and manufacturing processes are expected to conform to the environmental regulations of the country of origin.

A catalogue record for this book is available from the British Library.

A catalog record for this book is available from the Library of Congress.

10   9   8   7   6   5   4   3   2   1
16 15 14 13 12 11 10 09 08 07

Printed and bound in Great Britain by
Antony Rowe Ltd, Chippenham and Eastbourne

Contents

Foreword

Iver B. Neumann

After 15 years of scholarship on the importance of identity to international relations, here is the book on the place of identity politics in relations between regional organizations and their neighbors. Bahar Rumelili makes three contributions. First, she sums up and juxtaposes thin constructivist and post-structural identity scholarship within the discipline of International Relations. Secondly, she delivers a good that European Studies has aspired to deliver without success, namely a typologizing evaluation of EU relations with neighboring states. Thirdly, by delivering a contrasting case study of ASEAN's relations with its neighbors, she corroborates her findings in typical overall social science style.

In a seminal 1991 contribution, William Connolly argued that identity requires difference in order to be, and that, if threatened, identity may respond by turning that difference into otherness. The identity debate in IR has focussed on whether and under what conditions this hypothesis holds water. David Campbell argued in a book-length study about the US that its history was one of constant othering, which raised the question of whether difference stood much of a chance in a post-Cold War world. Campbell wrote this as an indictment of the US. He was soon joined by Samuel Huntington, however, who happily essentialized and embraced the othering processes in question. My own response was to try and sustain Connolly's hypothesis by delivering a series of empirical studies. Rumelili's response to Campbell and Huntington is also to uphold Connolly's hypothesis.

Alexander Wendt then joined the fray by arguing that difference was not analytically necessary for identity to exist; identity could be self-organizing. Rumelili retorts that "Wendt conflates two distinct processes here. The constitution of identity in relation to difference does not mean that the constitution of identity necessarily involves the agency and discourse of outsiders, but that it presupposes the existence of alternative identities. And no process can be self-organizing if it entails boundary-drawing because boundaries are by definition drawn between a self and an other – even though the other may not be actively participating in the boundary-drawing process" (p. 35 ms).

By the late 1990s, the key empirical site of this debate had become the EU. Rumelili rightly points out that, whereas thin constructivists who wanted to celebrate norms cascades and the spread of presumably universal liberal norms tended to study how the European Union embraced new Central and East European members, poststructuralists tended to focus on EU relations with states that were less integration-willing and to whom the social distance was larger, such as Russia and Turkey. Since each party focused on non-critical cases, this knowledge production about the EU thus became suboptimal as a source of theoretical insight into collective identity formation.

As a generalization, this certainly holds true, but it does not embrace one key debate which is also reviewed by Rumelili. In 1993, John Gerard Ruggie had argued that the EU was the first postmodern polity. Five years later, Ole Waever drew on this argument to make a new intervention into the debate on identity. Whereas it is true that identity needs difference and that difference may easily be turned into otherness, Waever argued, it does not follow that otherness needs to be located in one of the EU's neighbors. To Waever, on the contrary, the EU indeed has a key Other, but that Other is a former incarnation of the European self – a more conflict-prone one. Rumelili is supportive of this insight, but she sees it as supplementary rather than contradictory to extant insights. As she aptly puts it, "We have no reason to consider temporal and spatial differentiation as mutually exclusive; to the contrary, they are often mutually constitutive and sustaining. The widespread existence of an identity discourse that is based on differentiation from the past does not by itself make the EU a postmodern form of identity unless it can be demonstrated that external differentiation is (mostly) absent" (p. 75 ms).

Rumelili goes on to demonstrate that this is far from the case. True, the EU has an impressive series of interactions with neighbors who aspire to membership, but against this, Rumelili points to the case of Morocco, a state whose attempts to join the Union have been summarily dismissed. Furthermore, the case of Turkey before Turkey was granted candidacy status in 1999 demonstrates that there rages a fairly hefty intra-EU debate on what the nature of European identity should be. Rumelili analyzes these sequences in some detail, and usefully tops them up with three mini-studies of how they have served as preconditions of action for the handling of conflict between three pairs of EU/non-EU states. The conclusion she reaches is that EU identity is not threatened by relations either with integration-willing states such as the Central and East European ones, or with states that are represented by the EU as being inherently different, such as Morocco. By inherently different Rumelili the poststructuralist does not mean essentially different, but rather that the EU represents the difference in question as innate in the sense that it deems it so socially embedded that it cannot be changed other than in the very long haul. This conclusion is not interesting first and foremost because it tells us something new about the structure of identity, for Rumelili's "inherently different" may also simply be read as "other." The interest lies in what she has to say about the process of conflict, for as long as a neighboring state accepts the story told about it as other, and acts accordingly, it will not be represented by the EU as a threat to its identity. That, Rumelili demonstrates by turning to the case of EU/Turkey relations, only happens when the neighboring state deploys alternative and competing narratives of the identities in question. Specifically, it was Turkey's forging of counternarratives about the European self as an identity possibly exclusive of a Muslim state such as Turkey that first appeared as a potential threat to the European narrative of self, and then acted as catalyst of change to that narrative. In order to salvage an identity that emerged as inclusive of Turkey, the EU had to open the way for Turkish EU membership.

The wider implication of this is that a crucial site of study for relations between polities is the sequences of collective identity formation where well established narratives of self are challenged by narratives (internal or indeed, as here, external) which are new in drawing on new elements, or in blending extant elements in new ways. The key is not the degree to which external narratives are disparaging. A Moroccan narrative of European identity as old-style imperialist or a Russian narrative of European identity as hypocritically human rights-oriented has little potential to threaten European stories of self due to their character of being tiredly well-rehearsed. By contrast, when Turkey was convincingly able to tell a story of offering something new, the result was, first, that this was acted upon as a potential threat to European identity, and second, that this identity changed. Phrased in terms of Connolly's hypothesis, Turkey played up its difference. There followed an internal EU debate on whether this should be construed as a threat to European identity, in which case the appropriate response would have been to other Turkey, or whether Turkish difference could be accommodated by altering European identity. Whereas this debate is clearly ongoing (making the EU a late-modern rather than a postmodern entity in Rumelili's book), the dominant thrust since 1999 has been in the direction of making EU identity more inclusive of Turkey.

Rumelili demonstrates that this stylization of identity change has purchase beyond the EU by discussing ASEAN's responses to Australia's campaign to become an Asian country in the 1980s and 1990s. As did Turkey vis-à-vis the EU, Australia mixed elements of ASEAN's self-presentation with elements of its own narrative of self in order to tell a new narrative about ASEAN that would make that organization more inclusive of Australia. ASEAN's response to this playing up of difference was to fasten on its extant narrative of self and to other Australia as Western.

Rumelili's book is probably the best book on the place of neighboring states in European identity formation so far. However, identities do not stand still for their picture, which means that researching this phenomenon is an ongoing concern. Turkish–EU relations are work in progress. Rumelili underlines how important it is whether EU representations draw on what she calls "inherent" traits such as religion relative to "acquired" traits such as the adoption of human rights. Another set of sequences that may prove highly illuminating in this regard are relations between the EU on the one hand, and states like Albania, Bosnia, Macedonia and Serbia on the other. Here we have a clutch of cases where practiced religion and regard for human rights are varied in ways that should make them tasty food for further research. In this book, Rumelili is already working successfully with more cases than most other identity scholars. There is no reason why she should stop adding strings to her lyre.

Acknowledgments

In its earliest form, this book was a PhD thesis submitted to the University of Minnesota in August 2002. I want to express my special thanks to my advisor, Raymond Duvall, who guided me through the dissertation process with the right balance of support and challenge; to Richard Price (now at University of British Columbia), who has been involved in the project right from the beginning with his invaluable insights and encouragement; to Kathryn Sikkink for her constructive criticism and close personal attention, and to Helga Leitner for her enthusiasm and critical reading. My work has been greatly influenced by the writings of Iver B. Neumann, and I thank him for the inspiration and for his continuing generous support. David Blaney has also generously commented on many drafts and sharpened my thinking. My research and writing were facilitated by fieldwork fellowships and writing grants from the MacArthur Interdisciplinary Program on Global Change, Sustainability and Justice, and the University of Minnesota Graduate School.

I conducted further research on Europe and Greek–Turkish conflicts as a postdoctoral fellow for the European Union and Border Conflicts Project funded by the EU's Fifth Framework Program. I am grateful to all my colleagues in the project, especially to Thomas Diez, Stephan Stetter, Michelle Pace, and Kemal Kirisci for their inspiring comments and criticisms. My research for this project, which forms the basis of Chapter 5 in this book, is published in an expanded form in the *Journal of Common Market Studies* (March 2007).

Earlier versions of various chapters of this book have been presented at numerous conferences and published as journal articles. Chapter 3 draws on an article on identity and difference and the EU published in the *Review of International Studies* (January 2004). The case study on Greek–Turkish relations presented in Chapter 5 is partly based on an article published in the *European Journal of International Relations* (June 2003).

I am also thankful to Oliver Richmond, who read and commented graciously on various versions of the book manuscript.

Last but not the least, I would like to thank my mother and my husband for their unwavering support and sacrifice. I dedicate this book to my one-year-old daughter, Beste, in apology for the times I had to spend away from her.

List of Abbreviations

AFTA	ASEAN Free Trade Area
AKP	Justice and Development Party (Turkey)
APEC	Asia Pacific Economic Cooperation
ASEAN	Association of Southeast Asian Nations
ASEM	Asia Europe Meeting
CEES	Central and East European states
DIKKI	Democratic and Social Movement Party (Greece)
EAEC	East Asian Economic Caucus
EAS	East Asia Summit
EDN	Independents for Europe of the Nations
EEC	European Economic Community
ELDR	European Liberal, Democratic and Reformist Group
EMP	Euro–Mediterranean Partnership
ENP	European Neighborhood Policy
EP	European Parliament
EU	European Union
GUE/NGL	European United Left/Nordic Green Left
ICJ	International Court of Justice
INTERFET	International Force East Timor
IR	International Relations
MEP	Member of European Parliament
MP	Member of Parliament
NAFTA	North American Free Trade Agreement
OSCE	Organization for Security and Cooperation in Europe
PASOK	Pan-Hellenic Socialist Movement Party (Greece)
PCA	Partnership and Cooperation Agreement
PPE	European People's Party
PSE	Party of European Socialists
SEANWFZ	Southeast Asian Nuclear Weapon-Free Zone
SIT	Social Identity Theory
SLORC	State Law and Order Restoration Council (Myanmar)
TAC	Treaty of Amity and Cooperation
TGNA	Turkish Grand National Assembly

PMC	Post-Ministerial Conference
UN	United Nations
UNAMET	United Nations Mission in East Timor
V	Greens
Vert/Ale	Greens/European Free Alliance

1
Introduction

I. Regional organizations and community-building

In contemporary international relations, many regional organizations are "community-building"; they directly engage in, and serve as the reference points for, various practices that construct, promote, and sustain a sense of collective identity among their member states. For example, the institutions of the European Union frequently make references to the "European" identity that its member states share, and the ongoing debates on the institutions, scope, and policies of the European Union continuously re-define and negotiate the terms of that identity, but at the same time reinstate the collectivity. Likewise, the Association of Southeast Asian Nations claims that it unites "One Southeast Asia" and represents a unique "ASEAN way" to cooperation; the Gulf Cooperation Council claims to embody a distinct "Gulf identity"; and the Asia Pacific Economic Cooperation promotes the idea of a "Pacific region." This book argues that rather than being epiphenomenal rhetoric, these practices constitute crucial elements in the construction of regional orders, and consequently have impact on the global order.

Regional orders, broadly defined as "stable structures of regional intergovernmental relationships informed by common assumptions about the bases of interstate conduct" (Leifer 1987: 1), can take many forms, ranging from regional systems to regional communities (Ayoob 1999; Morgan 1997). In a regional "security community," interstate relations are governed by shared identity and mutual trust, and states do not expect or prepare to go to war against one another (Deutsch *et al.* 1957; Adler and Barnett 1998). The current wave of "new" regionalism is predicated on a marked increase in regional awareness and consciousness (Fawcett and Hurrell 1995), and community-building practices cultivate this awareness and consciousness to potentially transform regional orders into regional communities.

This book argues that regional orders are constructed. This does not mean that regions are invented or that regional orders can be re-grouped and re-designed merely through changing ideas and discourses (Vayrynen 2003). I do not deny that regional orders are shaped by material conditions, such as distribution of power, external threats, and economic conditions. But I argue simultaneously that regional orders are rooted in certain structures of meaning within which actors make sense of those material conditions. For instance, the contemporary trend toward regional institutionalization is rooted in a social/ideational context which favors regions as the context within which states conceive and pursue their political and economic interests. Moreover, these structures of shared meaning privilege "regional community" as the most desirable form of regional organization. It is within these structures of meaning that regional organizations have become the agents and the reference points for community-building practices.

There are multiple ways in which regional organizations construct and "build" regional communities. First of all, they articulate, claim to embody and act on behalf of a community of states.[1] Language of community – self references to a community, references to their members as a collectivity, construction of narratives about the community's past, present, and future – are widely employed in the various agreements and statements issued by these institutions. Recognized as actors in their own right in international affairs, and represented as such by significant "others," regional organizations embody and represent the sense of collectivity among their members.

These organizations also act as "region-builders" (Neumann 1994; Pace 2006); they politically process the geographical proximity among states so that it becomes relevant for and justificatory of community. Regions are not ontologically prior to community and do not have an objective existence apart from it, even though community-building often entails their representation as such. Instead, the social construction of regions and of collective identities are intertwined in a mutually constitutive and reinforcing relationship (Paasi 1996: 8). As community formation among states defines and constructs regions, the sense of mutual belonging in regions socializes states into collective identities. While constructing the region relevant for community, regional organizations also re-draw and re-shape neighboring regions, and endow them with special meanings (i.e. instability and threat) (Pace 2006).

Regional organizations also develop the similarities among member states by socializing them into community's norms and principles (Finnemore and Sikkink 1998; Finnemore 1993). Since norms specify the standards of appropriate behavior for a given identity, states abide by and internalize the norms of the community in order to validate their identities as members. In turn, the jointly agreed upon norms and principles constitute and legitimize the existence of the community, and define the content of its collective identity. It is necessary to note, however, that similarity and shared identity play a role but do not in and of themselves generate a sense of collective identity (Wendt 1999: 354–6). Institutions politically process similarities and differences so that they respectively become relevant and irrelevant for community (Neumann 1996: 166).

Moreover, regional organizations perform the crucial functions of arbitration and discipline. Members of a community may agree on their shared collective identity, while they define this identity according to different operating principles and values (Waever 1990). International institutions provide a site where these differences are arbitrated, and if necessary disciplined. Bially Mattern (2000: 305) argues that "community is an unstable social formation unless its members are forced to comply with a particular set of terms that define the community." Regional organizations constitute this site of discipline and stability; they define and enforce the terms of the community, through a variety of mechanisms that include expressions of collective criticism, economic sanctions, and, at the last resort, expulsion from membership.

Building on the premises of constructivist international relations theory, this book analyzes the implications of community-building practices for regional and global order. Community-building (re)constitutes relations of identity and difference among states, and shapes their conceptions of "self" and "other" and the appropriate means to relate to each other. These (re)constituted relations of identity and difference among states, in turn, shape relations of conflict and cooperation. This book will demonstrate the implications of community-building by developing a theoretical framework that analyzes how relations of identity and difference among states affect relations of conflict and cooperation. Then, it will demonstrate the empirical validity of this framework through a comparative study of the community-building processes in Europe and Southeast Asia.

II. Regional organizations and regional/global order

This book contributes to a long-standing literature on regional organization (Breslin *et al.* 2002). Karl W. Deutsch and his collaborators

(Deutsch *et al.* 1957) initiated the research agenda on regional organization by analyzing the emergence of a transnational "we-feeling" in regions where pre-existing relations of geographical proximity, cultural similarity, and economic interdependence generate dense transaction and communication flows among peoples. This "we-feeling," according to Deutsch, formed the basis of a "security community" where peoples entertain dependable expectations for peaceful change and hence neither expect nor prepare for war against each other.

This Deutschian research agenda was developed by a small group of integration theorists in the 1960s (Nye 1968, 1971; Haas 1958, 1964; Etzioni 1965; Jacob and Toscano 1964; Lindberg and Scheingold 1971). This "first wave" (Breslin *et al.* 2002) of research also historically coincided with a time when the number of regional integrationist arrangements rose rapidly and when regionalism was avidly promoted as "the next big step forward in international cooperation" (Nye 1968: v). Motivated by their belief that regional integration will have positive implications for international cooperation, these scholars sought to identify the functional "spill-over processes" that developed the European integration and apply it to different regions of the world. However, as integrationist initiatives in Europe and other regions of the world were stalled in the late 1970s, integration theories were increasingly discredited in favor of realist approaches, which were seen as offering the timeless truths, by acknowledging and emphasizing the systemic limits of anarchy (Puchala 1981).

The development and proliferation of regional arrangements since the late 1980s have re-ignited the scholarly interest in regions. Studies have underlined the characteristics that distinguish the "new" regionalism from the "first wave" (Fawcett 1995; Vayrynen 2003; Mansfield and Milner 1999; Breslin and Higgott 2000), focusing especially on the impact of globalization and the end of the Cold War, the role of non-state actors, wide variation in the level of institutionalization, and the importance of regional awareness and identity. While economists debate whether regionalism promotes or hinders multilateral liberalization (Mansfield and Milner 1999), New Regionalism Theory distinguishes between varying degrees of regionalization and regionness (Hettne and Soderbaum 2000), and regional security complexes approach analyzes the modes of conflict management in different regions (Buzan and Waever 2003, Lake and Morgan 1997).

In the midst of this growing interest in regionalism, two distinct bodies of literature have underscored collective identity as a key variable. The essentialist culturalist perspective advanced by Huntington

(1996) viewed regionalism as part of a broader trend toward alignments based on culture and civilization. Arguing that "regions are a basis for cooperation among states only to the extent that geography coincides with culture" (Huntington, 1996: 130), he predicted that cultural communities such as the European Union will outperform multi-civilizational groupings like North American Free Trade Agreement (NAFTA) and ASEAN. By asserting civilizations to be the broadest form of identification, Huntington assumed the incommensurability of civilizational identities and contended that the relations between these cultural communities will necessarily be conflictual.

On the other hand, the emerging constructivist approach revived the link between regional organization and community, advanced by the earlier Deutschian literature.[2] Defining itself in opposition to the rationalist approaches, constructivism effectively challenged the assumption that the ultimate unit of identity in international relations is the territorial state by making a convincing case for the possibility of collective identity among states. Wendt (1994, 1999) contended that state identities and interests are constructed by the intersubjective understandings that exist among states and not dictated by the logic of anarchy, and thus states can positively identify with each other, such that they see each other as "part of self" rather than "other." Also, distinguishing themselves from Huntingtonian cultural essentialism, constructivists have emphasized the situational and fluid nature of collective identification.

The possibility of collective identity among states formed the theoretical basis of a new generation of studies on international communities: Adler and Barnett (1998) explained the sustained absence of war in various *cognitive* regions of the world through the formation and institutionalization of security communities. Cronin (1999b) studied historically how political elites have constructed transnational communities through the formulation of common social identities and distinguished between different types of community-based security arrangements. Constructivist explanations of democratic peace focused on the sense of collective identity among liberal/democratic states (Risse-Kappen 1996; Kahl 1999). A plethora of studies appeared on the transformation of NATO from an alliance to a community of states (e.g. Cronin 1999a). More recent analyses have focused on the exercise of disciplining power within security communities (Bially and Mattern; Williams 2001) the effects of domestic instability (Nathan 2006), and the sources of tension within the transatlantic security community post 9/11 (Cox 2005; Pouliot 2006).

In all these studies, the concept of community has been used to explain the fact that war has become "unthinkable" among certain groups of states. According to the rationalist approaches in the discipline, the absence of war is either a product of short-lived alliance dynamics (e.g. Waltz 1979; Mearscheimer 1994/5) or of the increased communication and transparency in institutionalized security regimes (Keohane 1984; Krasner (ed.) 1983). More than the empirical absence of war, constructivists have argued, we are witnessing the non-expectation and unthinkability of war, the explaining of which necessitates close attention to ideational factors, such as shared norms, understandings, and sense of collective identity. Sense of community promotes sustained and dependable cooperation among states because "collective identity creates a basis for states to redefine their identities in terms of a broadened notion of 'self' that includes the co-identifying states" (Wendt 1994: 386). In the absence of community, cooperation among states is possible, but dependent on the interdependence or coincidence of individual "self-interests" of states, independently defined. In contrast, cooperation and peaceful relations are sustained among states within a community, not because their interests coincide, but because, as a result of collective identification, their interests have become inherently alike.

Constructivists contend that community-building discourses constitute a primary way in which international institutions construct collective identities. In analyzing the implications of community-building for regional order, this book builds on the constructivist literature but regards it as incomplete. A comprehensive analysis of the implications of community-building needs to take into account the intricate relationship between community-building and production of difference. While rightly underscoring the positive implications of collective identity for peace and cooperation within the communities, the constructivist literature has ignored the effects that community-building has in producing a sense of difference with outside states. In overall, the effects of community-building on regional order include both.

III. Community-building and regional order: a comprehensive analysis

Drawing on various literatures that have underscored the inherently relational nature of identity formation, this book conceptualizes community-building as a double-sided process such that the production of a sense of collective identity within the community inevitably entails the production of a sense of difference with states outside of the community. Collective identities among states, like all other forms of identity (individual, group, state, etc.), are constituted in relation to difference; it always "resides in the nexus between the collective self and its others, and not in the self seen in isolation" (Neumann 1998: 399). Hence, international communities do not have a self-generated and self-sustained existence; the inherently relational nature of identity inevitably implicates "others" in their production.

While establishing the theoretical link between collective identity formation and stable peace within communities, the constructivist scholarship has promoted an understanding of community-building as a self-generated and self-sustained process. The neglect of the role of difference in identity formation has also led scholars to misjudge the broader implications of community formation on regional and global order. While constructivism makes a convincing case on how a sense of collective identity generates the social conditions for peace among states within the community, it has not yet considered in comparable depth the possibility that, by virtue of the same logic, production of difference may perpetuate conditions for conflict in the external relations of the community.

This book argues that, in order to fully assess the implications of community-building for regional and global order, it is necessary to recognize three premises.

Collective identity formation produces difference with outsider states

Community-building is simultaneously productive of difference. Here, production of difference does not mean the fabrication of difference but rather the discursive practices of naming, marking, and articulating of another as different. International communities exist as a form of political identity only by virtue of an understanding on the part of the member states that they share certain characteristics, norms, and understandings, which are not shared by states outside the community, at least to the same extent. Community-building institutions constantly nurture and develop this understanding through discourses of difference that distinguish the collective identity from the alternative identities of others. In this book, I demonstrate both theoretically and empirically that production of difference is an integral part of community-building.

Under certain conditions, but not necessarily, the production of difference with outsider states is coupled with Othering

Community-building produces difference from outside states; however, it is important to note that this does not directly and necessarily entail the Othering of outsiders. In the literature, Othering is a concept that is indiscriminately used to denote a wide spectrum of self/other relations. By Othering, I specifically mean a behavioral relationship between self and other where the self perceives, represents, and acts toward the other as a threat to its identity. I argue that while production of difference always carries the potential for Othering, this potential is only realized under certain conditions. These conditions make up the constitutive dimensions of self/other interaction. Self/other interaction takes different forms depending on the nature of the identity, the social distance between self and other, and the response of the other to the construction of its identity. I develop a framework of self/other interaction, which defines the conditions under which production of difference is coupled with Othering. The empirical chapters of the book demonstrate that the interactions of community-building institutions with various outsider states are characterized by considerable diversity and variability.

Production of difference and Othering securitize conflicts with outsider states

This book underlines that production of difference and Othering are not simply externalities of community-building to be reckoned with but that they produce security implications beyond the community. Specifically, how international communities interact with difference affects conflicts between member and non-member states, and also shape the community's capacity to positively influence such conflicts. In re-constituting state identities, a community discourse characterized by difference and Othering leads insider and outsider states to conceive their interests to be conflicting and irreconcilable, and regard coercion as an appropriate means of relating to each other. As a result, the perception and representation of outsider states as threatening to community identity transform disputes on the periphery of the community into intractable identity conflicts. Thus, the security implications of community-building are not necessarily contained within the community; if a community-building process is "Othering" of outsiders, then it is productive of conflict beyond the community.

Similarly, the pacific effects of community-building need not be confined to the members of the community, international communities possess powerful means to diffuse the norms of their security community to their near-abroad. However, production of difference and Othering place constraints on their capacity to positively impact conflicts between insider and outsider states. Consequently, production of difference and Othering compromise the potentially positive effects of international communities on regional order beyond the community.

This book demonstrates the validity of these premises through a comparative study of the community-building practices of the European Union (EU) and the Association of Southeast Asian Nations (ASEAN). Europe and Southeast Asia are selected for analysis because they are two regions where a significant degree of collective identity formation among states has taken place. Western Europe is the most well known site of successful community-building in international relations. In a region that was the breeding ground of two major world wars in the last century, collective identity formation fostered by regional organizations has eliminated all expectations of war. Among the multitude of regional organizations in Europe, the EU stands out as the defining community-building institution in the region because it articulates the most author-itative discourse on European identity, such that EU membership is often unquestionably equated with Europeanness. Similarly, Southeast Asia stands out as the region in the non-Western world that most closely approximates a community. In this region, ASEAN has successfully fostered a sense of collective identity and reduced the likelihood of war among a diverse group of states with histories of conflict.

In terms of their institutional structures and the collective identities they profess to uphold, the EU and ASEAN are widely different from each other. The EU is a supranational organization, while the ASEAN is less formally institutionalized. In addition, while the EU promotes a partly inclusive/partly exclusive collective identity combining universalist norms of democracy and free market with a notion of "Europeanness," the ASEAN endorses a predominantly exclusive collective identity based on shared beliefs about regional norms and boundaries. The selection of these cases enables me to analyze the effects of these different collective identities on regional order and make generalizable claims about the implications of community-building.

The empirical chapters of the book analyze how these two regional community-building institutions produce and interact with difference, and the implications of these interactions for the broader regional order. In the case of the EU, I analyze the clusters of meaning that surround the interactions between the EU and Central and Eastern European states (CEES) (prior to 2004 enlargement), Morocco, and Turkey. I then investigate the implications of these self/other relations for the bilateral relations and conflicts between Poland/Germany, Morocco/Spain, and Turkey/Greece. In the case of the ASEAN, similarly, I analyze the meanings that surround the identity interaction between

ASEAN and Australia. I then investigate the implications of this identity interaction for Australian/Indonesian relations.

IV. Community-building and global order: a contingency framework

The conceptualization of community formation as a double-sided process, entailing both the construction of identity and interaction with difference leads us to a more comprehensive assessment of its implications for regional order. Consequently, it directs us to evaluate the implications of community-building for global order more in terms of a contingency framework. Since the founding of the United Nations (UN) at the 1945 San Francisco conference, the compatibility of universal and regional organizations and their appropriate division of responsibility in promoting peace and security have been debated (Wilcox 1965; Henrikson 1995). While proponents regarded regionalism as a stepping stone towards stronger international cooperation and world organization, critics argued that regional organizations will promote rivalries and undermine the UN and the principle of collective security. In this vein, Robert Gilpin (1975) has distinguished between benign and malevolent strains of regionalism, arguing that regionalism can either promote international economic stability and peace or promote mercantilist competition and international conflict. Similarly, during the resurgence of regional institutionalization in the 1980s and 1990s, economists have concerned themselves with the welfare implications of preferential trading arrangements both for their members and for the world as a whole (Mansfield and Milner 1999). Considerable attention has been devoted to identifying the conditions under which regionalism promotes or inhibits multilateral trade liberalization.

According to many scholars of "new regionalism," however, "the old controversy over the relative merits of regionalism and globalism has increasingly become obsolete" (Fawcett 1995: 19). In promoting peace and security, Henrikson (1995: 125) argues that "at least some UN action is always necessary, [first] to elicit regional-organizational efforts [and] then to make them fully accepted and effective; yet, without direct and deep regional involvement, international peacemaking is likely to lack continuity and consistency." Rather than being a "stepping-stone" or a "stumbling block,", new regionalism interacts with globalization in complex ways, mutually influencing each other as "two processes articulated within the same larger process of global structural transformation" (Hettne 2000: xxiii).

Within identity-based approaches that view regional organizations as communities and collective identity formation processes, a similar divide has also emerged with regard to their systemic implications. Wendt (1999) in particular has made explicit what is otherwise an implicit belief on part of many constructivist scholars that collective identity formation processes carry a system-transforming potential. In Wendt, the possibility of collective identity among states is embedded in a broader argument about cultural transformation at the systemic level. According to Wendt, "the international system is undergoing [a] structural change, to a Kantian culture of collective security" (ibid.: 314), and the formation of collective identities among states are "the instantiating processes" (ibid.: 336) of this cultural change at the systemic level. As more and more states represent each other as friends rather than enemies, "a tipping point" will be reached at which these representations take over the system (ibid.: 340). Although Wendt does not conceptualize collective identity formation as necessarily based on regional processes, he does not stipulate a universal process either. He does acknowledge several times in his account that collective identity formation remains at best a sub-systemic phenomenon, "limited mostly to the West, and even there it is still tentative" (ibid.: 314). He also argues that the Kantian culture can be "multiply realizable," by "Islamic states, socialist states, 'Asian way' states, and so on" (ibid.: 343).

The alternative to Wendt's systemic transformation scenario is the argument that processes of collective identity formation will end up reproducing the anarchical nature of the international system. This scenario comes in two variants. In *Clash of Civilizations*, Huntington (1996) argues that patterns of collective identity formation among states will ultimately coincide with civilizations and the relations among these civilizational groupings will necessarily be conflictual because their identities are inherently incommensurable. Unlike Huntington, Mercer (1995) does not make a prediction as to what patterns of collective identity will prevail in international relations. But, drawing on Social Identity Theory (Tajfel and Turner 1986), he argues that, whatever form they take, these collective identity formations will definitely be egoistic and resort to in-group/out-group differentiation, reproducing the anarchical and self-help nature of the international system (Mercer 1995: 230).

This book demonstrates that the implications of community-building for global order are more complex and contingent than acknowledged in either scenario. The reproduction of anarchy scenario builds on the assumption that collective identities will relate to others in an exclusionary and potentially violent fashion, what some have referred to as the "modern mode of differentiation" (Ruggie 1993). The anticipated result of such an interaction is that international communities will be productive of conflict with outsiders. The alternative, systemic cultural transformation scenario, on the other hand, builds on the assumption that such a relationship with others is not the *sine qua non* of international collective identity formation; we are dealing with postmodern or postnational collectivities (Buzan and Diez 1999; Cederman 2001a), whose identities can progressively expand to include others. The anticipated result of such an interaction is that the international communities will extend their norms and practices of peaceful conflict resolution beyond their boundaries.

Thus, implicit in these systematic scenarios are opposite assumptions about how collective identities relate to others and the security implications of those self/other relations. I argue that self/other interaction is constituted along several dimensions and continuously negotiated between self and other, which together make it impossible to reduce it to the ideal-types envisaged in the contending scenarios. How collective identities relate to others manifests considerable diversity and variability depending on the nature of the collective identity, the social distance between self and other, and the response of the other to the construction of its identity. Consequently, the implications of community-building for global order are contingent on the types of self/other interaction that materialize in the context of the existing community-building organizations.

Given that its empirical breadth is limited to two regional collective identity formation processes, this book cannot claim to provide an empirical proof for either systemic scenario. The objective, instead, is to develop a comprehensive framework which outlines the conditions under which either scenario can materialize. The book argues that the scenario of systemic cultural transformation is based on an incomplete assessment of the possible security implications of collective identity formation. The literature has focused exclusively on the positive security implications of collective identity within the collectivity and neglected the fact that community-building, as a result of the constitution of identity in relation to difference, is potentially productive of conflict with outsiders. Before reaching any conclusion about a systemic cultural transformation, it is necessary to recognize this potential, and analyze the conditions under which it materializes, and whether or not these conditions hold in contemporary patterns of community-building. On the other hand, both variants of the reproduction of anarchy scenario rest on assumptions about the nature of collective identities and/or the nature of their inter-relations, assumptions that are, this book argues, neither theoretically sustainable nor empirically validated by the contemporary patterns of collective identity formation.

Based on the track record of the two regional community-building institutions subjected to empirical analysis, this book deals with the question of "what kinds of communities to build?" for community-building to have positive implications on global order. Thus, instead of positing the validity of a systemic scenario, this book sets out to enumerate the conditions and identify the policy measures necessary to attain it.

V. Community-building and discourse

Identities are constituted in and through discourse and performed through representational practices that reproduce, negotiate, challenge, and subvert these broader discourses. Therefore, an empirical analysis of identity interactions, their constitutive dimensions, and implications for security relations necessitate the mapping of these discourses and the associated representational practices (Milliken 1999a; Hansen 2006). Such an analysis poses several conceptual and methodological challenges. First, it is necessary to conceptualize states and regional institutions as actors with identities, and assume that in their interactions they act upon those identities and these interactions in turn have constitutive effects on their identities (Banerjee 1998). While these assumptions inevitably lead me to anthropomorphize states and regional institutions, they do not necessitate a conception of those state and international institutions as essentially unitary actors. Following Ringmar (1996a: 452), the book adopts a "narrative" conception of the state that evades the question of what the state really is by asking the alternative question of how a state is narrated – how the state features in the stories told about it. "What we are is thus neither a question of what essences constitute us nor a question of how we are seen but a question of which stories are told about us."[3]

In this analysis, I am interested in how community actors such as the EU or the ASEAN and state actors such as Turkey are constituted through discourses and the shifts in these discourses through different temporal moments. A methodological challenge arises from the fact that there are always multiple narratives of the selves that I am interested in, articulated by the different actors that constitute the respective self. In this book, I have dealt with this challenge in several ways. One way is to immerse myself in the texts in which a particular "self" or "self/other nexus" is narrated as much as possible. This enables me to identify the dominant narrative based on preponderant usage and also the underlying discursive structure of distinct narratives. My empirical arguments are based on the analysis of as broad a range of texts as possible. I follow Milliken's (1999a: 234) suggestion to use grounded theory (Glaser and Strauss 1967) as a guide in the selection of texts. In grounded theory, the text selection is based on theoretical sampling: "The analyst jointly collects, codes and analyzes his data and decides what data to collect next and where to find them, in order to develop his theory as it emerges" (Glaser and Strauss 1967: 45). This unstructured form of text collection is guided and controlled by validity checks: The scholar generates provisional theoretical propositions from an initial empirical study, then tests these propositions against new cases and data, and if necessary reformulates the propositions so that they are empirically valid. Milliken (1999a: 234) argues that a discourse analysis "can be said to be complete when upon adding new texts, the researcher finds the categories she has generated in her analysis of previous texts."

Discourse is reflected in all the statements made about a certain topic, not necessarily only in the statements made by individuals who are authorized to speak on behalf of a specific institution. Therefore, in addition to official documents, such as conclusions of European Councils, reports of the European Commission, and declarations of ASEAN, I include texts of debates in the European Parliament and national parliaments, speeches by EU and ASEAN as well as national officials, and newspaper articles and commentaries in my analysis as well. Parliamentary debates enable me to identify the points of contention that do not make their way to official statements. The inclusion of newspaper articles and commentaries enables me to analyze the elements of common sense in societies (Milliken 1999a: 238). In attempting to render state discourses and practices intelligible, sensible and legitimate to broader societal audiences, representations in the national mass media presuppose, reflect and reproduce certain shared understandings in societies. Analysis of national mass media discourse enables me to identify these socially shared codes of intelligibility and standards of rationality and legitimacy. Such a broad textual base also facilitates the assessment of the hegemony and authority of official discourses (Hansen 2006: 61).

I analyze the statements made in these texts as representational practices that reflect, constitute, reproduce, and/or challenge broader discourses. I do not make an assumption about whether these representational practices constitute instrumentally driven rhetorical behavior or truth-seeking communicative behavior. In rhetorical action, actors use arguments instrumentally "to persuade others of the validity of one's selfish claims" (Schimmelfennig 2000: 129). In communicative action, actors are ready to change their perspectives and be persuaded by the better argument (Risse 2000). Discourse analysis requires that statements be evaluated not only to understand what they mean, but also to understand the structure of the discourse they embody and its effects, divorced from the intentions of speakers. Rather than the intentions of speakers that enter into a dialogue, discourse analysis is interested in their reproduction or contestation of a certain discourse. When engaging in representational practices actors can understand themselves to be voicing their sincere beliefs or acting strategically; but regardless of their intentions and beliefs, what matters primarily for discourse analysis is whether or not a particular discourse gets to be reproduced. Even when actors understand themselves to be acting strategically or instrumentally, their representational practices may have discursive effects that are contrary to their objectives.

Discourse, as a structure, has a complicated relationship to agentic representational practices. On the one hand, by determining what can and cannot be said, "discourse transcends the generative and critical capacities of any individual speaker or speech act" (Litfin 1994: 38). Discourse constitutes subjects, ascribes identities, and defines the terms of rational/irrational and legitimate/illegitimate behavior. No representational practice can be outside of discourse and hence totally contest a discourse without at the same time reproducing it. Quite often, oppositions and struggles against hegemonic practices end up reproducing the categories and hierarchies that are implicit in the dominant discourses that justify these practices in the first place. On the other hand, agentic representational practices continuously transform discursive structures, as each articulation adds new linkages to fluid discursive structures while subtracting others.

While noting the constitutive capacities of discourses on subjects, I adopt a structurationist approach that simultaneously sees the subject as agential in linguistic practices and instrumental in symbolic change (Diez 1999: 603). In line with Neumann (1998: 401–5), I use the concept of "identity-politics strategy" to denote representational practices of states that potentially have the effect of changing the constructions of their identities by others. The structurationist approach enables me to trace the processes of discursive change that occur in the negotiation and contestation of representations between actors. Discourse analysis has been unduly criticized for its inability to explain change. Sophisticated discourse analysis is able to demonstrate how representational practices simultaneously reproduce and transform discursive structures. Discursive change is always a gradual process of transformation through reproduction; change that is seemingly radical and sudden always occurs within a structure of continuity.

In the analysis of texts, this book seeks four empirical objectives. The first is to systematically analyze and categorize the substantive content of the self/other interactions between community-building institutions and outside states. For this, my method is predicate analysis, which "focuses on the language practices of predication – the verbs, adverbs, and adjectives that attach to nouns" (Milliken 1999a: 232). The second is to analyze the negotiation of representations between community-building institutions and outside states. For this, I map the discursive interdependencies (Diez 2001: 12) that exist between the representational practices of the self and those of the other and trace them over time. The third empirical objective is to demonstrate how representations at the community level constitute and constrain representations at the national level. This amounts to identifying relations of discursive "dependency" that stem from the symbolic authority the community discourse has over member state discourses. To demonstrate this dependency, I identify the similarities and complementarities in representations produced at the community level and those produced at the national level over time. A final objective is to demonstrate how representations shape policy-making by legitimizing one set of policy options over others. To demonstrate how representations matter for policy-making, I construct "counter-factual thought experiments" (Tetlock and Belkin 1996) of how in the context of an alternative set of representations the pursuit of the existing set of policies would have been precluded, made inappropriate, or harder to justify.

VI. Outline of volume

In Chapter 2, drawing on the constructivist literature on identity and difference, I develop a theoretical framework of self/other interaction which can be used to analyze how community-building institutions interact with difference. I argue that the existing literature forces us into an artificial choice between disregarding the constitutive role of difference in identity formation and assuming a relationship of Othering between self and other. After reviewing and refuting a series of counter-arguments raised in the literature, I argue that production of difference with external others is an integral part of identity formation. However, this does not necessitate that the self perceives and represents the other as a threat to its identity (i.e. Othering). Drawing on Todorov (1984) and the post-colonial studies literature, I deduce a multi-dimensional framework of self/other interaction that varies along three dimensions: nature of difference, social distance between self and other, and the response of the other to the construction of its identity. I analyze how the inclusivity–exclusivity of collective identities, relations of association– dissociation from the other, and the recognition–resistance by the other interact to produce different forms of self/other interaction, and identify the conditions under which self/other interactions are characterized by Othering. In the final section of the chapter, drawing on a communicative understanding of international conflict, I discuss how different forms of self/other interaction affect conflicts between states that are within and outside of an international community. I also identify how different forms of self/other interaction affect the international community's ability to positively influence those conflicts.

Chapters 3, 4 and 5 are devoted to the analysis of the EU. In Chapter 3, I comparatively analyze the interactions of the EU with states in Central and Eastern Europe (CEES, prior to 2004 enlargement), Morocco, and Turkey (prior to 1999) in terms of the three-dimensional framework of self/other interaction. I argue that in terms of the nature of its collective identity the EU promotes a partly inclusive/partly exclusive collective identity, and as a result its interactions with outsider states take different forms. Briefly, the EU constructed the CEES as different in terms of acquired characteristics, and associated with them. The CEES, in turn, recognized their deficiencies, and as a result the identity interaction was not characterized by the Othering of CEES. On the other hand, the EU constructs Morocco to be inherently different and dissociates from Morocco by ruling out the possibility of its membership. Morocco cannot effectively challenge the construction of its identity as such, and hence the construction of Morocco as an identity threat is not very prevalent in EU discourses. In contrast to these two cases, the EU's interaction with Turkey is characterized by forceful representations of identity threat. This is because the EU invokes both aspects of its identity in relation to Turkey, constructs Turkey to be different in terms of both inherent and acquired characteristics, and oscillates between association and dissociation. Turkey, on the other hand, effectively challenges and resists the construction of its identity as different. On the basis of these analyses, I conclude that the EU defies the binary classification of postmodern/modern collectivity, and is uncomfortably (or, alternatively, productively) situated in between.

Chapter 4 analyzes the process of identity negotiation between EU and Turkey that has made it possible for the EU to declare Turkey a candidate for membership in 1999, and start accession negotiations in 2005. I specifically show the ways in which Turkey sought to challenge the construction of the identities of Europe/Asia and Europe/Islam as mutually exclusive and inherently incompatible. In this ongoing process of identity negotiation, a fundamental element of continuity is the continued prevalence of discourses which construct Turkey as inherently different from Europe. At the same time, association with Turkey has become necessary to secure the inclusive aspects of European identity.

In Chapter 5, I discuss how the EU's differing institutional/identity relations with various outsider states have affected the broader regional order in Europe. I comparatively analyze how three sets of bilateral relations, Polish–German, Moroccan–Spanish, and Greek–Turkish relations, have been influenced by the EU. The cases of Polish–German relations and Greek–Turkish relations in the post-1999 period demonstrate that the EU has been able to positively affect conflicts involving outsider states with whom it has strong relations of association. On the other hand, the cases of Moroccan–Spanish relations and Greek–Turkish relations in the pre-1999 period demonstrate how the EU can perpetuate and aggravate conflicts between insider and outsider states.

Mirroring the analysis of the EU undertaken in the previous three chapters in a condensed form, Chapter 6 analyzes how ASEAN interacts with difference and the implications of these interactions for the broader regional order in Southeast Asia and beyond. As an exclusive community, ASEAN is different from the EU; it clearly distinguishes between self and other and is characterized by fixed boundaries. Yet, focusing on the case of ASEAN–Australia relations, I show how such fixed boundaries do not prevent the perception of certain outside states as an identity threat. In that respect, ASEAN–Australia relations constitute an analogous case to EU–Turkey relations. The efforts by Australian policymakers to contest the exclusive definition of the Southeast Asian collective identity in the 1980s and 1990s have produced forceful representations of Australia as an identity threat. In turn, the Othering of Australia has adversely affected Australian–Indonesian relations, especially during the 1999 East Timor crisis. Thus, I conclude that similar patterns govern the interactions of these two community-building institutions with outside states and their implications for regional order.

Chapter 7 summarizes the conclusions of this comparative analysis. I argue that the cases of both EU and ASEAN demonstrate that the implications of community-building for regional order are double-sided and more complex than previously acknowledged. Even though these two institutions are widely different from each other in terms of their institutionalization and collective identities, their community-building discourses produce outsider states as different. Their implications for regional order are mediated by their nature of self/other interaction with outsider states. Neither institution has been able to transcend self/other distinctions to constitute itself as a postmodern collectivity. Nor have they consistently produced conflict with outsider states. Thus, my findings do not lend support to either the systemic transformation or the reproduction of anarchy scenarios in terms of the implications of community-building for global order.

2
Self/Other Interaction in International Relations (IR)

As introduced in the previous chapter, in assessing the implications of community-building for regional and global order, the question of how collective identities relate to others is very important. This chapter seeks to address this question at the theoretical level. Despite a growing number of studies (for reviews, see Neumann 1996 and Hall 2001), the IR literature on self/other interaction remains mired in conceptual confusion. This is mainly because, in its conceptualization of self/other interaction, the constructivist literature in IR has drawn on diverse literatures in social theory – symbolic interactionism, poststructuralism, and social identity theory – in an unconsciously eclectic fashion, without recognizing their inherent incompatibilities. The failure to recognize the diverse roots of theorizing in IR theory has created a rather confused intellectual terrain, where the debates on the ontological foundations of self/other relationship have been conflated with the debates on the behavioral implications of the relationship. As a result, the literature forces us into an artificial choice between either disregarding the constitutive role of difference in identity formation or assuming Othering – perception and representation of the other as an identity threat.

In this chapter, I separate the debates on the ontological foundations and the behavioral implications of the self/other relationship. To stress the constitution of identities in relation to difference, I argue, does not entail an assumption that the behavioral relationship between self and other will necessarily be characterized by Othering. Conversely, to stress the potential variability in self/other relationship does not entail an assumption that relations of constitutive difference can entirely be transcended. An awareness that identities in international relations are constituted in relation to difference is not only conceptually correct, but also essential to recognizing the potential for distress and conflict in relations. The potential for transforming relations of difference into relations of threat and conflict is always there. However, recognizing the potential does not and should not amount to positing a necessity. One should instead analyze the social conditions under which this potential is realized.

The empirical chapters of this book will show that the interactions of community-building institutions with peripheral states exhibit a relationship of constitutive difference. Simultaneously, however, these interactions are characterized by considerable diversity and variability in their behavioral manifestations. This suggests that the behavioral relationship between self and other is constituted along multiple dimensions which allow for a wider range of possible interactions. In this chapter, drawing on a critical review of the literature, I deduce a tentative multi-dimensional framework of self/other interaction that varies along three dimensions: nature of difference, social distance between self and other, and response of the other.

For the sake of conceptual clarity and consistency, I follow certain rules in my usage of the concepts of "self" and "other." First, while it is possible to use self and other in reference to identity and difference in the abstract, in this book, self and other are used in reference to specific actors, to respectively denote the "bearer of identity" and the "bearer of difference." Hence, the term self/other interaction refers to the behavioral – and constitutive – interaction between the bearer of identity and the bearer of difference, not to the ontological relationship between identity and difference. When I am referring to identity and difference in the abstract (actors can have multiple identities), I use the terms identity and difference. Second, while self and other are perspectival and interchangeable concepts, in that who is self and who is other changes depending on whether you take the self's or the other's perspective, I maintain a consistency in my references by denoting international communities as selves and outside states as others. At some level, this conceptual consistency comes at a price, it forces me to approach the issue of identity formation from the perspective of international communities. However, as the discussion below will indicate, my conceptualization of self/other interaction attaches great significance to the role played by the other in identity formation.

I. Identity and difference

The main departure point for this book is that collective identities among states, like all other forms of identity, are constituted in relation to difference. Hence, I argue, the formation of collective identity among states inevitably entails the production of difference from states outside of the collectivity, resulting in a relationship of constitutive difference between the collective self and others. However, the presumption that identity requires difference in order to be is not an uncontested one in the literature, and therefore needs to be argued. As aptly demonstrated by Inayatullah and Blaney (2004), the discipline of International Relations itself is very much predicated on the interpretation of difference as an aberration. In this section, I present the different positions that constitute the debate on identity/difference, and make the argument that identity requires difference to be, but different types of identities are associated with different notions of difference. The following sections will demonstrate the significance of this distinction in producing different types of self/other relationships.

The divergent influences of symbolic interactionism and poststructuralist theory have created a division in the constructivist IR literature with regard to the import given to difference in identity constitution.[4] In symbolic interactionism (Mead 1934; Blumer 1969; Goffman 1959; for reviews Stryker 1987; Fine 1993) identity formation is depicted as a process of socialization through which an individual comes to see herself in the way that others do. Mead argues that an individual becomes a self by taking the attitudes of other individuals towards herself within a social environment. Society to the individual is what Mead calls the "generalized other"; it influences the behavior of individuals as individuals come to see, name, represent, and judge themselves from the perspective of the "generalized other" (Mead 1934: 225). Thus, in symbolic interactionism "other" does not denote difference, identities are constituted in interaction with others, but not necessarily in relation to difference that gets embodied in "others". "Other" simply represents other individuals, who constitute self's identity by naming, recognizing, and validating, but not by being the alternative and different identity.

Consistent with its symbolic interactionist roots, liberal constructivism has focused on processes of state socialization (Finnemore and Sikkink 1998; Checkel 1999). It has argued that there is a social structure to international politics, constituted by norms, institutions, ideas, and collective meanings (Jepperson *et al.* 1996). States acquire identities in the course of interaction with other states; they come to see themselves and each other in terms of the subject positions that are constituted by the social structure of international politics (Wendt 1999). For example, liberal constructivists would argue that democracy as an identity category is socially constructed; international norms, ideas, and collective meanings define the preconditions of a democratic state. States acquire identities as "democratic" through social recognition, only if the fulfillment of these conditions is recognized and validated by "other" states.[5]

In poststructuralist theory, on the other hand, production of difference is regarded as playing an integral part in identity discourses. Poststructuralists argue that, in Western thought, meaning is constructed through the "logocentric procedure, which differentiates one term from another, prefers one to the other, arranges them hierarchically and displaces the subordinate term beyond the boundary of what is significant" (Gregory 1989). Accordingly, a thing is known by what it is not. "What is" and "what is not" are not only differentiated, but also differently weighted; "what is" depends for its identity on a denigrated and excluded "what is not." Poststructuralism seeks to expose and undo this pairing and hierarchy as they are implicated in various social structures.

Accordingly, the constitution of identity and meaning in relation to difference forms the basis of the poststructuralists'/ critical constructivists' approach to international relations. In studying the social structure of international politics, they have emphasized that the discourses on international norms, such as democracy and human rights, are intertwined with such oppositional structuring (Doty 1996). This is because democracy, to be a meaningful identity category, presupposes the existence of its logical opposite, non-democracy. Therefore, the discourses on the promotion of democracy and human rights are inevitably productive of two identity categories, a morally superior identity of democratic juxtaposed to the inferior identity of non- (or less) democratic, thereby "constructing the very differences that transformation would ostensibly eliminate" (Doty 1996: 136). Poststructuralists/ critical constructivists also contend that identities are "performatively constituted" (Campbell 1992: 85) by practices of differentiation that distinguish the identity in whose name they operate from counter identities. For example, the performance of a democratic state identity entails representational practices that differentiate the democratic self from others constructed to be non- (or less) democratic.

To say that difference is constructed and produced is not to posit a pre-discursive state of similarity, nor is it to say that difference is fabricated. It may be argued that, since there are already existing differences among states in terms of democratic standards, discourses that indicate and articulate those differences cannot be said to be productive of difference. However, "to refer to something as socially constructed is not at all the same as saying that it does not exist" (Weldes et al. 1999: 12). Differences need to be politically processed to become relevant for identity, and the construction of difference refers to this political process of defining and fixing meanings so that the differences that "exist" become relevant to alternative identity categories. For example, while lack of meaningful opposition constitutes a state as non-democratic, low rates of voter turnout do not. Nor is production of difference reducible to strategically motivated rhetorical behavior of defiling the other to assert normative superiority. The point is that performance of identity entails production of difference regardless of actors' intentions or its presumed effects.

While poststructuralist theory underscores the discursive basis in the relation between identity and difference, another approach in social theory that has influenced the IR literature emphasizes the cognitive bases of intergroup relations. The main premise of social identity theory (SIT) is that individuals, once formed into groups, tend to accentuate their similarities with members of their own group and their differences from members of other groups (Tajfel and Turner 1986). It is argued that people distinguish between self and other because of the cognitive necessity of categorization, in order to simplify the social environment (Hogg and Abrams 1988). Categorization brings with it comparison and competition. Even in cases where individuals are randomly assigned to groups as in laboratory experiments, the consistent observation has been that individuals exercise in-group favoritism and out-group discrimination. SIT explains this tendency in terms of individuals' universal desire for self-esteem, which they seek to satisfy by maximizing the differences between their groups and the out-groups (Hogg and Abrams 1988). According to optimal distinctiveness theory, people want both to be unique individuals and to be included in a community; these opposing desires are balanced out by group membership. It is argued that, in differentiating itself from "out-groups," the "self" satisfies its need for self-esteem by constructing others' identities not only as different but also as (morally) inferior.

Distancing themselves from both poststructuralism and social identity theory, liberal constructivists downplay the role of difference in identity formation through various counter-arguments. One argument is that it is possible to distinguish between pre-social (corporate) and social identities of states and that corporate identities are "constituted by self-organizing homeostatic structures," and as such are "constitutionally exogenous to Otherness" (Wendt 1999: 224–5). According to Wendt (1999: 225), "if a process is self-organizing, then there is no particular Other to which the Self is related." To the criticism that the concept of corporate identity establishes states as "unequivocally bounded actors" and "brackets the struggle ... among many possible and rivaling selves" (Neumann 1996: 165), Wendt (1999: 74) responds by arguing that "the self-organization hypothesis does not deny the ongoing process of boundary-drawing" but simply states that this is an internally driven process that does not involve "the agency and discourse of outsiders."

Wendt conflates two distinct processes here. The constitution of identity in relation to difference does not mean that the constitution of identity necessarily involves the agency and discourse of outsiders, but that it presupposes the existence of alternative identities. And no process can be self-organizing if it entails boundary-drawing because boundaries are by definition drawn between a self and an other – even though the other may not be actively participating in the boundary-drawing process. The assumption of a self-organizing collectivity presupposes unequivocal boundedness. The empirical examples that Wendt provides to sustain his case makes it clear that he conceptualizes the self/other relationship in symbolic interactionist terms of recognition rather than post-structuralist terms of identity/difference: 'The Spanish state was a self-organized, objective fact for the Aztecs whether their discourse acknowledged this or not' (1999: 74). While it is patently true that the Spanish state did not require the recognition of the Aztecs for its existence, does Wendt really mean that Spain's corporate identity (as bodies and territory) was not re-constituted by the construction of Aztecs as inferior subjects to be conquered?

The assumption of a self-organizing collectivity whose corporate identity is not constituted in relation to difference is even harder to sustain in the context of international communities. The assumption of international communities as self-organizing collectivities is apparent if not explicitly stated in the liberal constructivist literature (e.g. Adler and Barnett 1998). Collective identity formation is treated as a self-generated and self-sustained process where shared norms, ideas, and understandings among states generate a sense of collectivity and mutual identity (Adler and Barnett 1998). By arguing that collective identities are constituted in relation to difference, I am not denying the significance of shared norms and understandings in the constitution of collective identity. What I am emphasizing is that an understanding of what is shared rests on a previously defined and bounded collectivity. Compared with state identities, there is an even greater necessity for discourses of difference to produce and sustain that sense of collectivity among states.

States enjoy relatively secure corporate identities, in the sense that their existence and boundaries are recognized by international law. In contrast, international communities exist as a corporate identity only by virtue of a sense of collectivity on the part of the member states. This sense of collectivity has to be constantly nurtured and developed through boundary-drawing practices that distinguish the collective self from others.

Liberal constructivists also argue that some state identities, such as democratic, are type identities that involve minimal interaction with "others" (only in the constitution of "membership rules"), and represent characteristics that are "intrinsic to the actors," such "a state can be democratic all by itself" (Wendt 1999: 226). Only "role" identities, such as enemy, friend, or rival are relational and require the existence of an "other" state. While it is true that democracy describes a state's internal system of rule and all states may become democratic if they fulfill the socially constituted criteria, democracy as an identity is constituted in relation to difference in two senses. First, its existence as an identity presupposes the conceptual possibility of non-democracy. Second, in a world where diverse regimes can claim to be democracies and the representativeness and accountability of democratic regimes are internally questioned, the "performance" of a democratic identity entails the discursive differentiation of the "fully" and "truly" democratic self from the "inadequately" and "falsely" democratic other.

Contemporary regional communities are being built around type identities, such as geographical region, political system, and economic system, as opposed to alliances that are based on the shared role identity of enmity. However, the production of these type identities also rests on external differentiation. The continuing debates on "who is European?" and "who is Asian?" indicate that the boundaries of these type identities are ambiguous and undefined. In this context, the construction and maintenance of the boundaries of a European collective identity entail the simultaneous marking of others as non-European. Similarly, the construction of a democratic collective identity rests on its differentiation from non-democratic identities, in a context where "who is sufficiently democratic?" is ambiguous and unclear.

Wendt argues that "collective identity brings the relationship between self and other to its logical conclusion" (1999: 229), indicating his belief that relations of difference are not inherent in the logic of identity, and can be entirely transcended. What he fails to see is that, while in case of collective identities certain states may begin to see each other as "extension[s] of self," the construction of difference remains integral to the production of the collective identity, itself. As Neumann (1998: 399) aptly puts it, "collective identity is a relation between two human collectives, that is, it always resides in the nexus between the collective self and its others." Hence, collective identity does not bring the relationship between self and other to its conclusion, but transforms it into a relationship between a collective self and its others. It is worth noting here that in no sense does the constitution of identity in relation to difference imply that the categories of self and other are fixed. It is perfectly possible that collective identity can expand to include what was previously its constitutive other; however, this expansion of identity will only reproduce the logic of identity in the now broader collectivity's interaction with a new constitutive other.

Other constructivist scholars have distinguished between self-reflexive differentiation practices that take a past condition of the self as their reference point, and outward oriented differentiation practices that are based on the denigration of external actors. Ole Waever (1998:100), for example, has argued that "despite the wish of various post-structuralists and critical theorists to catch the EU and the West 'Othering' various neighbors, the dominant trend in European security rhetoric is that the Other is Europe's own past (fragmentation)." Similarly, Thomas Diez (2004: 320) has argued that, in contrast to "otherings between geographically defined entities [that] tend to be more exclusive and antagonistic toward out-groups," the European Union "has opened up the possibility of the construction of a political identity through a less exclusionary practice of temporal difference."

Entering the debate from a more philosophical angle, Arash Abizadeh (2005) has argued that collective identity is different from individual identity in that it does not require an external other; the recognition required by a collective identity can come solely from its own constituent parts, that is, the individuals who make up the collectivity. Through this argument, Abizadeh seeks to refute the widespread particularist thesis that human collectives are necessarily bounded and demonstrate that a cosmopolitan political order based on solidarity with humanity as a whole is possible.

Such refuting of the role of the constitutive outside in identity formation leads constructivists down the dangerous path of essentializing collective identities and thereby undermining their very own constructivist premises. The arguments that are used to "absent" the outsiders in identity formation, such as the notion of a European identity that *solely* takes its own past as its Other, inevitably presuppose pre-given collectivities, with pre-given boundaries and uncontested histories. That difference is also located internally (i.e. temporally) does not mean it is not simultaneously located externally (i.e. spatially). (Hansen 2006: 49) Only when we assume that the questions of boundaries and membership are permanently settled can we talk about a collectivity having a shared past that it can take as a reference point in the construction of its identity. This is in contrast to those who see temporal othering as a characteristic of a post-sovereign and postmodern Europe that refuses to fix its identity and membership (Waever 1998; Diez 2004). However, even though Diez argues that temporal Othering requires a much "looser definition" of self, he also observes that the European Union increasingly resorted to geographical otherings after the 1990s, when the enlargement question became more prominent (2004: 321). To me, this indicates that whether temporal or geographical Otherings will dominate is not solely a question of whether European identity is endogenously loosely or strictly defined, but also a matter of how this European identity is constituted by outsiders.

Waever also argues that, in European security rhetoric "those further away from the center are not defined as anti-Europe, only less-Europe" (1998: 100). However, this is simply indicative of a different form of self/other relationship. While debating the role of difference in identity formation, constructivist IR has failed to pay attention to such variability in conceptions of difference. How different conceptions of difference produce different orientations towards the "Other" is best depicted by Todorov (1984: 146–67) in his discussion of the celebrated controversy between the philosopher Sepulveda and the Dominican bishop Las Casas during the Spanish conquest of the Americas. Sepulveda argues for the enslavement of the Indians by constructing Indians to be barbaric and thus inferior to the Spanish, and therefore to be dominated by them. Las Casas, on the other hand, argues for the colonization of Indians based on the egalitarian approach of Christianity, which embodies the belief that each man can become Christian. While their barbaric and non-Christian natures both make Indians into "Others" for the Spanish, they carry different implications in terms of how the Spanish should relate to the Other. This is because, whereas the civilized/barbaric dichotomy represents fixed and entrenched characteristics, the dichotomy of Christian/pagan embodies the possibility of conversion.

II. Negotiation of identity between self and other

In the existing IR literature, the discourse and identity performances of the other are rarely considered or acknowledged to play a role in the construction of identities (Neumann's analyses (1998; 1999) of EU applicants' rhetoric being a notable exception). The theoretical suppositions of liberal and poststructuralist/critical constructivist IR literatures lead them to neglect the role others play in the constitution of identity by reproducing, negotiating, or contesting the identity discourses of the self. Increased attention to developments and debates in postcolonial studies will strengthen IR theory in that regard.

While the constitution of identities in interaction between self and other is a major premise of symbolic interactionism, liberal constructivism has privileged a structuralist account of identity formation at the expense of an interactionist one. In symbolic interactionist theory, in addition to the assertion that intersubjective meanings that exist among actors construct their identities, there is an equal emphasis on the processes through which identities are negotiated. As Mead (1934: 254) argues: "One is continually affecting society by his own attitude because he does bring up the attitude of the group toward himself, responds to it, and through that response changes the attitude of the group." The existence of an overarching structure or a system of intersubjective understandings and meanings does not mean that the construction of the identities of self and other will go uncontested. The underlying premise of symbolic interactionist theory is that, from the perspective of the actor, the central problem in interaction is to create complementary and mutually compatible roles for self and others involved in interaction (Blumer 1969; Goffman 1959).

Neglecting this aspect of symbolic interactionism, liberal constructivism has been more interested in studying the constitution of state identities by intersubjective understandings rather than studying their contestation and negotiation between actors. In other words, it has placed the emphasis on the systemic variables that shape intersubjective meanings rather than on the symbolic efforts of states directed at shaping these structures. For example, liberal constructivism would be interested in studying the process through which intersubjective understandings of democracy are created and evolve, rather than how these understandings are maintained, negotiated or contested in the interaction between democratic states and those defined as non-democratic by them. In emphasizing the constitution of state identities by social structures, it should not be forgotten that states do not simply enact identities that are ascribed to them, but, in the course of performing their identities, actually act toward – with or without success – shaping and maybe even changing these ascriptions.

Liberal constructivists have paid attention to the interaction of collective identities with others only in the context of the expansion of the collective identity to others through the processes of normative diffusion, socialization, and imitation. Their accounts of expansion assume the prior existence of the collective identity (usually Western or European identity), as self-defined and self-sustained. Others (usually the Third World and the formerly communist states) enter the picture only because they intend to adopt this previously formed collective identity (Wendt 1999: 341; Schimmelfennig 2000). The only role the others play in this process is imitation; others become part of the collectivity if they manage to successfully adopt and implement the norms of the collective identity, and remain outside if they fail to do so. Liberal constructivists thus marginalize the input of others in collective identity formation and how collective identities are maintained, negotiated, and subverted in the interaction between the collective self and its others.

In its conceptualization of the self/other relationship, poststructuralism also denies effective agency to the other in structuring the relationship. Poststructuralist theory focuses on how identities are constructed and sustained by discourses of difference that create and maintain a moral hierarchy between self and other. It emphasizes that the relationship between self and other is one not only of difference, but also of power; hegemonic discourses structure self/other relationship in an asymmetrical fashion and deny the other effective agency. The critical task of poststructuralist theory is to deconstruct these practices and the constructions of the identity of the self to undo the hegemony of the self, and to grant the other effective agency. In the study of international relations, critical constructivism has sought to expose and deconstruct hegemonic discourses implicated in the production of identities.

Despite the intent to undo the hegemony of the "self," most poststructuralist studies end up empowering the self in relation to the other. This is because the power and the agency to undo the hegemony of the self and to construct a more desirable relation with the other is granted to the self only. For example, Todorov (1984) is very detailed in his exposition of the complexity of the ways in which the Spaniards have represented and related to the Indians. He is, however, virtually silent on the ways in which the Indians have represented and understood their relation to the Spaniards, and *most importantly* on the ways in which *their* perceptions and understandings have structured the Spanish/ Indian interaction. This inattentiveness to the agency of the other is also reflected in his understanding of the possibilities of change. By exposing the power and domination exercised by self over the other, Todorov calls for self-reflexivity on part of self. The power and the agency to undo the hegemony of the self and to construct a more desirable relation with the other – based on understanding and communication – is granted to the self only (1984: 247). The "other" is still conceptualized as a passive actor as the "self" denies or grants it agency by constructing or deconstructing hegemonic representations. Hence, his critique of the self ends up empowering the self in relation to the other.[6]

Connolly (1991: 65), on the other hand, presents a more sophisticated account of self/other interaction by conceptualizing identity as vulnerable to the tendency of others to "counter, resist, overturn, or subvert definitions applied to them." Thus, Connolly identifies the response of the other to the construction of its identity as a potential source of variation in the self/other relationship: "The bearer of difference may be ... one who incorporates some of its own dispositions into her positive identity while you insist upon defining them as part of her negative identity; or one who internalizes the negative identity imposed upon it by others." This book follows in Connolly's footsteps in identifying the response of the other as an important source of variation in self/other relationships.

Debates on the role and agency of the other in identity formation are most prominent in the postcolonial studies literature, but except for a few studies (Darby and Paolini 1994; Muppidi 1999), the international relations discipline has unfortunately not paid due attention. The postcolonial studies literature, especially during "the third movement" (Darby and Paolini 1994), has drawn upon and been influenced by poststructuralism, but, by looking at things from the perspective of the colonized, it has produced a far more sophisticated understanding of self/other interaction. In this conceptualization, the role of the other is not only passively constitutive (promoting and sustaining the identity of the self by embodying the alternative identity); the other through the performance of its identity is simultaneously put in an active position of consolidating, negotiating and contesting the identity of the self and its position as the "other."

While they disagree on the extent to which the hegemony of colonial discourse leaves room for meaningful autonomous resistance by the colonized, third movement scholars emphasized the "complicity" of self and other in maintaining colonial domination. That is to say, the colonial discourse of superior colonizer/ inferior native is made possible not only by the colonizer but also by the native "who internalizes the negative identity imposed on it by [colonizers]" (i.e. Connolly) to various degrees. It is in this sense that identity/difference is performatively constituted by self and other. According to Spivak, the project of imperialism, by inducing the natives to internalize what are essentially

Eurocentric modes of thinking, has eliminated any ground for resistance that is not in essence reproducing and strengthening the colonial hegemony (Parry 1995). Bhaba, on the other hand, through the innovative concept of mimicry, has uncovered grounds and strategies of resistance where Spivak saw none. According to Bhaba, the reproduction of the hegemonic European discourse by the natives in their own accents produced a "discursive system split in enunciation," enabling the ambivalent functioning of relations of power and knowledge. Having (seemingly) adopted the knowledge of the master, the native is at once complicit in its reproduction, but also free to misappropriate and pervert its meaning, and thereby able to circumvent, challenge, and refuse colonial authority (Parry 1995).

The debate between Spivak and Bhaba is useful in highlighting aspects one should be attentive to in asserting and discussing the agency of the other. In the name of empowering the other, my intention is not to adopt a naïve supposition that the other can exercise full autonomy in resisting and subverting the hegemonic discourses. Spivak's argument is a potent corrective in this regard. However, Spivak overstates her case by leaving virtually no room for resistance by the other. Bhaba, on the other hand, while acknowledging the limits of the Self's hegemony, also recognizes an autonomous space for the other in misreading, misappropriation, and mimicry.

Recognizing the discourses and agency of the other provides a more sophisticated understanding of the possibilities for change in collective identity. For example, this book shows how Turkey effectively resisted the construction of its identity as non-European, by producing counterarguments that represented Turkey as sharing Europe's collective identity. The production of these counter-arguments cannot be explained solely by a strategic motivation to secure a position in the EU, they were also part and parcel of the performance of Turkey's self-perceived identity as a European state. The discursive work of Turkey was consequential in changing the EU's stance with respect to Turkey by altering the discursive parameters within which debates on Turkey took place. Simultaneously, however, the performance of Turkey's identity ended up reproducing the dominant conceptions of identity/difference that the European collective identity rests upon.

III. Difference and Othering

Does a relationship of constitutive difference between self and other always and necessarily dictate a behavioral relationship where the self perceives and represents the other as a threat to its identity, and acts toward the other on the basis of discourses of fear and danger? In other words, are constitutive others always perceived, represented, and acted towards in terms of discourses of threat and danger? While acknowledging the ever-existing potential for difference to lead to such a behavioral relationship, in this book I seek to identify the conditions under which this potential is realized. This interest in conditions distinguishes me from both the liberal and the poststructuralist/critical constructivist approaches to self/other interaction in the literature. Liberal constructivists downplay the relationship of constitutive difference between self and other, but underscore the contingency and transformability of the self/other relationship. Poststructuralists/critical constructivists, on the other hand, have emphasized the ontological bases of the self/other relationships, but have not been attentive to the diversity of its behavioral manifestations.

In liberal constructivism, as the terms "self" and "other" are not used to denote actors in a relationship of constitutive difference, self/other interaction has been studied as relations between any two distinct states, not as the relationship between self and its constitutive other. Accordingly, liberal constructivists have conceptualized the behavioral implications of self/other relationship as a unidimensional continuum that ranges from negative identification to positive identification (Wendt 1994). Along this continuum, relations of identity and difference, and cooperation and conflict are assumed to co-vary. In negative identification, self sees the other as different, threatening, and inferior, and their relations are characterized by conflict and the ever-present possibility of war. In positive identification, the other is seen as similar, and as a non-threatening extension of self, and going to war with the other becomes a non-possibility. Scholars have formulated several variants of this continuum. The terms "amity" and "enmity" have been alternatively used instead of "positive" and "negative" identification (Bially Mattern 2000). Cronin (1999b:17) has divided the continuum up into six stages: hostility, rivalry, indifference, cohesion, altruism, and symbiosis.

The key point of liberal constructivists is the contingency and the transformability of the self/other relationship. The relationships of states can move along the continuum progressively towards positive identification, as relations of difference are transformed through the development of shared norms and understandings, into co-identification. With the demise of the communist Soviet Union, Russia and the United States have moved from a relationship of enmity towards rivalry. As a result of the community-formation process in Europe, the arch-enemies of the past, France and Germany, now share a collective European identity, and do not entertain expectations of war against each other. How self/other interaction will be situated on the continuum is shaped by their interaction, and also structurally determined by the prevalent culture of anarchy (Wendt 1999). While in the Hobbesian culture, the dominant form in which states relate to each other is as potential enemies and states are socialized into negative identification with each other; in the alternative possibility of a Kantian culture, states relate to each other predominantly as friends, and positive identification constitutes the norm of interaction.

By neglecting the constitution of identities in relation to difference, however, liberal constructivists are overlooking an important source of potential tension and distress in the relationship between self and other. In *Identity/Difference*, Connolly (1991: 64–6) argues that there is a "double relation of interdependence and strife between identity and difference," which constitutes the "paradox of difference" and makes identity "a slippery, insecure experience." On the one hand, because identity is constituted in relation to difference, it is "dependent on its ability to define difference." On the other hand, it is "vulnerable to the tendency of entities it would so define to counter, resist, overturn, or subvert definitions applied to them … The constellation of constructed others [is] both essential to the truth of the powerful identity and a threat to it. The threat is posed not merely by *actions* the other might take to injure or defeat the true identity but by the very visibility of its mode of *being* as other."

The paradox of difference–identity is dependent on difference, which is simultaneously threatening to identity – embodying the ever-present potential that the behavioral relationship between self and other may turn into Othering. This potential is not necessarily realized; difference is always ontologically threatening to identity, but the constitutive other, the bearer of difference, need not be perceived and acted toward as a threat to self and its identity. While the main objective of this book is to demonstrate that a relationship of constitutive difference between self and other does not always entail Othering, and to specifically identify the conditions under which it does, it is primarily important to be aware of the potential. By disregarding the relationship of constitutive difference between self and other, liberal constructivists are overlooking this potential.

While liberal constructivists downplay the potential for Othering, poststructuralists/ critical constructivists, on the other hand, overlook the fact that this potential is not always realized. Campbell (1992, 1998), for example, focuses on how the paradox of difference produces foreign policy practices that are dependent on discourses of fear and danger. In securing their identities, states engage in "boundary-producing political performances" (Campbell 1992: 69) that construct the external realm as different, inferior, and threatening. Because difference is omnipresent inside and outside the state, the externalization of difference and danger reproduces the distinction between the "internal" and the "external" by juxtaposing a unified and orderly "inside" to a chaotic and different "outside," and hence secures the state's existence. As Campbell (1992:70) argues, "the principal impetus behind the location of threats in the external realm comes from the fact that the sovereign domain, for all its identification as a well-ordered and rational entity, is as much a site of ambiguity as the anarchic realm it is distinguished from." Externalization also serves a disciplining function inside the state, by defining and representing dissident elements as "foreign" and "alien," and linking them to external threats.

Even though Campbell (1992: 77–8) concedes that he "paints a particularly negative picture of processes implicated in a state's identity," emphasizing "exclusionary practices, discourses of danger, representations of fear and the enumeration of threats," he justifies his position by "in so far as the logic of identity requires difference, the potential for the transformation of difference into otherness always exists." In the empirical examples that Campbell provides from US foreign policy, the logic of identity always and readily "succumbs to the temptation of otherness." In each encounter with difference, the securing of US identity entails the perception and representation of the constitutive other within discourses of danger and fear, resulting in Othering.

Campbell's argument depends on three suppositions on how the potential for the transformation of difference into Othering is realized in the case of state identities. The first is based on the nature of nationalist imaginary, which he argues "demands a violent relationship with the other" (Campbell 1998: 13). While he acknowledges that the practices of differentiation implicated in self/other interaction can have "positive and negative valences," he argues that foreign policy, understood as practices of differentiation which performatively constitute state identity, is more obviously dependent on discourses of danger and fear (Campbell 1992: 85). The second is a Darwinian supposition that in the domestic political contestation among different foreign policy practices, those strengthened by discourses of danger always have more appeal (Campbell 1992: 78). The third is an even weaker supposition

that relies on the force of historical continuity. He argues that representation of difference has historically more often than not involved a
negative figuration, as a result of the dominance of socio-medical discourse, within which danger has been construed as defilement (Campbell
1992: 99). As Hansen (2006: 39) notes, Campbell "does not seek to prove
that *all* foreign and security policies are always constructed through"
Othering, yet he does not pay particular attention to alternative
possibilities of self/other relations.

Other poststructuralists/critical constructivists have been more attentive to the varied representational practices that characterize self/other
relationships. For example, Milliken (1999b: 94) argues that the US Cold
War identity was also constituted in relation to the differences of the
non-US West and developing states that were part of the Free World and
that these relations of difference were represented in leader/partner and
guardian/children terms. In her analysis of (post) colonial encounters
between the North and the South, Doty (1996) also identifies the dominant representation of self/other as guardian/children. Hence, relations
of difference between the US self and the non-US West other and
between the Northern selves and the Southern others are based on more
complex notions of difference that are cast in less negative and zero-sum
terms. However, these rich descriptions of representational practices in
different self/other encounters are not supported by an analytical framework that explains how the relationship between a self and its constitutive other is in some cases characterized by discourses of fear and
identity threat and in other cases by less negative representations. Most
recently, Hansen (2006) has developed an analytical framework that
accounts for varying degrees of otherness by distinguishing between
spatial, temporal and ethical dimensions of identity.

Difference is simultaneously constitutive of and threatening to identity. However, in assessing the implications of this paradox of difference
for international relations, more attention needs to be devoted to how
the ontological relationship of identity/difference/threat shapes the
behavioral relationship between a self and an other. What I mean by the
behavioral relationship are not only acts of conflict and cooperation,
but also cognitive and discursive practices that include the perception
and representation of difference and threat. While the paradox of difference makes identities ultimately insecure, the performance and securing
of identity need not entail the reproduction of discourses of threat and
danger in relation to an external other. Even though identity is always
insecure, the question is whether the self's interaction with a particular
other makes that identity more insecure. To the extent that Campbell

draws behavioral implications, he overestimates the degree to which the paradox of difference produces foreign policy practices that construct the external realm as different, inferior, and threatening. Even though difference is always an ontological threat to identity, the bearer of difference need not be perceived, represented, and acted toward as an identity threat.

The application of social identity theory (SIT) to IR has been beset by a similar tendency to associate dynamics of in-group/out-group with intergroup conflict. Mercer (1995) has used SIT to counter constructivist arguments on the social constructedness of anarchy and the possibility of collective identity among states. According to Mercer, SIT provides a cognitive basis to self-help, to complement the structural basis of anarchy, which is impossible to explain away by constructivist arguments (1995: 230). Mercer does not deny the possibility of collective identity among states, but argues that "a group – however constituted – will be egoistic. This means that collective identity among some states brings us no closer to an other-help system; if anything, it takes us deeper into self-help" (1995: 249). Drawing on SIT, Mercer extrapolates that groupings of states, in the form of international communities, will be self-regarding and discriminating in their dealings with other communities and outside states. And because of this inherent tendency for groups to discriminate against out-groups, community formation among states will not lead to pacific relations between the communities. The in-group/out-group dynamics of differentiation, comparison, and competition translate into conflictual relations among human collectivities, be they in the form of ethnic groups, nation-states, or international communities. The con-flictual relations between states will be replaced by conflictual relations between communities, if and when such communities get to be formed among states, having no impact on the extent of conflict or on the culture of interaction within the international system.

However, as Mercer (1995: 243) himself admits, the link between the cognitive necessity to differentiate and the possibility for inter-group conflict is not that direct: "SIT is agnostic on the form that this compe-tition might take. How we compete and what values we think promote our social identity are socially constructed." Social psychologists have analyzed how different groups meet their identity needs by relating to out-groups in different fashions, and how the very processes by which groups are constructed can in fact reduce group conflicts. Hinkle and Brown (1990) have shown that low status groups often exercise out-group favoritism instead of in-group favoritism and out-group discrimi-nation. Also, according to the contact hypothesis, repeated contacts between groups over long periods of time reduce the propensity for intergroup conflict.

Constitutive dimensions of self/other interaction

The logic of identity allows for a great deal of variation in self/other relationships. Some of this variation is in the substantive, emotive, and normative content of representational practices. What I am particularly interested in, however, is the variation in self/other relationships in terms of the degree to which the other is perceived and represented as a threat to self's identity. Needless to say, this is particularly important in international relations because of its potential security implications; the construction of the other as threatening to self's identity may produce conflict and legitimize violence towards the other.

While itself a representational practice, the construction of the other as threatening to self's identity is an outgrowth of the identity interaction that self and other engage in. Some interactions between self and other make self's identity more insecure; hence there is a greater need to reproduce and re-inscribe the self's identity in relation to the other, strengthening the tendency to represent the differences of the other in terms of discourses of fear and danger. In contrast, other possible interactions between self and other are securing of self's identity, lessening the necessity for the representation of the other as threatening to self's identity. In this section, I tentatively identify three important constitutive dimensions of these identity interactions

1. Nature of difference: The terms of the Las Casas–Sepulveda controversy can be applied to contemporary international relations by drawing a distinction between inclusive and exclusive collective identities. Inclusive identities, such as liberal or democratic, that can possibly be acquired by any state if it fulfills certain criteria, embody a conception of difference based on acquired characteristics. Other identities, such as European (in a strict geographical sense) or Islamic, are by definition bounded and exclusive, and assumed to be based on some inherent characteristics.[7] By drawing this heuristic distinction, I am not claiming that there is an objective yardstick by which identities can be classified as inclusive and exclusive. Taking note of the fact that understandings about the nature of an identity as inclusive or exclusive are socially constructed and politically contested, I am solely pointing to the ways in which these understandings are associated with different kinds of discourses of difference. If difference is constructed to be deriving from inherent characteristics (the other as non-self), then the

possibilities for change in the "other" are by definition non-existent, and the other is placed in a position of permanent difference. If, on the other hand, difference is constructed to be deriving from acquired characteristics (the other as less self), then, by definition, there is the possibility that the other will become like self one day, so the other is only in a position of temporary difference.

The collective identities of international communities can be inclusive or exclusive, and this affects whether the difference of outsider states is constructed as based on inherent or acquired characteristics. In contemporary international relations, most community-building institutions manifest a hybrid character in terms of the nature of collective identities they promote. The fact that they are regional in scope makes them bounded and exclusive; even though the boundaries of Europe are uncertain and contested, this ambiguity is still within limits. On the other hand, the content of their collective identities may embody characteristics that are universal in aspiration, such as democratic and capitalist. As a result, their conceptions of difference are based simultaneously on inherent and acquired characteristics.

Different community-building institutions emphasize inclusive and exclusive identities to varying degrees. For example, as I will later demonstrate, the EU promotes a more inclusive collective identity than ASEAN, in that it emphasizes acquired characteristics in its self-definition more than ASEAN. On the other hand, the Organization for Security and Cooperation in Europe (OSCE) could be said to be more inclusive than the EU in that it has adopted a less strict definition of Europe that is based on self-identification as European, rather than European in an exclusively geographical and/or cultural sense (Adler 1998). Inclusive and exclusive identities set the bases for different forms of self/other relations. The potential for Othering is present in inclusive as well as exclusive identities; however, the context of its realization is different.

2. Response of other: A second dimension is the response of the other to the construction of its identity. By response of the other, I do not mean willful acts that are necessarily directed back at the self. The discourses and practices that the other adopts in the course of performing its identity may have reproductive or undermining effects on the identity claimed by the self and the difference attributed to the other. For example, a state constituted as non-democratic, in the course of performing its identity, can produce discourses that accept or challenge the moral superiority of democracy as a system of rule. The identity discourses and performances of the other can lend recognition to or

resist the construction of its identity as non-democratic. Alternatively, the identity discourses of the other can undermine the democratic states' identity claims by pointing to flaws in their practices. Any one of these "responses" by the other will shape the social definition of democracy and the notions of difference it depends on.

Recognition by the other is securing of the identity of the self, and because the identity discourses and performances of the other reproduce the self's identity, there is no longer the need to reassert the self's identity in relation to the other. The other is not perceived, represented, or acted toward as an identity threat. In contrast, resistance by the other makes the identity of the self more insecure, and therefore creates a greater necessity to reinscribe the identity of the self and the differences of the other. In this alternative ideal-type situation, the behavioral relationship between self and other is marked by representations of threat and danger, as the self tries to secure its identity. An extreme example would be Sweden's intervention in the Thirty Years' War, where Ringmar (1996b) argues Sweden acted to defend a particular constitutive story of itself that was denied recognition by significant others.

Recognition and resistance by the other are associated with different identity discourses and performances in response to inclusive versus exclusive identities. In response to inclusive identities, such as democratic, recognition by the other takes the form of acknowledging self's superiority and aspiring to become like self. For example, if the state that is constituted as non-democratic acknowledges its shortcomings, engages in efforts to promote democracy, and refers to the democratic state as a model, then such a response is securing of the democratic state's identity. If, on the other hand, it questions the status of democracy as a desirable system of rule or claims to be equally democratic, then its response would be undermining of self's identity. In the context of exclusive identities, such as European, recognition and resistance take different forms. Recognition entails the acknowledgement of separateness by the other, that it can never be like self. On the other hand, resistance entails a claim by the other to the identity of the self. While recognition reproduces the clear boundary between identity and difference that the exclusive identity depends on, resistance threatens the exclusive identity by blurring the boundary.

One can give numerous examples from contemporary and past encounters among states that support and justify these analytical distinctions. How was the Soviet Union threatening to US identity? How is it that the Cold War with the Soviet Union became a matter of producing US identity? The answer has less to do with the extent of Soviet

Union's difference and more with the nature of US identity. Because the US claimed an inclusive capitalist identity, its identity was threatened by others who did not aspire to become like the US. Had capitalism been somehow an exclusive and bounded identity – say, limited to states of the Western hemisphere – then the existence of an alternative economic system outside the bounds of that identity would not have posed a threat, but rather would have helped secure the Western capitalist identity as exclusive.

Similar possibilities exist in the interactions between community-building institutions and outside states. Outside states may either recognize the construction of their identities as different (either inherent or acquired) as legitimate, or resist by seeking to negotiate the construction of their identities. Such interactions usually play out in the context of enlargement debates. The material and social benefits of membership usually attract membership applications from states on the periphery of the community. Through these applications, these outside states make a claim that they identify with the collective identity of the community. For example, all applications for membership within the European Union are accompanied by a common applicant discourse that the applicant is a "European" state and can therefore meet all the requirements and obligations of membership. If these applications are from states differentiated from the community on the basis of acquired characteristics, then these applications are securing of the community identity; they constitute recognition because they indicate that the outside states are aspiring to the community identity. However, if coming from states differentiated from the community on the basis of some inherent characteristics, these applications constitute resistance; they make the collective identity more insecure because they have the effect of blurring the boundary between identity and difference.

In Chapter 3, I use this analytical distinction to explain how it is that the EU's interaction with Turkey is characterized by perceptions and representations of threat, whereas its interaction with the CEES is not. While both (groups of) states are engaging in the same behavior – application for and pursuit of membership – given that the community discourse emphasizes the acquired differences of CEES and both the inherent and acquired differences of Turkey, the CEES' pursuit of membership constitutes recognition, while Turkey's constitutes resistance.

3. Social distance: A third dimension is the social distance maintained between self and other. One way states perform and secure their identities in international relations is through associating with or

dissociating themselves from other states. States associate by participating jointly in various international organizations, signing treaties of mutual understanding, and engaging in collective action on issues of mutual concern. All these acts are undertaken to symbolize the co-belonging of the states within the same identity community. Here it is important to note that association is different from cooperation because it entails a notion of society that cooperation does not necessarily possess. States may cooperate on matters of mutual interest, but choose not to engage in acts that symbolize their co-belonging within the same identity community. For example, while there are strong ties of cooperation between the United States and Saudi Arabia, their relationship is characterized by a relatively low degree of association. Or states may completely dissociate themselves from other states that they see as different, by refusing such engagements. An example of substantial dissociation would be the United States' relationship with the Castro regime in Cuba.

Inclusive identities allow for association between self and other. Because inclusive identities, i.e. democratic or capitalist, construct the differences of the other to be based on acquired characteristics, such identities are secured by others who aspire to become like self. In this context, association with the other communicates the recognition that the other may, and indeed is willing to, become like self, and provides the self with the institutional means to influence the evolution of the other's identity. This sustains a relationship between self and other, which is not characterized by the perception and the frequent representation of the other as a threat to self's identity. Dissociation, on the other hand, makes the inclusive identity more insecure, by leaving undefined whether the other aspires to self's identity, and depriving the self of institutional means of control.

On the other hand, dissociation is securing of exclusive identities. Because exclusive identities, i.e. European or Islamic, construct the differences of the other to be based on inherent characteristics, such identities are secured by clear boundaries between self and other. The self dissociates from the other, the non-self, to inscribe clear boundaries that indicate that the other may never become like self. For example, as will be discussed in the next chapter, Morocco's relationship with the European Union is an example of how dissociation is securing of exclusive identities. Once Morocco is constructed as non-European, hence inherently different, association with Morocco makes the exclusive identity of Europe insecure, by indicating the possibility that Morocco can eventually become a part of Europe. If what is constructed as inherently different becomes a part of self, then the exclusive identity would be diluted, and the boundary between the European self and the non-European other would be blurred. The following chapter will argue that this is why the European Union's response to Morocco's membership application just had to be an unequivocal no, unlike all other cases where the possibility of membership was left open.

Community-building institutions in general determine their social distance toward outsider states through policies of inclusion and exclusion. These institutions usually employ a gradation of relationships with outsider states that represent differential degrees of association; other than member states, there are candidates, associates, partners, and non-members. If the difference of the outsider state is perceived to derive from inherent characteristics, the community-building institution adopts a relationship that represents a lower degree of association. If, on the other hand, the difference of the outsider state is perceived to derive from acquired characteristics, the institution may associate at a higher level.

Self perceives and represents the other as a threat only when its interaction with the other is not securing of its identity. The above discussion on the constitutive dimensions indicates that often self/other interactions are securing of identities. Only in cases where the other engages in practices that resist the construction of its identity as different, either in terms of inherent or acquired characteristics, and when self cannot set the appropriate social distance in relation to the other, self/other interaction becomes a source of insecurity.

Finally, I do not propose these constitutive dimensions discussed above as an exhaustive list. Hansen (2006), for example, has distinguished between spatial, temporal, and ethical dimensions of identity in her analysis of the Western discourse on Bosnia. I would like to suggest, however, that my conceptualization is rooted in an understanding of identity as co-constituted between self and other, and particularly developed for the analysis of "discursive encounters" (ibid.: 76) between self and other.

IV. Self/Other interaction and external relations

The forms of self/other interaction carry important implications for the external relations of community-building institutions. In this regard, the nature of collective identity is an important determinant. Community-building institutions promoting inclusive identities can grant or withhold relations of association on a conditional basis and thereby promote change in their near-abroad. Especially in those institutions whose membership is highly coveted, the enlargement process functions as an important foreign policy tool. On the other hand, community-building institutions with predominantly exclusive identities lack this capacity because they grant membership to regional states more or less as an automatic right because of their inherent characteristics.

As has been noted before, however, the form of self/other interaction is not wholly determined by the nature of identity; and other constitutive dimensions such as social distance and response of the other also shape the external relations of community-building institutions. For example, community-building institutions promoting inclusive identities can face further complications in their external relations beyond their immediate spheres of enlargement. Because inclusive community-building institutions associate with outsider states in order to validate their identities, the boundaries of such institutions are not absolutely fixed. The ambiguity of boundaries legitimizes possible claims of belonging to the community raised by various outsider states. Each wave of enlargement is followed by the emergence of a new group of aspirant states on the boundaries of the community. This results in a continuous challenge to the community identity, which, in order to validate itself, needs to build relations of association. If the building of such relations does not prove possible for various reasons, then this leads to charges of discrimination and exclusion, which are threatening to the inclusive community identity. Such an identity interaction creates the basis for a relationship of Othering between the community-building institution and outsider states.

Community-building institutions promoting predominantly exclusive identities, while limited in their capacity to promote change in their near-abroad through membership conditionality, generally have to confront fewer aspiring outsider states. Especially when the constructed categories of self and other come to be socially accepted as fact by insiders and outsiders, there is less of a need to continuously reproduce and enforce them through the articulation of outsider states as different. Regional institutions promoting exclusive identities are thus able to divorce their external relations from the pressure of enlargement, entering into various flexible institutional arrangements with outsider states as a community.

The track record of community-building institutions on conflicts involving member and non-member states is fundamental to assessments of their implications for regional order. If community-building produces implications for regional order beyond the community, then these implications are most likely to be manifested in the bilateral relations between insider and outsider states. Such bilateral relations are directly affected by community-building, as one party is constituted an insider and the other an outsider, by definition. Hence, the bilateral relationship is under the influence of the community discourses of identity and difference. Community-building institutions may also affect relations between non-member states; however, those relations are not directly, or as much, affected by the discourses of community-building. If a community-building institution is able to diffuse the logic of security community beyond its borders, to positively affect relations between member and non-member states, then we can conclude that its overall effects on regional order are positive. If, on the other hand, community-building only aggravates conflicts between member and non-member states, then its effects on regional as well as global order are more equivocal.

The pacific effects of community-building need not be confined to the members of a community; community-building institutions can potentially positively affect conflicts on their external borders and in their near-abroad through various mechanisms. Diez, Stetter, and Albert (2006) have listed four pathways through which the European Union can potentially positively affect conflicts, and these pathways can be generalized to all community-building institutions. First, as part of their enlargement policy, they can stipulate the resolution of disputes to be a condition for membership (*compulsory influence*). Accordingly, states are induced to resolve their disputes in order to gain membership of the institution. Secondly, under certain conditions, institutions can indirectly diffuse their norms of peaceful conflict resolution, by providing an ideational/normative structure for the rationalization and legitimization of alternative foreign policy options (*enabling influence*). Thirdly, institutions can materially support non-governmental initiatives which are advocating conflict resolution (*connective influence*). And fourthly, the institutions can provide a discursive structure (i.e. the discourse of a common identity) that allows for the rewriting of the identity and conflict discourses at the societal level (*constructive influence*).

The framework of self/other interaction indicates, however, that these pathways are only likely to work and be effective under certain conditions. Inclusive identity and the accompanying relations of association greatly facilitate these pathways of influence. They reinforce the logic of security community, and promote the development of institutional relations, trans-governmental and transnational links, and positive identification between the insider and outsider states. The possibility of granting or withholding membership to states that fulfill certain conditions raises the stakes and strengthens the institution's hand in the application of its conditionality instrument. Secondly, inclusive identity and relations of association foster positive identification with the regional institution at both the governmental and societal levels, and thus make it easier to legitimize the policy changes. As a result, the reform process in the outsider state acquires its own domestic dynamics.

The eventual possibility of co-membership in the regional security community empowers moderate domestic actors in both conflict societies, who would like to use the regional institution as a means of reconciliation. Thus, inclusive identity gradually incapacitates the hardliners in the insider state who value the regional institution as a means of power against the outsider state. The instruments of power possessed by virtue of institutional membership increasingly become less convenient and more costly to use in terms of prestige for the insider state. Consequently, in the outsider state, the defensive perception that the regional community is captured gradually gives way to a growing willingness to use the community norms and principles to settle the differences with the insider state.

Relations of association also strengthen the community's *connective and constructive impact* on the conflict. Transgovernmental and transnational links multiply between the two countries, undergirded by the shared interest in community co-membership and the growing mutual trust. And finally, inclusive identities construct the less oppositional distinctions between insider and outsider states and thereby gradually weaken the conflict enhancing, oppositional discourses of self versus other in both societies.

On the other hand, exclusive regional institutions that construct hard boundaries end up exacerbating the differences between member and non-member states. Exclusive identities and relations of dissociation also harden the boundaries between the insider and outsider states and impede the development of institutional relations, transgovernmental and transnational links, and positive identification at the bilateral level. In effect, they reinforce the logic of alliance rather than the logic of security community along the external borders of the community. First of all, relations of dissociation severely circumscribe the community's *compulsory impact*. Though it is possible for the community to offer low-level institutional relations without the possibility of membership, the stakes involved are usually not high enough to induce or coerce meaningful change in the outsider state. Secondly, exclusive identities reinforce a low level of identification (or possibly even negative identification) between the community and the outsider state. Under these conditions, the community's *enabling impact* is also debilitated because it is difficult to legitimize new policies in the outsider state, when the reference point is an external actor, with whom the level of identification is low.

Within the insider state, exclusive identities serve to empower those domestic actors who approach and view the community as a means of power *against* the outsider state rather than as a means of reconciliation *with* the outsider state. The clear lines of inclusion/exclusion drawn by the exclusive identities provide the insider state with institutional instruments to use against the outsider state, instruments which are simply too convenient to pass. The corollary of this from the perspective of the outsider state is that the already low level of identification with the community is further worsened by the perception that the community is captured by the insider state.

Exclusive identities also incapacitate the community from having positive *connective and constructive impact* on the conflict. It is difficult to encourage transnational contacts when the community border functions as a barrier. In addition, the willingness of societal actors to engage in meaningful transnational contacts declines when the level of identification is low. Furthermore, exclusive identities reinforce the conflict-enhancing self versus other identity distinctions between the conflict parties.

Thus, in terms of the nature of identity, community-building institutions promoting inclusive identities are better equipped to have a positive influence on conflicts involving member and non-member states. However, nature of identity is only one of the constitutive dimensions of self/other interaction, and social distance and response of the other also affect the capacity for conflict resolution. As has been noted before, both types of collective identities carry the potential for the Othering of outsiders, which is realized under different conditions.

The construction of the outsider state not only as different but also as threatening to community identity, and the associated practices of securing community identity by repeatedly articulating its differences, have a compounding effect on the conflicts between member and non-member states. They legitimize and accentuate the sense of identity threat that member states perceive from outside states. In other words, what is constituted as threatening to the community becomes legitimized as an object of threat to those who identify with the community. The presence of Othering fundamentally affects the capacity of the community-building institution to promote conflict resolution in its near-abroad, by specifically undermining its enabling and constructive influences. Consequently, an inclusive regional community that is otherwise well-equipped in terms of its compulsory and connective influences may actually exacerbate conflicts involving a specific outsider state because of Othering. Conversely, an exclusive regional community, which is lacking in terms of possible pathways of influence, may have a relatively more positive impact.

In conceptualizing the relationship between Othering and conflict, I rely on a stage model of conflict development, proposed by Diez, Stetter, and Albert (2006). This model is based on an understanding of conflict as discursively constructed, through "articulation(s) of the incompatibility of subject positions" (ibid: 565). Conflicts escalate as these articulations become more frequent, structured, widespread, and securitized (Buzan *et al.* 1998). Particularly relevant for my analysis is the transition from an "issue conflict" to an "identity conflict," which entails the explicit invocation of identities as part of the conflict (Diez *et al.* 2006: 568).

Therefore, Othering does not "cause" conflict *per se*, but it transforms existing conflicts into "identity conflicts" and hinders their de-escalation. The perception and representation of the other as a threat to one's identity promote the understanding that the disagreements between self and other cannot be resolved through negotiation and persuasion. They legitimize a coercive relationship with the other based on (threats of) physical harm and sanctions. They ultimately make going to war against the other possible and permissible. In the absence of Othering, conflicts are not automatically resolved, but such understandings and legitimizations would become unsustainable, paving the way for de-escalation of the conflicts to "issue conflicts." Issue conflicts are based on the articulation of the incompatibility of specific interests, and are limited to specific issue areas, and thus lend themselves more easily to conflict resolution efforts.

It should be kept in mind that the relationship between representational practices, such as Othering, and policy practices is a mutually constitutive one of "conceptual dependency" (Wendt 1998: 105–106). Constitutive explanations account for the properties of things by reference to the structures in virtue of which they exist. Wendt (1998) argues that "the effects of constitutive structures might be said to vary with their constituting conditions, but the dependency reflected in this variation is conceptual rather than causal. When constituting conditions vary, then so do their constitutive effects, by definition." Certain ways of representing actors make certain ways of acting towards them possible and legitimate. In addition, particular framings of issues make particular policy responses rational and appropriate. This relationship of conceptual dependency between representational and policy practices is different from a causal relationship in that it does not assume that representational practices exist independently of or temporally precede policy practices (Wendt 1998).

V. Conclusion

Through a critical engagement with the literature, this chapter advanced four arguments. First, within a constructivist ontology, identities are constituted in relation to difference, and the construction of identity necessarily entails the production of others as different. Arguments to the contrary, such as that certain layers of identity are exogenous to Otherness, self/other distinctions can be transcended through collective identity formation, or identities can be constructed through self-reflexive differentiation, end up essentializing identities and undermining their very own constructivist premises.

Second, identities are always negotiated between self and other and the identity discourses and performances of the other are as much entailed in the construction of identities as those of the self. A critical approach towards dominant discourses of identity should entail a recognition of the ways in which those constituted as "others" reproduce, negotiate, challenge, and subvert those very discourses.

Third, the constitution of identities in relation to difference does not necessitate that the self perceives and represents the other as a threat to its identity (i.e. Othering). While Othering has been discussed as a potential in major works on identity/difference, such as Connolly (1991), poststructuralists/critical constructivists, such as Campbell (1992), have misrepresented this potential as a necessity. I argue that relations of difference are transformed into relations of Othering only under certain conditions, which make up the constitutive dimensions of self/other interaction. Certain interactions between self and other are securing of identities and hence are not coupled with the representation of the other as a threat. Only in cases where the nature of identity, the social distance, and the response of the other are not in congruity, self/other interactions are characterized by Othering.

Finally, despite a growing number of studies that seek to explain relations of conflict and cooperation by reference to identity and difference, there is not a framework in the literature that links the two. This chapter suggested such a framework by drawing on an understanding of conflicts as communicatively produced. I argued that the presence of Othering escalates conflicts into identity conflicts, where identities are explicitly invoked as part (and the cause) of conflict. Alternatively, the absence of Othering de-escalates conflicts into issue conflicts, which are articulated as incompatibility of interests.

3
Identity/Difference and the EU

I. Introduction

As the prime example of community-building in international relations, how does the EU interact with difference, and with what implications for regional and global order? While some scholars argue that the EU has succeeded in constructing a postmodern community where self/other distinctions are blurred not only within the community but also in relation to its outside, others contend that the EU replicates the nation-state form in terms of externalizing difference and legitimizing a violent relationship with others. By applying the three-dimensional framework of self/other interaction, this chapter argues that the EU promotes a partly inclusive/partly exclusive collective identity, and as a result its identity interactions with outsider states are characterized by considerable diversity and variability. Thus, the EU defies such binary classifications as postmodern/modern or postnationalist/pan-nationalist and is uncomfortably (or, alternatively, productively) situated in between. While some of its interactions with outside states are securing of its identity, others are not, and the EU, as an example of a collective identity formation beyond the state, has not been able to supersede Othering. As empirical evidence, the chapter comparatively analyzes the cases of the EU's interaction with CEES (prior to 2004 enlargement), Morocco, and Turkey (prior to declaration of its candidacy in 1999).

II. EU and difference: contending views

Following Ruggie's (1993) characterization of the European Union as "the first 'multi-perspectival polity' to emerge since the advent of the modern era," many international relations scholars have stressed the "postmodern" or "post-Westphalian" nature of the EU as a polity and collectivity (Wendt 1994, 1999; Waever 1998, Buzan and Diez 1999; Cederman 2001a). In most such analyses, the EU's "postmodernity" is argued to derive from how international politics is conducted among the community members. Identities in the modern nation-state system rest on the construction of clear and unambiguous inside/outside and self/other distinctions. In contrast, a postmodern collectivity entails "moving beyond the hard boundaries and centralized sovereignty characteristics of the Westphalian, or 'modern' state towards permeable boundaries and layered sovereignty" (Buzan and Diez 1999: 56). Ruggie (1993) has argued that the conduct of international politics among EU members is remarkably different from modern nation-state politics and rather resembles the medieval system of rule with its "overlapping forms of authority" and "nonexclusive forms of territoriality." Wendt (1994) has characterized the EU as an example of a "collective identity formation" in international relations, where states begin to see each other as an extension of self rather than as other.

There have not been sufficient analyses of whether the EU constitutes a postmodern collectivity in terms of its relations with its outside. While clear-cut self/other distinctions may have been replaced within the EU by overlapping and mutually constitutive identities, the EU as a collectivity may be replicating the modern, Westphalian "mode of differentiation" (Ruggie 1993) in terms of its external relations. In response to how the EU relates to its outside, some scholars (e.g. Neumann 1998, 1999) have presented arguments on the side of a modern mode of differentiation, arguing that the European collective identity has entailed the construction of its outside as different, inferior, and threatening. Others (e.g. Waever 1998) have presented evidence of a "post-modern mode of differentiation," arguing that the European collective identity is founded not on the fear of "others" but on the shared fear of disunity, and that the EU does not erect firm lines of boundary around itself, but large zones of transition (frontiers).

However, it has been impossible to adjudicate between these rival claims on the basis of the empirical record. Scholars have drawn on cases of interaction selectively to find empirical support for their claims. While the cases of Morocco, Turkey, and Russia have supported claims of a modern mode of differentiation (e.g. Neumann 1999), the EU's interactions with CEES have been used as empirical evidence that the EU is becoming (or has become) a postmodern collectivity (e.g. Schimmelfennig 2001a). By conceiving of differentiation in terms of the polar opposites of modern and postmodern, the literature is unequipped to explain the diversity in the EU's interactions with various states on its periphery. How is it that, with respect to certain states, the EU constructs firm lines of boundary between self and other, and with regard to others, fluid and ambiguous frontiers? Scholars have failed to develop a theoretical account that can explain how and why these different ways of relating to difference coexist in the context of the EU.

The EU as a post-modern collectivity?

The argument that the EU constitutes a new, postmodern form of identity in international relations is advanced in three fashions. As also discussed in the previous chapter, one claim is that while the construction of a European collective identity entails discourses and practices of differentiation, these operate across the historical rather than the spatial realm, constructing as its other Europe's past, rather than its current neighbors (Habermas 1995; Waever 1998; Diez 2004). It is hard to deny that the discourse on European unity has from the very beginning derived its legitimacy from Europe's war-torn past. However, the existence of an identity discourse based on temporal differentiation does not rule out the simultaneous and sometimes mutually sustaining existence of another discourse that is based on spatial differentiation. We have no reason to consider temporal and spatial differentiation as mutually exclusive; to the contrary, they are often mutually constitutive and sustaining. The widespread existence of an identity discourse that is based on differentiation from the past does not by itself make the EU a postmodern form of identity unless it can be demonstrated that external differentiation is (mostly) absent.

Second, the argument that the EU constitutes a postmodern collectivity also rests on the claim that it constructs the identities of outside states as less rather than as anti-self (Waever 1998). According to Schimmelfennig (2001a: 174), the European collective identity promoted by the EU is a liberal one. "A liberal identity is universalistic, acquirable, and changeable. Neither adherence to liberal values and norms nor their rejection is regarded as a 'natural' or 'immutable' characteristic of a state. The liberal identity is based on values and norms that can be taught and learned, adopted and rejected."

The EU's interaction with CEES is often pointed to as corroborating the claim that the EU constitutes a postmodern collectivity (Schimmelfennig 2001a). It is true that, in relating to the CEES after the fall of the Iron Curtain, the EU has refrained from constructing their differences as antithetical, irreconcilable and threatening, the characteristics of the modern mode of differentiation. Rather, motivated by a sense of kinship-based duty, the EU has adopted an inclusive approach toward these states, extending an offer for membership conditional on their adoption of liberal norms in economy and politics (Sjursen 2002; Smith, K. 2004). The interaction has succeeded in promoting the progressive expansion of the sense of community, culminating in the membership of eight Central and Eastern European countries in 2004 (and of Bulgaria and Romania in 2007).

However, other observations cast a shadow on the claim that its liberal identity constitutes the EU as a postmodern collectivity. While the EU has espoused a liberal collective identity ever since its inception, its interaction with the CEES had a different character prior to the fall of communism in those states. What has changed is not the nature of the EU's identity, but the response of the other towards the construction of its identity. The postmodern mode of differentiation is made possible only through the willingness of the CEES to adopt a liberal identity. Ever since the fall of communism, their interaction has been based on a discourse of superior/inferior, where the EU claims the superior identity, and the CEES are accepting of their inferior status.

This observation reaffirms the importance of response of the other as a determining dimension of self/other interaction. A liberal collective identity makes a postmodern mode of differentiation possible only to the extent that others are accepting of the construction of their identities as less. The EU is constituted as a postmodern collectivity not only by the nature of its collective identity, but also by the response of others. A liberal collective identity carries a potential for Othering as much as non-liberal identities. The universalistic mission of liberal identities opens up the possibility for a non-threatening interaction between self and other only to the extent that others recognize their inferior status.

The EU's relations with the states in North Africa also cast doubt on the claim that the EU constitutes a postmodern collectivity because of its liberal collective identity. In contrast to Central and Eastern Europe, the EU's relationship with the states in North Africa has been characterized by their clear exclusion as outside of Europe (Pace 2004). In other words, the EU constructed the identities of those states as primarily non-European, not as less but as anti-self, ruling out the possibility that they may become part of self, one day. In relation to the states in North Africa, the EU clearly adopted the modern mode of differentiation. In this chapter, I devote a lot of attention to the case of Morocco, which is symbolic because it is the only state that got an unequivocally negative answer to its membership application. All other membership applications have led to the building of institutional relations that promised the possibility of eventual membership.

How do we explain the differential treatment of the states in North Africa in comparison with those in Central and Eastern Europe? Scholars who contend that the EU constitutes a postmodern collectivity either argue that their exclusion is normal because their differences are simply too great, or adopt an essentialist definition of Europe to contend that these states are situated outside of Europe (Schimmelfennig 2001a: 174, 182). These explanations are both problematic. If liberal identity goes with a postmodern mode of differentiation, then it should be the case regardless of the extent of difference. The possibility of membership should have been offered to Morocco on the condition that it fulfills its requirements. To contend that the states in North Africa are definitely situated outside of Europe is to overlook the fact that the geographical demarcation of Europe has been and still is a political process. And to fall back ultimately on essentialist criteria is to vitiate postmodern sensibilities.

Third, the argument that the EU constitutes a postmodern collectivity rests on the claim that it constructs fluid and ambiguous frontiers around itself rather than strict lines of boundary (Zielonka 2002; Christiansen *et al.* 2000). The modern mode of differentiation requires a clear demarcation of the self from the other, whereas fluid and ambiguous frontiers indicate that the differences between self and other are blurred. While it is true that at least in the east, the boundary of the EU is far from defined, I argue that this does not necessarily ensure a non-threatening relationship with difference. To the contrary, the non-definition of the boundary creates sites of ambiguity and liminality that may be perceived and represented as especially threatening.

In this chapter and the next, I use the case of Turkey to illustrate how states caught within the ambiguity of frontiers can emerge as sites of threat rather than experiencing a smooth and progressive expansion of the collective identity. Even though Turkey had expressed its interest in becoming a member of the European Economic Community (EEC) ever since its inception, its status as a potential member remained at best ambiguous until 1999, and controversial thereafter. Unlike the CEES, the EU hesitated in extending the conditional offer of membership to Turkey. But also, unlike Morocco, it refrained from an outright rejection that would amount to the declaration of Turkey as "non-European." While the EU declared Turkey to be a candidate in 1999 and started accession negotiations in 2005, the process is still fraught with tension and conflict, as evident in the EU's decision to stall eight negotiating chapters in December 2006.

Buzan and Diez (1999: 42) argue that "the game between Turkey and EU (and indeed between the EU and all of its periphery) has been played too much according to strict inside/outside understandings about which relationships are desirable within the EU framework. Putting too much emphasis on being wholly 'in' and 'not in' has narrowed political visions in an unhelpful way and runs counter to the EU's increasingly postmodern character." Put differently, Buzan and Diez contend that half-way institutional positions (neither "wholly in" nor "wholly out"), such as the one Turkey finds itself in, attest to the fact that EU is becoming a postmodern collectivity that does not construct clear boundaries between self and other. In this chapter, I demonstrate how, quite to the contrary, constructing an ambiguous and fluid frontier with Turkey has not constituted the EU as a postmodern collectivity because a close inspection of the discourses surrounding the EU's interaction with Turkey reveals widespread representations of threat.

The EU as a modern collectivity?

Other scholars argue that the EU simply replicates the Westphalian nation-state form at a higher level of aggregation. First of all, the EU promotes a collective European identity that draws its inspiration from the idea of "Europe," which has a very exclusionary and ethnocentric legacy. Delanty (1995) argues that the idea of Europe always remained tied to ethno-cultural values, and as a result does not constitute an alternative to the nation-state: "The nation-state, far from being its enemy, is the condition of its possibility." Similarly, Harle (1990) has highlighted what he refers to as the "darker side" of European values. According to Harle, European political thought contains a strong element of dualism, the tendency to make a distinction between "us and them," "friend and enemy," that is widely reproduced in the debates on European identity. Neumann and Welsh (1991) have explored how European identity, especially before 1856, was tied to the construction of the Turk as Other and how the "logic of culture" continues to be an important dynamic in the interaction between European and non-European societies. Shore and Black (1994) underline how the definition of European cultural heritage encompassing Greek thought, Roman law, Christianity, Renaissance, Industrial Revolution and social democracy is ethnocentrist and potentially racist. According to Shore (2000), despite claims of postnationalism, Europe is being constructed on the same symbolic and cultural terrain as nation-states.

While the idea of Europe certainly has an ethnocentrist and exclusionary legacy, the European identity constructed by the EU may be evolving as a more inclusive and civic identity. When the reformulation of the collective European identity became an imminent necessity after the end of the Cold War, the inclination of policymakers was to turn to the historical and cultural idea of Europe. However, there may have been a learning curve, as the dangers associated with cultural exclusion became more apparent. As argued by some scholars, it may be that the idea of Europe as a political identity came to be emphasized by policymakers at the expense of the idea of Europe as a cultural identity. Cederman (2001a) argues that the declaration of Turkey as a candidate of the EU in 1999 indicates the EU's sensitivity against the charges that it is practicing cultural discrimination in its external relations.

While the emphasis on the idea of Europe as an ethno-cultural identity may be waning, the construction of a European collective identity is still intertwined with practices of exclusion. Many scholars argue that this intertwining constitutes the EU as a modern collectivity. In external relations, the practices of exclusion employed against states in North Africa are the most pronounced. Foucher (1998) has argued that the EU's frontiers on its southern flank from Morocco to Turkey resemble Roman "limes." The border serves as a line of defense against migrations and citizenship from the South, but is open to trade, ideas, and languages in an asymmetrical relationship that remains a permanent source of tension. Migration is another issue area where discourses and practices of exclusion are very prominent. The abolition of internal border controls within the EU has been accompanied by attempts at strengthening the external border controls. The issue of migration has been politicized and securitized to such an extent that it has been constructed into an existential threat to European identity (Huysmans 2001).

III. Understanding the EU's mode of differentiation

As the above discussion illustrated, the EU simultaneously displays characteristics of what have been referred to in the literature as modern and postmodern modes of differentiation. With respect to certain outside states, the EU constructs firm boundaries between self and other, while with respect to others it employs an inclusive stance that allows for the progressive expansion of the community. The diversity and complexity of the EU's interactions with outside states can only be explained once it is recognized that the relationship between self and other is constituted along three dimensions.

In this section, I use my theoretical framework to arrive at a better understanding of the EU's mode of differentiation. As a statement of

European identity promoted by the EU, I take the Treaty on European Union, which states in Article 49 that "any European State which respects the principles set out in Article 6(1)" – liberty, democracy, respect for human rights and fundamental freedoms and the rule of law – "may apply to become a member of the European Union." Among the identity criteria listed in this statement, being European (i.e. being geographically situated in Europe) is bounded and exclusive, thus embodying a conception of difference that is based on inherent characteristics. It is not that the boundaries of Europe are ultimately fixed or objectively pre-given, but that they are constructed and represented as such. As a result, the identity category of European (in a geographical sense) confronts states as an objective fact; there is no possible way in which a state can alter its geographic situation, except for invasion or colonization of other territories. The other identity criteria, being democratic, respecting human rights and fundamental freedoms and the rule of law, are, on the other hand, inclusive and universal in aspiration. Any state can possibly become democratic, if it successfully adopts the necessary institutions.

In geographically demarcating Europe, European community formation has been productive of inherent difference. Because only European states can become members of the European community, questions of where Europe begins and ends have been fundamental to constructing a European collective identity (Wallace 1990; Neumann 1998; Anderson 1998). However, these questions have never had definitive answers: Europe is merely a geographical construct, with no natural or pre-given boundaries; the geographical perimeters of Europe have shifted not only throughout the centuries but also within the short history of the European community. Therefore, demarcating a certain geographic area as Europe has only been possible by discourses and practices of differentiation that have also historically shifted and changed.

Each attempt at demarcating the community has produced discourses of inherent difference. In objecting to Britain's membership in the EEC, De Gaulle had argued that the "maritime" Britain was inherently different from "continental" Europe.[8] Opponents of Turkey's membership in the EU argue that its history and culture make it inherently non-European. The boundary dividing North Africa from Europe is also maintained with discourses of inherent difference. Nothing could be stronger evidence of this than the Community's outright rejection of Morocco's membership application in 1987 on the grounds that it is not a European state. No other state's application to the EU has received such an unequivocally negative response; all other applications have led to different institutional arrangements that left the possibility of full membership open (Neumann 1998: 398). The maintenance of the community's southern boundary necessitated that Morocco be treated so differently.

On the other hand, in defining the European identity as democratic, the EU has been productive of acquired difference. The institution of candidacy is a good example of how European identity is constituted through discourses and practices of differentiation. By making applicant states candidates before they can be members, the EU constructs them as inadequate in these characteristics that define the European identity. The 1993 Copenhagen European Council stated three conditions, known as the Copenhagen criteria, which candidate countries had to satisfy: stable institutions guaranteeing democracy, the rule of law, human rights and respect for and protection of minorities; a functioning market economy that has the capacity to cope with competitive pressure and market forces within the Union; and the ability to take on the obligations of membership, including adherence to the aims of political, economic and monetary union (European Council 1993). Consequently, the EU differentiates its member states as the natural possessors of these morally desirable qualities. The institution of candidacy also grants the members of the community, as natural possessors, the authority to monitor and evaluate the progress of these outside states towards these moral ideals.

The different identity criteria of European community (i.e. European, democracy, capitalism) are secured by different social distances from the other. As Europe defines itself as the community of European states, the community relates to difference by exclusion. An exclusionary approach towards the other is necessary because bounded and exclusive identities need a clear-cut boundary that defines the other as not self. On the other hand, as Europe defines itself as the community of democratic states, it relates to difference by inclusion. Inclusion, or rather the prospect of inclusion, is appropriate because, in order to be sustained, inclusive and universalist identities need others that aspire to become like self.

Central and Eastern Europe: inclusive identity/ association/recognition

While, during the Cold War, European integration had become synonymous with Western European integration (Dinan 1999: 185–6), the end of Communist rule in Eastern Europe challenged the EU's assumptions about the meaning and definition of Europe. Participating in the challenge were the intellectuals and governments of the Central and Eastern European countries, who effectively pushed the cognitive boundaries of Europe to the East to group themselves with their Western neighbors. Their successful identity-politics strategies (Neumann 1998) emphasized their common history and civilization with Europe and the importance of developing the European identity. For example, in his address at the European Parliament on March 8, 1994, the Czech President Vaclav Havel stated that

> the Czech Lands lie at the very center of Europe and sometimes even think of themselves as its very heart … The European Union is based on a large set of values, with roots in antiquity and in Christianity, which over 2,000 years evolved into what we recognize today as the foundations of modern democracy, the rule of law and civil society … The most important task facing the European Union today is coming up with a new and genuinely clear reflection on what might be called European identity. (http://old.hrad.cz/president/Havel/ speeches/1994/0803_uk.html)

The community-building discourse of the EU lent recognition to their claims to a European identity, by constructing Eastern enlargement as the (long awaited) unification of Europe. As the President of the European Commission, Jacques Santer, put it, "the collapse of the Iron Curtain ended the Cold War and presented us with a unique opportunity to unite Europe in peace and freedom almost after five hundred years. We have a historical and moral duty to seize this opportunity" (Santer 1998). Any argument in favor of enlargement routinely referred to the CEES' European outlook, culture, history, and geography. Underlining the "Europeanness" of CEES became a standard practice in the speeches and policy documents (Sjursen 2002: 503). In the Copenhagen European Council in 1993 it was agreed that "the associated countries in central and eastern Europe that so desire shall become members of the Union" (European Council 1993). In July 1997, the Commission released Agenda 2000, which included opinions on all membership applications and a comprehensive report on the impact of enlargement on the EU. The Commission recommended that the EU begin accession negotiations in early 1998 with the five most advanced CEES: the Czech Republic, Hungary, Poland, Estonia, and Slovenia (Dinan 1999). In December 1999, accession negotiations with the remaining five CEES began. In 2004, in a big-bang enlargement (Smith, K. 2004), eight CEES became EU members, and the remaining countries of Bulgaria and Romania joined in 2007.

It may be argued that the EU's planned enlargement to Central and Eastern Europe was made possible by shared identity (Schimmelfennig 2001b) and a kinship-based duty (Sjursen 2002), and therefore did not entail production of difference. However, while the CEES are constructed as similar on the basis of inherent characteristics, such as geography and culture, production of difference on the basis of acquired characteristics, i.e. democracy and capitalism, continued to play an important role in the interaction between the EU and Central/Eastern Europe. Throughout the course of the enlargement process, the EU constructed a space of superior/inferior in relation to Central and Eastern Europe, where it claimed the superior identity of having stable and mature democratic and capitalist institutions. The dominant representations of CEES often contrasted the recentness of their transition to democracy and market economy with the stability and maturity of those institutions in Europe. "Throwing open the doors of the Union to those countries ... [means] helping the young democracies to consolidate and recover a spirit of solidarity and friendship" (EP 1997a).

Constructed as similar in terms of inherent characteristics, but different in terms of acquired ones, the European collective identity was secured in relation to CEES through association. The EU related to the acquired differences of CEES through the institution of candidacy. The institution of candidacy helped to maintain the space of superior/ inferior between the states within the community and Central and Eastern Europe, by constructing the latter as lacking and inadequate. In addition, the institution of candidacy furthered the belief in the ability of CEES to develop strong and stable institutions, if rightly incorporated in the EU, thereby reproducing the understanding of European identity as inclusive and universalist.

Because they were constructed as different, the CEES were potentially threatening to European identity. However, in the enlargement process, this potential has not materialized because the CEES were largely accepting of the construction of their identities. Even though the pros and cons of EU membership were subjected to debate within these states (Cichowski 2000), Central and Eastern European governments did not resist the construction of their identities as relatively inferior. The detailed pre-accession plans adopted by these governments basically stated their agreement with the EU on their deficiencies and the mechanisms of improvement. In their rhetorical practices, they "depict themselves as industrious students and list all the norms they have internalized" (Schimmelfennig 2000: 129). If the CEES had not applied for membership in the EU after the fall of communist regimes, or if, in the performance of their identities, they had contested the superior democratic and capitalist identities of the EU states, then their differences would have set the basis for their perception and representation as threats to European identity. As Schimmelfennig (2000: 124–5) aptly puts it: "The developments in Central and Eastern Europe are not without repercussions on the international legitimacy of the Western community. A failure of the CEES to develop into consolidated liberal democracies and market economies would severely weaken the Western claim that its system of rule was universally applicable and successful."

At times, some CEES diverged from the reform path, such as Slovakia under Meciar, but these did not amount to a wholesale challenge to the discourse of European identity underpinning the enlargement process. That the EU did not perceive and represent the CEES as an identity threat is demonstrated in the various European Parliament debates on the human rights situation in the CEES. For example in 1998, even when the situation especially in Slovakia was particularly alarming,[9] we do not encounter statements representing the CEES as a threat to European identity. Instead, the primary threat to European identity is presented as the failure of enlargement which "would not only undermine the economic and democratic development of Eastern Europe, but it would also do serious damage to the image of the Union as a model of peaceful, economic and political integration." In the representations of Slovakia, the main theme is that "Slovakia is a European nation," and that the problem is arising from "a handful of people in the Slovakian government … [who are] interpreting the will of the Slovak people … in a very one-sided way" (EP 1998).

Morocco: Exclusive identity/dissociation/recognition

In 1987, King Hassan of Morocco applied for membership in the EC with a letter that stressed the extent to which his country had liberalized its economy and adopted democratic practices, the "sensitive" security aspect of the western Mediterranean, and the consistently pro-Western orientation of his government (*The Guardian*, July 21, 1987). The response of the EC was an absolute no. The application was not even forwarded to the European Commission for an opinion as is the regular procedure. The Danish President of the EC's Foreign Ministers' Council was quoted as saying that he regarded the application as absurd. (*Financial Times*, July 30, 1987). Rabat was told that EC membership is open to Europeans only, and that Morocco is not part of geographical Europe. Morocco is not an oft-told story of European enlargement; however, it marks the first moment when the EU clearly took an exclusionary stance against an outside state based on its inherent characteristics. All other membership applications had led to institutional arrangements that left the possibility of future membership open. By marking Morocco as inherently non-European, the EU left no possibility that Morocco might one day become a member.

It may be argued that in its reply the EC merely stated an objective fact – Morocco is clearly in Africa and not in Europe – therefore, this cannot be considered as the *production* of difference, it is merely a *statement* of difference. Such an argument, however, omits several important points. First of all, the Spanish enclaves of Ceuta and Melilla on the North African coast already challenge the claim that the Mediterranean constitutes a natural clear boundary between the European North and the non-European South. If anything, the European community had already enlarged into North Africa with Spanish membership; however its territories in North Africa had not entered into considerations of Spain's eligibility of membership. Hence, the outright rejection of Morocco's application was not a straightforward statement of existing difference, but entailed the *production* of difference.

Second, the incident demonstrates that what the EC sees to be an objective fact, Morocco's non-European location, is not recognized by the other side as such. Clearly, the Moroccan state did envisage a possibility, however remote, that it might one day form a part of a community of European states and was willing to risk ridicule to try that possibility. It may be argued that Morocco's application and rhetoric were purely instrumental; however, that ignores their continuing resonance. For years, Morocco has defined itself as a bridge between Europe and Africa, a self-conception that the country seeks to realize with a massive 17-mile tunnel between Spain and Morocco. As the king's economic adviser recently stated: "Geographically, historically and culturally, Morocco is closer to Western Europe than most of Eastern Europe. The Strait of Gibraltar is just a geographical accident" (*The Economist*, January 9, 1993). Turkey's attainment of candidacy status in the EU in 1999 has encouraged Morocco to renew its membership bid. During his state visit to France in March 2000, Moroccan King Mohammed VI sought French support for Moroccan application. The king's spokesman Hassan Aourid stated: "After the acceptance of the Turkish candidature, EU membership for Morocco is no longer taboo" (*BBC News*, April 3, 2000).

Hence, in relation to Morocco, the EU invokes predominantly exclusive aspects of its identity and constructs Morocco to be inherently different. This relationship of identity/difference is secured by the EU's dissociation from Morocco. Dissociation is not only apparent in the rejection of Morocco's application for membership, but also in the nature of institutional relations. (To repeat, dissociation does not mean the absence of relations, but rather indicates not belonging in the same identity community.) As a key state in the EU's Euro–Mediterranean strategy, Morocco has signed an Association Agreement with the EU in 1996, and finalized an Action Plan in 2005 as part of the new European Neighborhood Policy. Still, the institutional relations that the Community has established with Morocco have been those that repro-duce the construction of Morocco as an absolute other. First of all, it was mainly security concerns, the fear of religious fundamentalism and uncontrolled migration that have prompted the establishment of these institutional relations. This rationale underscores Morocco's inherent difference. Secondly, the relations established within the Euro–Med framework are highly asymmetrical, giving the EU the authority to penalize failures concerning democracy and human rights in Morocco and elsewhere in the South Mediterranean, while denying the latter the opportunity to comment on practices inside the EU, for example regard-ing the civil rights of migrants (Junemann 1998).

Morocco is also constructed to be different from Europe in terms of acquired characteristics, because of its monarchical rule, illegal occupa-tion of Western Sahara since 1975, and human rights issues. However, given that Morocco is already marked as non-European, these deficien-cies are in some sense considered normal, and Morocco is subjected to lower standards. For example, in a debate in the European Parliament on the situation of human rights in Morocco, von Habsburg from European People's Party (PPE) noted: "Of course, there are human rights abuses in that country ... The fact is that there are various levels of culture and development. We should not simply say that everything has to be done in accordance with our standard" (EP 1996a). Similarly, the 1995 Barcelona Declaration, which started the Euromed Program for the EU's cooperation with North Africa and the Middle East, recognizes "the right of each of [the partners] to choose and freely develop its own political, socio-economic, and judicial systems" (Haddadi 2003: 80). Unlike in Central and Eastern Europe, deterioration in Morocco's human rights condition is not considered to be a failure of Europe in providing the right incentives, but as further evidence of its non-European character. Therefore, the EU's dissociation from Morocco does not make the inclusive aspects of the European identity more insecure.

As different, Morocco is always potentially threatening to Europe. Yet, Morocco is often not perceived and represented as a threat to European identity because it has not been able to resist the construction of its identity as different. Because the inclusion of a non-European state would dilute the identity of the community, claims by Morocco to a European identity would elicit from the EU representations of Morocco as wholly unlike and threatening to European identity. However, despite several attempts, Morocco has so far not been able to successfully resist the construction of its identity as geographically non-European. The fact that Morocco's application is rarely mentioned in the narratives on European enlargement attests to that.

This was clearly demonstrated, for example, during the June 1996 European Parliament debate on human rights in Morocco. In debating whether the EU should conclude an association agreement with Morocco, the members of the European Parliament (MEPs) made no reference to Morocco as threatening European identity and/or the need to defend European identity in relation to Morocco. Even though the condition of human rights in Morocco was clearly below European standards, Morocco's difference was not perceived or represented as a threat to European identity. Instead, the MEPs talked about "the need to respect the different points of view with regard to pace, content, or intensity [of progress in human rights]," "the desirability of mutual understanding between two cultures – European and Moroccan," and Morocco "as a fundamental piece in the consolidation of a stable southern frontier [for Europe]" (EP 1996a).

The liminal: Turkey

Turkey first expressed interest in eventually becoming a member of the EU in 1959, right after the community's inception. This has led to a series of different institutional arrangements between Turkey and the EU, but Turkey's status as a potential member has continuously evoked heated debate within the EU and remained at best ambiguous. In 1963, Turkey signed an association agreement with the EEC, which stipulated a 22-year period of mutual tariff reductions, with the end result of a customs union between Turkey and the EEC. By recognizing Turkey as a European state, this agreement confirmed Turkey's eligibility for full membership in the future. Turkey applied for full membership in April 1987. The Commission rejected Turkey's application in December 1989, and recommended that Turkey pursue a customs union first. The Customs Union Agreement between Turkey and the EU was finally effected in March 1995. Turkey always regarded the Customs Union to be a step towards full membership, even though the European Union never made such an indication. Therefore, the 1997 Luxembourg

European Council which did not proclaim Turkey as a candidate caused considerable disappointment in Turkey, and in response Turkey suspended its institutional relations with the EU. Turkey finally attained candidate status at the Helsinki Summit in December 1999.[10] The developments in EU–Turkey relations following the declaration of Turkey's candidacy will be discussed in the following chapter.

Nearly all analyses of Turkey–EU relations acknowledge at some level that "identity" plays a role, but there are not many studies that provide a theoretically informed analysis of how "identity" plays a role. If the EU is not a club where prospective members are chosen on the basis of costs and benefits but a community that possesses and asserts a collective identity, what do its interactions with Turkey say about the nature of the EU as a community?

According to Cederman (2001b: 235), the EU's interaction with Turkey in the end demonstrated the postnational character of the EU: "The participants of the Eastern enlargement debates have overwhelmingly subscribed to a post-nationalist logic ... The Helsinki Summit's decision in December 1999 to allow Turkey as a candidate for admission to the European Union allays the fears that the EU is becoming a Christian club." Similarly, Schimmelfennig (2001a: 182) argues that "it is perfectly justifiable from a liberal community perspective that the EU treats Turkey differently from the CEES: Turkey's human rights record is far worse than that of the associated CEE countries." According to this liberal constructivist perspective, Turkey's continuing deficiencies in human rights and democracy alone explain why Turkey is still at the end of the queue for membership. In relation to Turkey, the EU is just stating the standards that Turkey has not yet fulfilled; there is no production of difference, let alone cultural discrimination against Turkey. Unless Turkey fulfills the necessary conditions, it cannot become a member of the EU, and the strict application of standards only attests to the fact that the EU is a community of shared liberal norms and values.

Subscribing to an essentialist understanding of identity, Huntington (1996) devotes a lot of attention to the case of Turkey–EU relations. He argues that Turkey is a torn country because while it essentially belongs to the Islamic civilization, its governments claim to be a part of the Western civilization, and aspire for membership in the EU. A Turkish scholar, Muftuler-Bac (1997), also agrees with Huntington that some aspects of the troubled relationship between Turkey and Europe could be explained by a culturally deterministic perspective: "An analysis of the relations between Turkey and Western Europe should take into consideration the rift between Islam and Christianity."

Neumann and Welsh (1991), on the other hand, represent a post-structuralist/critical constructivist position on Turkey–EU relations. Their argument is that the "logic of culture" is an important dynamic in the interactions between EU and non-European states. Like all identities, the European identity is constituted in relation to difference, and the Turk has historically been the Other that the European identity was constituted in relation to. According to poststructuralists/critical constructivists, that Turkey is still at the end of the queue for joining the EU is a reflection of how European perceptions of Turkey are colored by Turkey's historical role as Europe's Other. While noting the significance of the "logic of culture," the poststructuralist/critical constructivist position is not culturally deterministic like Huntington. Rather than viewing the contents and boundaries of cultures and the differences between them as objective facts, poststructuralists/critical constructivists are interested in how certain understandings of European culture came to be dominant and reproduced at the expense of others, with a view that things could have been otherwise. For example, Robins (1996: 64) argues that "coming to terms with 'the Turk' is a crucial aspect of the cultural re-ordering and re-association that must be undertaken in the European space."

Neither the liberal constructivist nor the poststructuralist/critical constructivist accounts can wholly capture the complexity of the identity interaction between the EU and Turkey. Unlike Morocco or the CEES, Turkey is differentiated from Europe on the basis of both inherent and acquired characteristics. As I noted before, the European collective identity promoted by the EU is hybrid in terms of embodying both inclusive and exclusive aspects. This hybridity produces competing discourses on Turkey's identity in relation to Europe. The discourses that emphasize the exclusive aspects of European identity based on geography and culture construct Turkey as inherently different; Turkey cannot ever become a European country (like Morocco) because 97% of its territory is geographically in Asia and because it is a Muslim society. On the other hand, the discourses that emphasize the inclusive aspects of European identity construct Turkey as different from Europe solely in terms of acquired characteristics. These underscore that, while exclusion of Turkey is racist and hence incompatible with European identity, Turkey is significantly different from Europe because it is economically under-developed, has an unstable political system marked by pervasive military involvement, and a bad human rights record. If and when Turkey develops economic and political institutions in line with European values and standards, it will rightfully become a member of the EU, despite what others may claim to be its inherent differences.

The coexistence of these competing identity discourses on Turkey can be seen at every encounter in EU–Turkey relations. After Turkey lodged its formal membership application to the EC in 1987, during a subsequent debate on Turkey in the European Parliament, an independent MEP, Antony, for example, listed the inherent qualities that make Turkey non-European as:

> It has to be understood that Turkey is not part of Europe. Turkey has its own history, with its moments of glory and its dark moments, but its history is not our history ... From time immemorial, Turkey – or the states that preceded it – was the threat against which Europe was able to unite ... Spiritually, morally, and even physically, Turkey is not Europe. (EP 1987)

The European Commission's Opinion on Turkey's membership application, on the other hand, based its recommendation on not starting accession negotiations with Turkey on Turkey's acquired differences, underlining "the need to bear in mind substantial political problems, such as the expansion of political pluralism, the continuation of the positive trend with regard to human rights and the rights of minorities, the persistence of disputes with a member state, and the lack of a solution to the Cyprus problem" (European Commission, 1987).

Similarly, in 1995, when the conclusion of a Customs Union Agreement with Turkey was on the EU's agenda, this dual construction of Turkey's identity as different on the basis of both inherent and acquired characteristics persisted. During the European Parliament Debate on Turkey on December 13, 1995, Fabre-Aubrepsy from the nationalist Independents for Europe of the Nations (EDN) political group argued that:

> It does not seem possible to me, given its geographic position, its culture, and its religion, to envisage Turkey forming an integral part of the European Community with its Judeo-Christian heritage. (EP 1995)

On the other hand, Green, from the Party of European Socialists (PSE), noted that the reservations of the MEPs belonging to that political group to concluding the Customs Union Agreement with Turkey were based on Turkey's acquired differences:

> We have a healthy skepticism, born out of experience that Turkish reform is often short-lived and expedient. We find it difficult to countenance such a close and sensitive relationship with a nation

that continues to violate individual rights in a well-documented and shameful way. (EP 1995)

In the lead-up to the 1997 Luxembourg European Council, some leading political figures emphasized Turkey's inherent differences. In February 1997, Dutch Foreign Minister Hans van Mierlo remarked to a committee of the European Parliament: "There is the problem of a big Muslim state. Do we want it in Europe? It is an unspoken question. It is time that we, Europeans, are honest" (Wood 1999: 109). In March 1997, Wilfred Martens, the former Prime Minister of Belgium, stated during a meeting of European Christian Democratic leaders that "European Union is a civilizational project. Turkey is not a candidate to be a member of the EU, short-term or long" (ibid.: 109).

While these remarks received a great deal of negative publicity in the European press, their authoritative sources also legitimized the more detailed articulation of similar views. In *De Standaard*, Christopher Boval underscored the importance of religious difference, which was aggravated by the election of the Islamist Welfare Party to power (*De Standaard*, March 8, 1997). In *Le Figaro*, Jean Claude Casanova drew attention to the dangers of "denying" the historical difference between Europe and Turkey, which entails "forcing it to hide only to resurface with rage and passion" (*Le Figaro*, February 19, 1997). In *Die Welt*, Heinrich Lummer argued that "European identity would be endangered with massive Muslim immigration" (*Die Welt*, March 25, 1997).

On the other hand, others were pointing to Turkey's acquired differences. Luxembourg's Prime Minister Jean-Claude Juncker stated in 1997 that a country "where torture is still a common practice cannot have a seat at the table of the European Union" (Phillips 2004). In a Topical and Urgent Debate on Turkey in the European Parliament, Green (PSE) also based his objections to Turkey on Turkey's acquired differences, specifically in its foreign policy towards Cyprus.

It is not normal to retain 35000 occupying troops on the sovereign territory of an independent state … This behavior is barbaric, medieval, and cannot be tolerated. (EP 1996b)

I argue that, as a consequence of these competing discourses, EU–Turkey relations are uniquely embedded in an identity interaction in which Turkey occupies a liminal position with respect to the European collective identity. Turner (1995: 95) defines liminals as "entities that are neither here nor there; they are betwixt and between the positions assigned and arranged by law, custom, convention, and ceremonial." According to Turner, liminals appear as threatening to those concerned with the maintenance of structure, because, as entities that fall in-between, they challenge the categories and hierarchies embedded in that structure (Turner 1995: 109). Along similar lines, Norton (1988) has argued that liminal groups, such as subcultures, minority groups, dissidents, have a two-fold function or significance in the constitution of national identities. First of all, by being at once other and like, they serve as mirrors for nations, and provide the occasion for their initial definition. Secondly, and after they have prompted the polity to make a clear differentiation between self and other, liminals undermine that differentiation "by providing an illustration of a condition in which the like and unlike, the alien and the appropriate are inextricably entangled" (Norton 1988: 54). The likeness of the liminal threatens the dissolution of the self in the other, and according to Norton (1988: 55), this gives rise to the identification of the liminal as wholly unlike and threatening.

In the late 1990s, Turkey–EU relations were characterized by various scholars as "a complex, tense, at times mutually disappointing relationship" (Onis 2000: 466), as following "an uneasy cyclical trajectory" (Onis 2000: 468), as "relations [that] have gone badly wrong" (Buzan and Diez 1999), as "a roller coaster relationship" (Yesilada 2002: 95), and as a "relationship under fire" (Wood 1999). In this chapter, I show that in the late 1990s it was Turkey's liminal identity position which formed the basis of the meanings and understandings that have made EU–Turkey relations complex, tense and cyclical. After the 1999 Helsinki decision to grant Turkey candidacy status, Turkey's liminality, as will be explained in the next chapter, has become modified and less pronounced, and this has facilitated important changes in Turkey's domestic politics and relations with the EU. However, it is important to recognize that Turkey's liminal identity position continues to shape the meanings and understandings that govern EU–Turkey relations.

In the context of these competing discourses, EU has kept a fluctuating social distance towards Turkey. This ambivalent orientation resulted from the fact that different social distances (association–dissociation) are securing of different aspects of European identity (inclusive–exclusive). While complete dissociation from Turkey, in the form of marking Turkey as ineligible for membership, secures the exclusive aspects of European identity as a bound civilizational and cultural project, it does make its inclusive aspects more insecure. Conversely, while conditional association with Turkey secures inclusive aspects of European identity as champion and promoter of democracy and human rights, it does make its exclusive aspects more insecure. At the same time, non-conditional association with Turkey also makes inclusive aspects of European identity insecure as long as Turkey's deficiencies in democracy and human rights continue.

As a result of the intricate relationship between these competing identity discourses, EU–Turkey relations have had a cyclical, two-step forward, one-step backward trajectory. The relations were stalled in 1989 in response to the negative response of the European Union to Turkey's membership application, received a boost with the 1995 Customs Union Agreement, slowed down again when Turkey was excluded from the list of candidate states by the 1997 Luxembourg European Council, moved ahead with the 1999 Helsinki European Council's decision to grant Turkey candidacy status, were held up when the 2002 Copenhagen European Council postponed the decision to start accession negotiations, accelerated with the 2004 decision to start accession negotiations without delay, and were hindered with the 2006 decision to stall negotiations in eight chapters due to Turkey's failure to honor its commitments to Cyprus in the Additional Protocol to the Customs Union. While it is true that the EU's Eastern enlargement also did not proceed as quickly as the CEES had hoped (K. Smith 2004), the delays and set-backs in Turkey's membership quest were always tinged with a skepticism regarding Turkey's place in Europe altogether.

At each encounter in EU–Turkey relations, decisions on furthering/stalling relations were closely interlinked with alternative discourses on European identity. When the Customs Union Agreement with Turkey was being debated in the European Parliament, Green (PSE) warned that "a no vote can only harm those very people on the ground in Turkey who fight to give their dignity and respect to the concept of Turkish democracy" (EP 1995). In other words, Green argued against dissociating further away from Turkey because that would disable the EU from serving as a reference point for the human rights struggles in Turkey, damaging the EU's inclusive identity credentials as a promoter of democracy and human rights. On the other hand, Roth, speaking on behalf of Greens, justified their affirmative position on the Customs Union with the argument "for us there is no question that Turkey is a part of Europe and our Europe must not and cannot be the stronghold of the Christian West" (EP 1995). With this statement, Roth rightly expressed the concern that dissociation from Turkey would strengthen exclusive aspects of European identity.

Aware that the pending decision of dissociation from Turkey would be framed as validating an exclusive identity for the EU, Luxembourg's Prime Minister Juncker, as the holder of the EU's rotating presidency in the latter half of 1997, found it necessary to make the following distinction to explain the Union's decision not to grant Turkey candidacy status: "We want Turkey to understand that we are not a club of Christians but we are, to use the same terminology, a club with certain rules" (EP 1997b). Juncker represented the prevailing view in the European Union at the time that further association with Turkey would dilute the values and rules of the European Community, and thereby threaten "Europe" as an inclusive identity. As the Luxembourg European Council concluded, Turkey had not satisfied the political and economic conditions for candidacy, including "human rights, respect for minorities, stable and satisfactory relations with Greece, and a political settlement in Cyprus" (European Council 1997).

Yet Roth (V) believed that with the exclusion of Turkey from the list of candidate states, the EU is constructing itself an exclusive identity, based on Christianity. As she remarked in the same debate in the European Parliament:

Is not the true background to the exclusion of Turkey the question of the identity the European Union claims? The issue of the Christian occident versus the Islamic Orient; religion as the new element which builds entirely new walls. (EP 1997b)

And those who advocated an exclusive European identity argued that the "real reasons" behind the exclusion of Turkey must be explicitly stated. As an independent MEP, Vanhecke, remarked during the debate in the European Parliament:

Europe has never gone so far as to say, or never wanted to say, that Turkey cannot qualify for membership of the European Union because it is simply not a European country ... This ambiguous attitude is the crux of the problem. (EP 1997)

An exchange between Luxembourg's Foreign Minister Jacques Poos and Roth at the end of the debate in the European Parliament well indicates how the liminal identity position of Turkey makes it difficult for the EU to settle on a certain social distance with respect to Turkey that would be securing of European identity. Poos remarked that "one of the curious things" about the debate "was the reaction from Mrs Roth of the Green Group ... It was rather surprising for me to hear criticism with regard to this from a group which I thought cared about human rights and international law" (EP 1997). While Roth frames the decision of the Luxembourg European Council as racist, Poos argues that such criticism is actually undermining the principles of human rights and international law that European identity is based upon. Thus, Turkey is not securing of European identity either when it is associated with or dissociated from.

Following Luxembourg, the view that dissociation from Turkey undermined the inclusive aspects of European identity began to regain prevalence. In a European Parliament Debate on Turkey in October 1999, Martinez from the Party of European Socialists expressed his concern that "Europe" has lost its credibility in its interaction with Turkey:

> We need Turkey ... to regain the credibility and universality of the Project of European construction. A large secular state with a majority Muslim population will prove that the Europe we are building is not a Europe with a Christian outlook. (EP 1999a)

Echoing Martinez, Duff from the European Liberal, Democratic, and Reformist group (ELDR) argued in a following debate that "where Europe stops should not be a matter of geography but of liberal values and democratic practices" (EP 1999b). Yet others pointed out that association with outsider countries to validate an inclusive European identity has to have a limit. The President of the European Commission Prodi concluded the debate on a cautionary note that the EU will soon need to decide on the "nature" of Europe before it is pressured with new demands of inclusion:

> We cannot respond to the albeit reasonable requests of countries asking to join Europe. Where would these requests end? Why should countries in Asia, for example, not apply? (EP 1999b)

As another dimension of Turkey's liminal identity position, Turkey's sustained resistance to the alternative constructions of its identity makes it more difficult for the EU to settle on a certain social distance with respect to Turkey. Successive Turkish governments have actively resisted constructions of Turkey's identity as inherently different from Europe by producing counter-arguments that construct Turkey as sharing Europe's collective identity. For example, they emphasize that the Ottoman Empire was a European empire and long regarded to be part of the European states system, that modern Turkey has consciously adopted a European vocation, and that it is the most secular and democratic Islamic country. In campaigning for the conclusion of the Customs Union Agreement, the Turkish Prime Minister Tansu Ciller

(1995) argued in the Washington Post:

> A Europe without Turkey would be a continent that is in denial of its
> 3000 year history and culture. Turkey and the Turks have been a part
> of the continental way of life for centuries. What is new is the idea
> that Turkey is not European.

This statement is in direct contrast to the arguments, including those
previously cited in this chapter, advanced by the proponents of an
exclusive European identity that Turkey is historically and culturally
non-European. Turkish political leaders have also resisted the constructions of Turkey's identity as different by framing such constructions to
be racist and exclusionary on religious grounds. They have thereby
sought to appeal to the sensitivities of the proponents of an inclusive
European identity based on universal principles. For example, in the
period leading to the Luxembourg European Council, Turkey's Foreign
Minister Ciller called on European leaders "not to build a cultural Berlin
Wall" (*De Standaard*, March 8, 1997). Following the EU's decision not to
include Turkey as a candidate, Turkish Prime Minister Yilmaz
commented to the New York Times:

> Even if we satisfy all their conditions, they will not change their
> minds about our membership. The reasons they put forth do not
> reflect the true reason behind Turkey's exclusion, which is religious
> discrimination. (*Milliyet*, December 16, 1997)

In contrast to Morocco's, Turkey's counter-arguments resonate more
strongly in Europe, making Turkey's resistance noticeable. Following the
1997 Luxembourg European Council, the fear that, by excluding Turkey,
Europe was turning into a neo-Christendom was widely articulated in
various circles in Europe. It was argued, for example, in a leading article
in *The Independent* that Europe should "wrestle with the long shadow of
Hassan," the leading Janissary who stormed the walls of Constantinople
in 1453:

> Why is Turkey different from Estonia, Slovenia, Bulgaria and
> Romania? The first, and very important answer is human rights. But
> this is not the whole story, and it is worth pursuing further the reluc-
> tance to admit Turkey even into the EU's waiting room. For many,
> "not yet" is code for "never," and the issue of human rights usefully
> postpones facing up to other reasons. What, then, is the real

difference? It is that Turkey is a Muslim country ... Europe, as the region bordering on the Mediterranean, has a much longer history than the land-mass of north and west Europe. It is a history divided by religion, but it is a division like the division of Europe by communism which the EU could overcome. (*The Independent*, March 13, 1998)

Turkey's resistance to the construction of its identity makes the EU's dissociation from Turkey more difficult to legitimize. Through its resistance, Turkey upsets the establishment of clear boundaries between Europe and non-Europe, and has a subversive impact on the exclusive aspects of European identity.

Until 1999, Turkey also resisted the construction of its identity as different on the basis of acquired characteristics. While resisting the construction of Turkey's identity as non-European, Turkish governments have, unlike their counterparts in Central and Eastern Europe, displayed an ambivalent attitude towards the EU's conditions for membership. There is a well-established identity discourse in Turkey that constructs Europe as a threat, flourishing on memories of the Ottoman Empire's dismemberment by European powers at the end of World War 1. Paradoxically, this identity discourse is reproduced by those who seem to advocate a closer relationship with Europe, to question the legitimacy and validity of Europe's conditions for membership, such as minority rights for Kurds or the settlement of the Cyprus problem.

Every time the European Union has stalled relations with Turkey on the grounds of human rights and democracy, this construction of Europe as a threat has been activated in Turkey. For example, in December 1994, the European Parliament suspended Customs Union negotiations with Turkey following the sentencing of MPs from the pro-Kurdish Democracy Party on the charges of separatism. On December 15, the European Parliament issued a resolution "condemning all aspects of the trial and the verdict ... as a persistent violation of the principles of Turkey's representative and pluralist democracy and of fundamental human rights" (EP 1994).

In response to the suspension of the negotiations, Ismail Cem, who was later to serve as Turkey's Foreign Minister between 1997 and 2002, wrote in his column in the Turkish daily *Sabah*:

Have we really spent all this effort in vain? Did we pay all this price for Westernization so that its doors would be shut to our face one day? ... The reason for [Turkey's] rejection is the further degrading charge of 'human rights violation'. Human rights violations, democracy deficit, Kurdish problem, etc. What is the place of all these in the Western mind? The Western mind takes all factors into account when making a decision, but this process is always removed from emotional considerations. The presence of economic interest always rules out other considerations. If EU decides not to initiate the Customs Union with Turkey, that means that plans are being made for re-structuring the balance of power in the Middle East and the redrawing of its map. Only if there is such a motive, can the Western mind decide to give up on a market like Turkey for human rights. (Cem 1994)

This reaction by Cem well illustrates the prevalent perception of the EU's human rights concerns in Turkey at the time, which was that these conditions, cloaked in humanitarian and normative terms, actually represent Europe's strategic agenda of excluding, weakening or even disintegrating Turkey (Onis 2000; Yesilada 2002). As evidence of Europe's ulterior motives, the articulators of such views pointed to the uncertainty surrounding Turkey's membership in the Community. At the time, an MP from the opposition Motherland Party similarly argued that Europe is being hypocritical in posing the Democracy Party trial and human rights as reasons: "If these were not the case, they would have found other reasons. Christian fundamentalism is at the root of all Western hypocrisy" (*Dunya*, December 22, 1994).

In the period leading to the 1997 Luxembourg European Council, the pro-Islamist Welfare Party MPs submitted an inquiry to the Turkish Grand National Assembly (TGNA), where they questioned the "ulterior motives" of the European Union, and Turkey's continued insistence on becoming a member:

Even though our country is much more developed economically and politically, it has been placed behind the states in Central and Eastern Europe. The real cause of this double-standard – and I think differently on this issue from my fellow MPs – is the cultural and religious factor. The aim is not human rights or democratization, but to obtain concessions. Southern Cyprus does not want to join the EU for economic reasons. Its aims are political, it wants to achieve Enosis [union with Greece] indirectly through the European Union. They want to encircle Turkey from the South. (TGNA 1997)

Thus, in the late 1990s, Turkey's liminality served as a discursive position within which Turkey could rationalize not fulfilling the conditions, while fervently pursuing membership in the EU. The debates about the Europeanness of Turkey were widely perceived as evidence of Europe's reluctance to accept the country as a member, of the double standards the Union applied, and even of an inherent historical animosity. This allowed those in the elite who had no interest in change to fend off legitimate criticisms of its shortcomings in human rights and democracy. It also tied the hands of reformers (Diez and Rumelili 2004). Once Europe had been constructed as hostile and hypocritical towards Turkey, the defense of European criticisms as legitimate would have brought charges of complicity in this hostility and hypocrisy. As a result, apart from some half-hearted changes, the EU's membership conditionality failed to instigate a reform process in Turkey as it had done throughout much of Central and Eastern Europe. While it may be argued that the representation of EU–Turkey relations within the discourse of conspiracy constituted merely instrumental use of rhetoric by the political elite to deflect criticism, it is necessary to note that this strategy would not have succeeded had Turkey not been in a liminal position with respect to Europe. In the absence of a European discourse that constructed Turkey as inherently different, the construction of Europe as hostile would not have so widely resonated.

By questioning and resisting the conditions of the European "community," while aspiring for membership, Turkey had a subversive impact on the inclusive aspects of European identity. Turkey's resistant stance towards the conditions placed on its membership made association with Turkey more difficult to legitimize. Thus, liminality also explains how the EU could justify dissociation from Turkey when it has largely failed in socializing Turkey into its norms, in comparison with its success in Central and Eastern Europe. Perceptions and representations of Turkey as an identity threat to Europe justified dissociation from Turkey, which in turn reinforced perceptions and representations of Europe as an identity threat to Turkey that justified the non-fulfillment of the EU's conditions for membership. In the late 1990s, EU–Turkey relations were thus caught in a vicious circle that disabled the EU from exerting positive influence on the political and human rights situation in Turkey.

As will be explained in the next chapter, an important implication of the 1999 Helsinki European Council's decision to grant Turkey candidacy status has been the breaking of this vicious circle by discrediting the perceptions of double standards and enmity that the status quo elite relied upon. Turkish policymakers and opinionmakers began to acknowledge and recognize the construction of Turkey as different from and inferior to Europe in acquired characteristics, and undertake rounds of sweeping reforms to attain European standards. This has modified – but not eliminated – Turkey's liminal position as Turkey's practices became securing of inclusive aspects of European identity and legitimized association with Turkey.

But in the period prior to 1999, which has been the focus of this chapter, the interaction of the EU with Turkey was situated in the three dimensional framework of self/other interaction simultaneously in two ways: inclusive identity/acquired difference–resistance–dissociation and exclusive identity/inherent difference–resistance–dissociation. Demonstrating the validity of my framework of self/other interaction, these interactions were both characterized by Othering, the perception and representation of Turkey as an identity threat. Discourses of threat are very prevalent in all encounters between the EU and Turkey in this time period. This can, for example, be clearly seen in the December 1995 European Parliament debate, where the human rights situation in Turkey was perceived and represented as threatening to European identity. In commenting on the human rights in Turkey, the MEPs underscored how Turkey "threatens ... our [Europe's] cohesion, the basis of our moral authority," how they "find it difficult to countenance such a close and sensitive relationship [with Turkey]," and the need to defend "the ideals, visions, and struggles of the peoples for dignity and democracy" (EP 1995).

Turkey's liminal position created a greater necessity to clarify and articulate the differences between Turkey and Europe. Its liminal position also made possible the representation of Turkey as threatening to European identity, both when it is potentially included in and when it is excluded from the EU. The EU's relationship with Turkey was almost always represented in terms of "defining the frontiers" and "defending the borders" of Europe. All possible responses towards Turkey were hence enveloped within discourses of danger and served to underscore Turkey's differences from Europe. Even the case for Turkey's inclusion is a negative one based on the potentially undesirable consequences of its exclusion. In relation to Turkey, we see a defensive EU that fears losing its credibility and the basic principles and values of its civilization by associating with Turkey. In other words, the non-definition of its boundary in relation to Turkey did not turn the EU into a postmodern collectivity, but in fact reinforced its modern character.

Beyond enlargement

The EU conducts its relations with states outside its immediate sphere of enlargement on a variety of bases. The EU's proximity policy with the Mediterranean and the Middle East is conducted through the Euro–Mediterranean Partnership (EMP), which now compromises 25 EU members and 10 Mediterranean partners, Algeria, Egypt, Israel, Jordan, Lebanon, Morocco, Palestinian Authority, Syria, Tunisia and Turkey. Within the EMP, the EU negotiates bilateral association agreements with various characteristics with each Mediterranean partner state, and initiates political, economic, and cultural dialogue at the regional level.

With the states in Eastern Europe and Central Asia, the EU has negotiated Partnership and Cooperation Agreements (PCAs), which are "legal frameworks, based on the respect of democratic principles and human rights, setting out the political, economic and trade relationship between the EU and its partner countries." There are currently PCAs in force with Armenia, Azerbaijan, Georgia, Kazakhstan, Kyrgyzstan, Moldova, Mongolia, Russia, Ukraine, and Uzbekistan. In addition, the EU has adopted Common Strategies to structure its relations with Russia and Ukraine. Also, implemented within the framework of the EU's PCA with Russia, the Northern Dimension aims to address specific challenges and opportunities in the Baltic and Arctic Sea regions and develop cross-regional cooperation to prevent "the emergence of new dividing lines in Europe."

Since 2004, the Mediterranean partners as well as Moldova, Ukraine, and Belarus have been included in the new European Neighborhood policy (ENP), whose objective is to forge greater political, security, economic, and cultural cooperation with the EU's neighboring countries after the recent enlargement.

Despite their variety, these institutional arrangements structuring the EU's external relations all produce a hierarchy between the European "selves" and non-European "others." While the EMP produces a clear distinction between members and partners, the ENP similarly reiterates a distinction between members and neighbors, and these institutional arrangements, while furthering contact and cooperation, also serve to reproduce the boundary and foreclose its future contestation. In addition, the EU's external relations are predicated on security concerns broadly defined, and serve to construct the non-EU space as a source of instability, poverty, crime and illegal immigration. According to Pace (2004: 303), "the nature of the EU's security discourse on the Mediterranean raises an identity division between those included in the European project and those excluded from this process." Therefore, these institutional arrangements may serve to heighten, rather than remedy, the sense of exclusion and discrimination of outsider states, especially in spaces where the EU boundary is not socially accepted from within and without and is subject to contestation.

There is an ongoing debate in official and scholarly circles regarding the costs and benefits of defining the EU's borders or leaving them as fuzzy (Smith 2005; Christiansen *et al.* 2000; Zielonka 2002). The EU's ambiguous frontiers actually function as a double-edged sword. On the one hand, the ambiguity of the boundaries serve as an inducement to outsider states – even if they are outside the immediate sphere of enlargement – to undertake certain reforms to fulfill the inclusive identity criteria and possibly re-define the boundaries of the community. Therefore, ambiguous frontiers enable the EU to extend its influence beyond its immediate sphere of enlargement. On the other hand, the ambiguity of boundaries legitimizes possible claims of belonging to the regional community raised by various outsider states. Because the boundary is not fixed, each wave of enlargement is followed by the emergence of a new group of states on the boundaries of the community. If their claims of belonging are not met with a perspective for membership, this potentially leads to charges of exclusion and discrimination and creates the basis for an identity conflict.

Liminality is not a condition that is unique to the case of Turkey. In fact, the EU's hybrid identity as partly inclusive and partly exclusive creates ample potential for states to be situated in liminal positions with respect to the EU. Another candidate could be Russia (Neumann 1999: 67). According to Neumann (1999), historically, Russians have been simultaneously regarded as Europeans because of their Christianity, but deemed contaminated and Asiatic by virtue of the existence of Muslim peoples within Russia. With the end of the Cold War, Russia has been put in an ambiguous position with respect to the community formation process in Europe; while no longer the enemy, neither is it grouped with the CEES deemed to be parts of the future European self. A widespread assertion in European identity discourse that "Russia is in Europe but not of Europe" attests to Russia's partly self/partly other status.

Although those in Russia advocating a closer relationship with the EU and NATO have tried to resist the ambiguous positioning of Russia's identity by producing counter-arguments that situated it unequivocally in Europe,[11] Russian leaders have not sought EU membership. This constitutes the fundamental difference between the cases of Turkey and Russia. Russian officials in fact seek to restructure their relations with the EU on an equal basis in the form of a strategic partnership. As a result,

Russia does not contest the construction of its identity as different and dissociates itself from Europe.

IV. Conclusion

Does the EU replicate the nation-state form in terms of externalizing difference and legitimizing a violent relationship with others or has it succeeded in constructing a post-modern community where self/other distinctions are blurred not only within the community but also in relation to its outside? Building on the framework developed in the previous chapter, this chapter has demonstrated that the EU's interactions with various states on its periphery demonstrate a diversity that cannot be captured in terms of the two alternatives of modern and postmodern modes of differentiation. The EU promotes a partly inclusive/partly exclusive collective identity. In all of the EU's interactions with outside states, there is production of difference, but, while the CEES are distinguished on the basis of acquired characteristics, others like Morocco are constructed as different on the basis of their inherent characteristics. The potential for Othering is realized in the case of its interaction with liminals, states that are distinguished on the basis of both inherent and acquired characteristics, such as Turkey. While the CEES recognize the construction of their identity as different on the basis of acquired characteristics and Morocco cannot effectively resist the construction of its identity as inherently different, Turkey resists and challenges the construction of its identity. Because its interactions with outside states all carry the potential for Othering, the EU does not qualify as a postmodern collectivity. At the same time, the EU cannot be said to be characterized by a modern mode of differentiation because it invokes an inclusive identity in relation to some states.

In the previous chapter, I had argued that self/other interactions are not static, they are continuously negotiated between self and other. The next chapter of this book, therefore, focuses on the significant case of Turkey, with which the EU has an interaction that is characterized by Othering. It analyzes how Turkey negotiated its liminal identity position so as to make it possible for the EU to declare it as a candidate in 1999 and how Turkey's liminality has been modified in the course of EU–Turkey relations after 1999.

4
Negotiating "Europe": EU and Turkey

I. Introduction

The institutional relations between the EU and Turkey intensified after the declaration of Turkey's candidacy in 1999 (Muftuler-Bac 2005). In line with the pre-accession strategy for Turkey, the Commission prepared an Accession Partnership Document in November 2000, which the European Council adopted in March 2001. In turn, Turkey submitted its National Program for the Adoption of the EU acquis in March 2001. The 2002 Copenhagen European Council decided to review Turkey's candidacy in 2004, committing itself to starting accession negotiations with Turkey "without delay" if the Copenhagen political criteria had been fulfilled. In May 2003, the European Commission adopted a revised Accession Partnership Document for Turkey. Also in July 2003, the Turkish government revised its National Program on the Adoption of the Acquis, reflecting the political reforms already adopted. The European Commission's Progress Report of October 6, 2004 recommended the opening of Turkish accession negotiations (European Commission 2004). In line with this report, the 2004 Brussels European Council decided to start accession negotiations with Turkey on October 3, 2005, provided that Turkey signed an Additional Protocol, extending the Customs Union Agreement to the ten new member states, including Cyprus.

Extending the Customs Union Agreement to Cyprus was a difficult political move for Turkey, given its position in the Cyprus conflict. With the 2004 Annan Plan for the reunification of the island having been approved by the Turkish Cypriots and rejected by the Greek Cypriots, and Greek Cypriots having become EU members in spite of that, Turkey considered further concessions on the Cyprus question to be unfair and politically unviable. Turkey nevertheless signed the Additional Protocol on July 29, 2005, but simultaneously issued a declaration that the Protocol did not amount to the official recognition of Cyprus. The negotiating framework for Turkey's accession contained special provisions that indicated the EU's ambivalence with respect to Turkey's full membership. It was underlined for example that the negotiations would be open-ended, which meant that their outcome could not be guaranteed beforehand. The framework also allowed for the possibility that the EU might include long transition periods, derogations, specific arrangements, and permanent safeguard clauses (European Commission 2005). The negotiations were formally opened on October 3, 2005, and began in practice in July 2006. Meanwhile, Turkey did not ratify and start to implement the Additional Protocol with respect to Cyprus, and showed inadequate progress and even regress on issues of freedom of expression and minority rights. On November 29, 2006 the Commission recommended to partially suspend membership negotiations with Turkey due to lack of progress on the Cyprus issue (European Commission 2006). On December 11, 2006 EU foreign ministers decided to follow the Commission's recommendations and suspend talks with Turkey on eight of the 35 negotiating areas.

This chapter analyzes the process of identity negotiation that has made these intensified relations between EU and Turkey possible. If the discourses of difference and threat were so prevalent in EU–Turkey interaction prior to 1999, how was it possible for the EU to declare Turkey as a candidate at the Helsinki European Council in 1999 and start accession negotiations with Turkey in 2005? It is hard to explain this policy change if one focuses solely on the reproductive aspects of discourse. As I had argued in the previous chapter, this decision has modified, but not eliminated, Turkey's liminal identity position as Turkey came to be constituted as less threatening to inclusive aspects of European identity. This chapter traces the process whereby the discursive practices of the EU and Turkey simultaneously reproduced and transformed the discursive structure governing their interaction, as each articulation added new linkages to fluid discursive structures while subtracting others. The chapter also analyzes the ways in which and the extent to which Turkey's liminality continues to structure EU–Turkey relations in the period since 1999. Finally, I return to the question raised in Chapter 3 and discuss whether the changes in EU–Turkey relations have constituted the EU as a postmodern collectivity.

II. Negotiating liminality

Liminality is a historically contingent discursive position. That liminality is not an objective structural condition is an important point to make, especially with regard to the case of Turkey, because the much-too-frequent representation of Turkey as a "torn" state and society makes it seem as if Turkey's liminality is inherent (Huntington 1996). Turkey is often represented as a country of contradictions; one that is geographically situated both in Europe and in Asia, where a predominantly Islamic society coexists with a staunchly secular westernizing state, which is founded on the rejection of its Ottoman and Islamic heritage. Turkish society is represented as divided between Islamic fundamentalists and secularists, Westernizers and those seeking closer relations with the Islamic and Turkic countries. "The most accurate way to describe Turkey," according to Muftuler-Bac (1997: 18), "is as a country caught between two continents, between two traditions, two trends of history."

What is important to note here is that "torn" is an ascribed condition, that presupposes the existence of a discourse that constructs these characteristics as incompatible and mutually exclusive, such that one is either European or Asian, Islamist or Westernizer, but cannot simultaneously be both.[12] According to Robins (1996: 65), Europe is unable to come to terms with Turkey's "hybridity," which is "so equivocal in Turkish culture" but simultaneously "so unsettling for Europe." Turkey is constituted as torn and divided only through the reproduction of a discourse that constructs Europe/Asia, West/East, and West/Islam as inherently incompatible and mutually exclusive identities.

As the following analysis will show, such a construction of Europe/Asia, West/Islam as inherently incompatible and mutually exclusive identities has been very prevalent in EU–Turkey interaction, and indeed has formed its very basis. Actually, EU–Turkey interaction carries a lot of potential with regard to the transcendence of these very entrenched identity dichotomies. As both like and unlike, within and without, betwixt and in-between categories, liminals are sites where the dichotomies of identity/difference and inside/outside break down, and therefore they hold the discursive opportunity for the recognition of the liminal as simultaneously other and like. Turkey as the liminal exposes a space of overlap that challenges the exclusivity of the self/other, and thus provides the opportunity for a creative response to the identity/difference predicament (Inayatullah and Blaney 2004). The recognition of the liminal as simultaneously other and like would develop when, in the negotiation of the liminal position between self and other, the identity discourses come to reflect the ambiguous position of the other and be "at home" with this ambiguity. However, as the following analysis will show, such a recognition has not developed in EU–Turkey interaction, even after the declaration of Turkey's candidacy. The construction of Europe/Asia and West/Islam as inherently incompatible and mutually exclusive identities is the fundamental barrier to the elimination of Turkey's liminality as it forms the basis of the construction of Turkey as inherently different from Europe.

Dating back to the very beginning of institutional relations between Turkey and the EU, the question of whether Turkey is in Europe or in Asia has been posed as a dichotomous question. In Europe and in Turkey, the advocates of closer relations have sought to situate Turkey in Europe, and the opponents in Asia; however, neither have been willing to acknowledge that the answer is actually both. During the signing ceremony of the 1963 Ankara Agreement, the President of the European Commission, Walter Hallstein, declared that "the main significance of this event is to underscore that Turkey is a part of Europe. This is not a simple restatement of historical and geographical facts, but the contemporary way of confirming a reality that goes much beyond." However, when the President of the European Council, Joseph Lunz, was pressured during the press conference with the question "is the territory we are in right now Europe or Asia?" he replied "yes, this is Asia. But political and economic agreements go beyond geographical boundaries" (*Cumhuriyet*, September 13, 1963).

Commenting on the Ankara Agreement in the Turkish daily *Aksam*, commentator Vecdi Unal wrote:

> Our association with the EEC testifies our Europeanness, our will to Westernize, and the recognition of that will by Europeans ... Membership in the Common Market will save us from admiring Europe from afar and as an outsider, but will enable us to fully partake in its way of life. Integration with the Common Market will resolve the question of whether we are European or Asian, that is still being debated internally and externally, even today. (*Aksam*, September 13, 1963)

In his remarks, Turkey's deputy Prime Minister, Turhan Feyzioglu, also agreed:

> The significance of our association with the EEC goes beyond its short-term benefits. With this agreement, Turkey's long-term efforts to become a European state have recorded yet another victory ... With this agreement, it has been once more affirmed that the boundaries of Europe pass from our eastern and southern borders. (*Aksam*, September 15, 1963)

However, contrary to the expectations of commentators, the question of whether Turkey is European or Asian must not have been resolved, for twenty-two years later, the conclusion of the Customs Union Agreement was celebrated in Turkey with very similar commentary. The leading article of the national daily *Sabah* argued that: "Turkey is becoming a first league European country after 150 years of going back and forth between the East and the West as a Third World country on Europe's periphery" (*Sabah*, December 14, 1995). Another daily, *Yeni Yuzyil*, expressed similar themes: "Be it by conquest during the times of the Ottoman Empire, or by its self-chosen vocation in its republican history, Turkey has been in Europe and its European identity is about to be accepted by the West" (*Yeni Yuzyil*, December 13, 1995). In 2004, the commentaries on the EU's decision to start accession negotiations were similar, if not more cautious: "We have turned a critical corner on our way to entering Europe" (Akyol 2004).

The question of Turkey's Europeanness was not resolved in Europe either. Contrary to the debates on CEES, one cannot encounter an unequivocal statement that Turkey is "European in outlook, history, culture, and geography." While, according to van den Broek, Prague is "the center of Europe," according to Verheugen, Istanbul is "a crossroad of cultures and civilizations" (Sjursen 2002: 504). In 2000, it was still argued that closer relations with the "will establish Turkey's European identity" (Solana 2000 cited in Sjursen 2002: 505). In objecting to the possibility of Turkey's membership in 2002, former French President Giscard D'Estaing argued that: "Turkey's capital is not in Europe, 95% of its population lives outside of Europe and it is not a European country" (BBC News, November 8, 2002). According to Koenig *et al.* (2006: 150), in the representations of European mass media, "Turks may be acknowledged as being in Europe, but as long as they are Muslims, they are not accepted as being of Europe."

In addition to the Europe/Asia dichotomy, the discourses underlying EU–Turkey relations also construct Europe and Islam as inherently incompatible and mutually exclusive identities. As perceptions of the threat of Islamic fundamentalism rose after the mid 1980s, strategic arguments made to propagate closer EU–Turkey relations always portrayed Turkey as a bulwark against Islamic fundamentalism. For example, in 1995, Turkish Prime Minister Tansu Ciller chose to build Turkey's case for the Customs Union Agreement as such:

> A strong and prosperous Turkey that is well-integrated in the European way of life will become a foothold of stability in a region

torn by religious and ethnic hostilities, a model against the widespread hatred and extremism. Certain movements in the Middle East are still a source of anxiety. One of them is religious fundamentalism. I believe that Turkey can make an important contribution on that point. Turkey has a devout Muslim population. But this population is at the same time European and very much moderate'. (Ciller 1995)

This argument has resonated very strongly with the European public opinion. In the European Parliament debate on the Customs Union Agreement with Turkey, Schwaiger (PPE), the rapporteur on Turkey, underlined the very same point: "Turkey plays a central stabilizing role in the economic development of the Mediterranean region and acts as a natural counterbalance to the medieval structures and behavior of its fundamentalist neighbors" (EP 1995). Schwaiger's ideas were shared by many other commentators, who, in various European newspapers, have underscored the strategic benefits that Customs Union would bring by curbing Islamist pressures in Turkey. While Martin Peter argued in *Die Presse* that Turkey–EU Customs Union will halt the Islamists (December 12, 1995), Caroline Sauthey observed in the *Financial Times* that the members of the European Parliament are voting under the shadow of Islam (December 13, 1995).

Although the "shadow of Islam" has succeeded in swaying the European public opinion in favor of the Customs Union Agreement, it is misplaced and self-defeating as an identity-politics strategy. First of all, it makes a case for Turkey based not on its similarities but on the threatening possibility of its further differentiation. It reproduces an understanding of Islam as potentially threatening to Europe. Even though the threat is qualified as "fundamentalism," the Middle East is equated with Islam and characterized as having a propensity for extremism. In contrast to the potentially extremist Islam in the Middle East, the Islam in Turkey is presented as moderate and "European." Therefore, repeating a common pattern in applicant rhetoric (Neumann 1998), Turkey constructs itself as similar to (or less different from) Europe by differentiating itself from its neighbors to the East. However, within this discourse, while more similar to Europe, as a Muslim country Turkey is constructed as always vulnerable to fundamentalism.

As a result of this construction of Europe and Islam as antithetical identities, Turkey came to be constituted as a country torn between its European orientation and Islamic identity. Yet, after approving the Customs Union Agreement as a guarantee against Islamic fundamentalism in Turkey, the European politicians were shocked that, in the early parliamentary elections in December 1995, the Welfare Party known for its Islamist stance got the plurality of votes. The Parliament resolution issued in response to the elections stated that "notwithstanding the vote registered by Islamic fundamentalists, the results of the election clearly showed that a vast majority of the population rejected political extremism and opted for maintaining relations with the European Union" (EP 1996c). As a result of the thin distribution of votes across political parties, the coalitions not including the Welfare Party proved to be unsustainable. After a series of failed minority governments, Tansu Ciller, who had presented the Customs Union Agreement as a guarantee against Islamic fundamentalism, ended up building a coalition government with the Welfare Party in July 1996. This came as a shock to the members of the European Parliament:

> Today there is an Islamic government in Turkey although we were told that by voting in favor of the customs union we would prevent the Islamic faction from coming to power. (EP 1996d)

The dominant reasoning behind the approval of the Customs Union and the reaction to the Islamist government in Turkey reflected in the above quote represent a dichotomous understanding of identities, such that one is either a European or an Islamist. It is important to note that this understanding was not only produced in Europe. Tansu Ciller reproduced the same dichotomy in the identity-politics strategy she pursued towards the EU, and it was also reflected in the Welfare Party's policy position with respect to the EU. To appeal to an Islamic constituency in Turkey, the party's leader, Necmettin Erbakan, saw it necessary to criticize the Customs Union, and vow to establish an Islamic common market:

> Of course, we will hold those who put Turkey in the Customs Union with this slavery accord responsible. Look at them! They look like the infidels who greeted the British troops with flowers during Istanbul's occupation. (*Milliyet*, December 14, 1995)

Thus, through the discursive constitution of Europe and Islam as inherently incompatible and mutually exclusive identities, Turkey became constituted as an imaginary battlefield for the zero-sum conflict between Europe and Islam. In this understanding, Turkey could become either more European or more Islamist, but could not be both. After Turkey was excluded from the list of candidate states at the Luxembourg Council, *The Times* ran the headline of "Kohl's notion of Christian

Europe leaves Turks turning to Mecca" (March 9, 1998). *The Daily Telegraph* warned that if Ankara turned its attention eastwards and "orientalized," this would have enormous geopolitical implications for the balance of power between the West and the emerging Muslim nations (June 17, 1998). Comments such as these are clearly structured by a discourse that constructs Europe and Islam as distinct identities that are in opposition.

Liminal positions contain a great deal of discursive space for the negotiation of identities. Only after the 1997 Luxembourg decision, Turkey and advocates of Turkey's accession to the EU began to make greater use of this discursive space to challenge the dichotomous construction of Europe/Asia and Europe/Islam. And it is only as a result of this identity negotiation process that the progress made by Turkey on democracy and human rights could be interpreted in a way to justify granting to Turkey the candidacy status in 1999. After 1997, Turkey negotiated the construction of its identity and in turn the European identity in three ways. First, Turkey successfully invoked the "specter of Huntington" and reproduced the discourse of "Christian Europe." Second, Turkey began to emphasize that it is simultaneously European and Asian, and thereby presented itself as a contribution to the making of Europe into a multicultural space and collectivity. And finally, the fact that by 1999 the Islamic party became one of the strongest advocates of democratization and integration with Europe in Turkey has challenged the dichotomy of Europe/Islam.

Christian Europe and the specter of Huntington

As discussed in Chapter 3, European identity discourse in relation to Turkey, its liminal, does not lend itself easily to categories of who is for or against closer relations with Turkey and of who is for or against a certain notion of European identity. This ambiguity opens up room for strange bedfellows, intra-group disagreements, and for a great deal of rhetorical maneuvering. For example, dissociation from Turkey would be advocated both by proponents of an inclusive European identity – because Turkey fails to fulfill conditions on human rights and democracy – and by proponents of an exclusive identity – because Turkey is inherently non-European. Under these circumstances, defending a particular notion of European identity entails not only setting an appropriate social distance with respect to Turkey, but also justifying why. This was exemplified in the previous chapter by the exchange between Roth and Poos in the European Parliament debate on the Luxembourg European Council decisions, where Roth accused the Council of using human rights as a pretext and Poos accused Roth of not caring for human rights.

In this ambiguous discursive setting, Turkey successfully employed the identity-politics strategy of reproducing the discourse on Europe as a "Christian club." This placed the burden of proof on those who advocate an inclusive European identity to demonstrate that they are not actually proponents of an exclusionary Europe and using human rights concerns as a pretext. It also marginalized those who were against Turkey's accession because they did not want to be associated with religious exclusion and racism. Despite the denials from EU officials, Turkey's identity-politics strategy reproduced the understanding that, if the EU were not to grant an accession perspective to Turkey, it would be doing so for cultural and religious reasons. In March 1997, Turkey's Foreign Minister Tansu Ciller called on European leaders "not to build a cultural Berlin wall" in Europe by excluding Turkey (*De Standaard*, March 8, 1997). In November 1997, the Prime Minister Mesut Yilmaz made a similar warning: "Some states openly – while some quietly – are thinking that Europe belongs only to Christian countries. If they want to erect a cultural Berlin wall, they can go ahead. But they would have to deal with its consequences" (*Milliyet*, November 26, 1997). In July 1999, Turkey's Prime Minister Ecevit argued that the "EU countries are conspiring to do down Turkey and turn the EU into a Christians-only Club" (*The Daily Telegraph*, July 12, 1999). In 2005, the Prime Minister Recep Tayyip Erdogan objected to the addition of new conditions to Turkey's accession process by resorting to the same argument: "If you really claim that the EU is not a Christian club, if you believe this, then you should take Turkey among you" (Casanova 2006: 236).

The charges of Christian exclusivism had a certain degree of resonance especially among the secular circles in Europe. The fear that, by excluding Turkey, Europe was turning into a neo-Christendom was widely articulated in various commentaries on Turkey–EU relations. It placed the burden of proof on those Europeans to demonstrate that the EU is indeed not a Christian Europe, and the process of Turkish accession emerged as a way of doing so. For example, De Keyser, representing the Party of European Socialists, argued in a 2006 European Parliament debate on Turkey's Progress Towards Accession:

> Our long term aim is to have Turkey join because we believe – and this is a genuine political project – in a Europe that is multicultural, secular, but multi-faith, peaceful and open to the rest of the world. (EP 2006)

The question of Turkey's belonging in Europe also got embroiled in the intra-European debates on whether Christianity (or Judeo-Christianity, to be more precise) should be explicitly acknowledged as a defining element of European heritage in the European Constitution (Menendez 2005). At a 2004 debate on Turkey in the European Parliament, Ainardi from the European United Left – Nordic Green Left (GUE/NGL) complained that "certain political elements, moreover, are still trying to exert pressure to have the so-called Judeo-Christian foundations of Europe enshrined in the draft Constitution in order to make it difficult or even impossible for Turkey to accede to the Union" (EP 2004).

That said, it has to be acknowledged that the politics of religion in Europe around the question of Turkey's accession are rather complex and cannot be reduced to a simple equation of seculars being for and non-seculars being against (Hurd 2006; Gole 2006). According to Hurd (2006: 407), the debates on Turkey very much reflect the unsettled nature of the relation between religion, politics, and European identity. Some arguments made in the name of a secular Europe question the compatibility of the Turkish version of secularism with European versions and object to Turkey's accession on that basis. For example, in October 2004, Jean Pierre Raffarin, then Prime Minister of France, in an article written for the Wall Street Journal spoke of the difficult prospect of the "river of Islam" flowing into the "riverbed of secularism" (Koenig *et al.* 2006: 160). It is argued by some French and German intellectuals, such as Heinrich August Winkler, that the European version of secularism originated within a Judeo-Christian cultural and historical context, and that experience is not replicable in an Islamic society (Le Gloannec 2006).

The events of September 11 placed the charges of Christian exclusivism in Europe in the spotlight, and elevated the question of identity compatibility between Turkey and Europe to a strategic concern. While previously the discourse on the EU as a Christian club provoked European fears of a racist and exclusionary Europe, after September 11th, it also raised the specter of a clash of civilizations. Among advocates of Turkey's EU accession, Turkey's relations with the EU came to be framed as a test case of the possible dialogue between civilizations. According to Tony Blair, the decision to start accession negotiations with Turkey taken in December 2004 "show[ed] that those who believe that there is a clash of civilizations between Christians and Muslims are wrong" (*Sunday Express*, December 19, 2004, cited in Koenig *et al.* 2006: 162).

When framed as the accession of a Muslim country into an international community formed by Christian states, the EU's relations with Turkey emerge as a critical element of European foreign policy in the post-September 11th period. The possible membership of Turkey in the

EU becomes an important way to show how the EU's "normative power" (Manners, 2002) can make a critical difference at a time when the US' military power is failing to reach its objectives in the Middle East. Thus, after 2001, countering charges of Christian exclusivism acquires strategic significance for the EU, and the arguments by EU officials on Turkey routinely make note of that.

At a 2003 European Parliament debate on Turkey, the then Enlargement Commissioner, Guenther Verheugen, stressed that:

> The advantages for the European Union of having a Muslim country standing firmly by its side are becoming ever clearer, providing living proof that it is perfectly possible for such a country to share our values. One of the great questions of the 21st century will be how we shape the relationship between the West and the Islamic world. Turkey has a key role to play here. (EP 2003a)

Following the same line of thinking, the current Enlargement Commissioner, Olli Rehn, argued at a 2006 European Parliament debate on Turkey:

> It is in our mutual interest for Turkey to pursue its democratic, societal and economic transformation with the goal of joining the EU. If Turkey succeeds, with our consistent support, it can become an eversturdier bridge between civilizations, at a moment when the relationship between Europe and Islam is the greatest challenge of our time. (EP 2006)

Thus, Turkey's repeated reproduction of the discourse on "Christian club" Europe and the invocation of the specter of Huntington were successful and timely as identity-politics strategies. They resonated well with European concerns over racism and religious exclusion and with strategic concerns following 9/11. They placed the burden of proof on Europe to demonstrate that the EU is indeed not a "Christian club," and in turn allowed Turkey to present the prospect of Turkish accession to the EU as a way of doing so. This identity politics strategy also enabled the framing of EU–Turkey relations as a critical element of European foreign policy in the post-9/11 period.

Muslim and European

A second and related way in which Turkey negotiated the construction of its identity and in turn Europe's identity is by challenging the construction of Europe and Asia as mutually exclusive identities. As discussed above, Turkey began to challenge this construction only after the disappointing results of the Luxembourg European Council. The most important aspect of this identity-politics strategy has been the representational shift to portray Turkey as both European and Asian. This is in marked contrast to the previous encounters, when Turkish officials chose to emphasize over and over that Turkey is a European state without acknowledging the existence of other aspects to Turkey's identity. The Foreign Minister Cem's statement below made to *La Libre Belgique* represents Turkey's hybridity as an asset rather than a handicap:

> Is Europe's future going to be based on ethnic, racial, and religious discrimination and exclusion or will Europe open itself up with a pluralist and unifying approach? We consider ourselves both European and Asian and consider this dual identity to be an asset. (Cem 1997)

In this new identity-politics strategy, there is a change in emphasis from what could happen to Turkey if Turkey is excluded from the EU to what would happen to Europe. Rather than appealing to the strategic fears of Turkey's fall to Islamic fundamentalism, this new strategy seeks to promote the understanding that association with Turkey would help turn Europe into a truly multicultural space and collectivity. The following statement by Cem reflects this sense of confidence:

> What Turkey can provide to EU is a historical experience of a different kind; a dimension that only a country that for centuries was the representative of a huge geography and a genuine civilization can provide … Being the only country with a predominantly Muslim population which has the ideals and practices of a pluralist democracy, secularism, rule of law, human rights, gender equality, Turkey enjoys the privilege of constituting a paradigm of modernization. (Cem 2000)

After Cem, this representation of Turkey's hybrid identity as an asset for Turkey and Europe has been embraced by the incoming pro-Islamist Justice and Development Party (AKP) government, which was elected to power in November 2002. As will be discussed later, despite its pro-Islamist roots, AKP has wholeheartedly embraced the goal of Turkey's EU membership and taken the political reform process in Turkey the farthest. In this process of Europeanization, an identity discourse that emphasized the Muslim heritage and identity of Turkey was appealing to AKP to maintain the support of its original constituency. In addition, in the post-September 11th international context, such a discourse on Turkey's identity was reproduced by the United States and the West, and served to underline Turkey's strategic significance. Thus, although initially, the secularist circles in Turkey were against the construction of Turkey as a "Muslim democracy," eventually it became a standard discourse of Turkish foreign policy.

As Recep Tayyip Erdogan underlined at a speech given in the US:

> Turkey is the most successful Muslim country in putting together Islamic culture, democratic order, and the principles of secularism ... Turkey not only has proven false the idea that the [West and Islam] represent two incompatible worlds, but also provided an example for why these two can't even be separated by definite lines. (Erdogan 2005)

There is an important way in which the identity politics strategy of underscoring Turkey's hybrid dual identity differs from the previously discussed discourse on "Christian club Europe," While the latter represents Turkey as predominantly Muslim and Europe as predominantly Christian, the former refers to the existence of a hybrid dual identity in a single site. And even though the desirability of including a Muslim state in Europe has been more widely accepted for strategic and other reasons, the possibility of a state being Muslim and European at the same time has been harder to swallow. As Casanova (2006: 237) notes:

> Turkey is adamantly staking its claim to be, or its right to become, a fully European country economically and politically, while fashioning its own model of Muslim cultural modernity. It is this very claim to be simultaneously a modern European and a culturally Muslim country that baffles European civilizational identities, secular and Christian alike.

While taking into account the diversity of European opinions on this subject, it would be fair to say at least that Europeans perceive this duality in Turkey's identity not as an asset but as a handicap to Turkey's modernization process. As will be discussed later on in the chapter, the discourse on Christian-club Europe has marginalized arguments advocating Turkey's outright exclusion because of cultural difference. The emerging broad consensus on the desirability of the accession process with Turkey, however, masks fundamental differences of opinion on Turkey's capacity to fulfill the conditions for membership. These differences of opinion are rooted in perceptions of Turkey's cultural difference as an insurmountable obstacle to its full Europeanization, and have emerged more clearly as Turkey has advanced in political reform. Turkey's progress in the fulfillment of the so-called more objective

Copenhagen criteria has triggered pronouncements of new and vaguer criteria that conflate the division between political and cultural. For example, the European Parliament's rapporteur on Turkey, Oostlander (PPE) stressed in his 2003 report that the European values are rooted in a Judeo-Christian and humanist culture, but this forms no barrier to the accession of an Islamic majority country (EP 2003b). During a follow up debate in the European Parliament Oostlander specified further his expectations from Turkey:

> The changes we want are revolutionary. What matters is that the candidates should fit in with the European Union in terms of the political values they uphold. Until such time as they do, they should not consider membership. This is not simply about correcting a number of specific abuses, but also about the legal and *social* basis from which abuses arise. (EP 2004, emphasis mine)

Thus, considering the absence of European values as rooted in a Judeo-Christian culture as a handicap to Turkey's modernization and reform, Oostlander and others are stipulating a broader process of social and cultural change as a condition for Turkey's membership. Whether such a vague condition can ever be objectively satisfied is debatable. Le Gloannec (2006) also notes the pre-eminence of values in discussions about Turkey. Those who stress the importance of European values underscore that the problem does not lie in Turkey's religious difference but in the way religion shapes political culture and mental habits, which are very hard to change.

In short, representations of Turkey's hybridity have failed to undermine the construction of Islam and Europe as mutually exclusive identities. European audiences have not recognized Turkey as simultaneously Muslim and European, and in fact, representations of Turkey's hybridity have been counter-productive to the extent that they have allowed for the conflation of inherent and acquired characteristics in debates on Turkey's EU accession criteria.

Justice and Development Party (AKP)
and the reform process

Following the declaration of Turkey's candidacy in 1999, the fact that a political party of an Islamist orientation has been at the forefront of completing the political reforms necessary to start the accession process has further confounded the construction of European identity. First, the enactment of a sweeping set of reforms, mostly on controversial and politically costly issues, in a very short time frame surpassed the expectations of even the most ardent supporters of Turkey. Between 2001 and 2004, Turkey has adopted nine constitutional packages and a new civil and penal code in view of fulfilling the Copenhagen criteria in order to begin accession negotiations with the European Union. With these legal changes, Turkey has abolished the death penalty, revised its anti-Terror law, allowed for broadcasting in languages other than Turkish, abolished the State Security Courts which had a military judge, and allowed for the retrial of all cases, strengthened the legal measures directed toward the prevention of torture, ratified the International Covenant on Civil and Political Rights and the International Covenant on Economic, Social, and Cultural Rights, gave civilians numerical majority in the National Security Council and appointed a civilian as its Secretary-General, and recognized the priority of international treaties ratified by the Turkish parliament over the rulings of Turkey's constitutional court (Muftuler-Bac 2005).

These sweeping reforms have strengthened the belief that the EU's decision to grant Turkey candidacy status was the right one. European leaders as well as the European Commission gave due credit to Turkey's progress and the 2004 European Commission report on Turkey's Progress towards Accession declared that the Copenhagen political criteria have been fulfilled (European Commission 2004). In fact, the continuation of the reform process was the strongest argument and the main motivating factor behind the EU's decision to start accession negotiations with Turkey in December 2004.

The political reform process in Turkey is one of the main factors behind the modification of Turkey's liminal identity position in relation to Europe. As mentioned in the previous chapter, until 1999, EU–Turkey relations were caught in a vicious circle regarding the EU's impact on Turkey's democratization. While Turkey's poor democracy and human rights record justified dissociation from Turkey for the proponents of an inclusive European identity, EU's dissociation lent legitimacy to constructions of Europe as a threat in Turkey. The 1999 decision to grant Turkey candidacy status broke this vicious circle in two ways. First, it made the EU's membership carrot more credible and thereby legitimized the fulfillment of the associated conditions, discrediting constructions of Europe as a threat to Turkey. Second, Turkey's progress in fulfilling the conditions, in turn, legitimized further association with Turkey for the proponents of an inclusive European identity. Previously, there was an uneasy alliance between proponents of inclusive and exclusive European identities with regard to their Turkey policy; the former advocating dissociation from Turkey because of its poor human rights record, and the latter because of its inherent differences. With the political reform process in Turkey, this uneasy alliance came to an end, and Turkey came to be constituted as securing of the inclusive aspects of European identity, which justified association with Turkey.

The fact that an Islamist political party, the Justice and Development Party, AKP, was leading Turkey in this period of almost revolutionary political change also challenged European identity discourses. As Casanova (2006: 240) puts it, "the paradox is that only the rise in Muslim democracy has created the conditions for real democratization in Turkey." It was also paradoxical from the point of view of Turkish politics. The AKP is the latest offspring of the National View Movement, which traditionally was based on a critical stance on the westernization and secularization of Turkey. Because of its anti-secular stance, several political parties originating from this movement were previously banned, re-established under different political names. However, as Dagi (2005) observes, Turkish Islamists have departed in recent years, from their conventional position of anti-westernism and begun to advocate the importance of meeting EU standards on democracy. According to Dagi (2005:30), the AKP "can best be described as a post-Islamist movement: keeping its ties with Islam in the social realm but abandoning it as a political program."

The fundamental reason for this change of heart was the domestic political pressures faced by Turkish Islamists in Turkey. After the Welfare Party was removed from government and banned in the Constitutional Court due to its anti-secular stance, Turkish Islamists came to realize that their political survival could only be guaranteed through the full institutionalization of political and human rights in Turkey. The turning point in the Turkish Islamists' approach to Europe was their taking of Turkey's decision to ban the Welfare Party to the European Court of Human Rights. However, in both the Welfare Party case and the 2005 decision of the European Court of Human Rights to uphold the ban on headscarves in Turkish universities (the Leyla Sahin case), the rulings of the Court were contrary to the expectations of Turkish Islamists.

The AKP's embrace of the goal of EU membership and the associated reform program challenged the construction of Islam and Europe as incompatible identities both in Europe and in Turkey. After the landslide victory of AKP in the November 2002 elections, Peter Hintze, spokesman of the German Christian Democrats said: "It is now out of the question that a date be set for the beginning of membership negotiations" (*The Times*, November 6, 2002). Yet, such prejudicial views were marginalized in the light of Turkey's unforeseen success in fulfilling the Copenhagen criteria. In a 2004 debate on Turkey, there remained only the insinuation that "there may be some in this House who, precisely because it is an AKP government that is making progress, believe that Turkey should no longer be a candidate" (EP 2004).

Though the secularists' bureaucracy and the military in Turkey remained suspicious of AKP's real intentions, i.e. pursuing democratization and human rights in order to use them later on to institute an Islamic state, the business world and the liberal circles have given their support to the AKP reform program. The tension between these two views surfaced in the spring of 2007, with mass protests against AKP's presidential nomination supported by a declaration from the Turkish military. Despite this mobilization, in the July 22, 2007 elections, AKP registered a decisive victory, garnering 47% of the national vote. As a Turkish academic and journalist explained in the New York Times:

> It appears to be one of modern history's ironies that the Turkish party most willing and able to enter the European Union on Europe's terms, as stated in the party's platform, would be an Islamist one. But this should be seen as an immense opportunity for Europe. The extension of an invitation to Turkey, led by Justice and Development, to start negotiations will consolidate the liberal changes that have gained such momentum in Turkey. It would also begin reducing the so-called civilizational barriers between Muslim countries and the West. (Ozel 2002)

Thus, as a result of the AKP government's rigorous pursuit of the political reform agenda with a view to starting accession negotiations with the EU, Turkey came to be securing of inclusive aspects of European identity. This, as will be discussed in the following section, fundamentally modified Turkey's liminal identity position. While initially raising concerns, the party's Islamist heritage ceased to be a factor that undermined the credibility of its reform agenda. The pursuit of EU membership by an Islamist party attained a level of normalcy within Europe and Turkey, undermining to some extent the construction of Islam and Europe as antithetical identities.

III. Liminality modified

The negotiation of European identity in the ways discussed above has not eliminated but has nevertheless modified Turkey's liminal identity position. A fundamental element of continuity is the continued prevalence of the construction of Turkey as inherently different. In fact, the very fact that such representations of Turkey's identity have continued to be voiced by top European political figures even after the declaration of Turkey's candidacy attests to Turkey's liminal status. Gole (2006) points to the irony of the fact that in France a debate on the legitimacy of Turkish membership started the moment Turkey accomplished many of the requirements, getting closer to the standards set by the EU. Validating the relationship stipulated between identity, social distance, and perception of threat in the conceptual framework of self/other interaction, Gole argues that it is the increasing proximity [of Turkey] which is the source of conflict and controversy.

There are many examples of such representations, which have been widely publicized in the Turkish and European press. For example, in November 2002, the former French President and the President of the European Convention, Giscard D'Estaing, told the *Le Monde* newspaper his personal view that the inclusion of Turkey in a future wave of enlargement would be the "end of Europe." In justifying his claim, Giscard D'Estaing resorted to geographical arguments and characterized the people who supported Turkey's accession as "the adversaries of Europe" (*BBC News*, November 8, 2002). Former West German Chancellor Helmut Schmidt suggested that Turkey should be excluded from the EU due to its unsuitable civilization (cited in Hurd 2006: 406). Similarly, invoking the image of Turkey as the historical enemy of Europe, the Dutch Commissioner for the European Union, Frits Bolkenstein, argued in 2004 that Turkey entering Europe would mean forgetting 1683, when the siege of Vienna was lifted and the Ottoman army was defeated (Gole 2006).

Similarly, in the European Parliament, such representations of Turkey continued to be employed, though with less frequency than before. As an Independence and Democracy (IND-DEM) parliamentarian, Rogalski, argued during a 2006 debate on Turkey:

> I do not agree that Turkey can play the role of a bridge between Europe and the Muslim world. On the contrary, I think that Turkey could become a gateway for terrorism. Turkey is part of a world that is alien to us in terms of its culture and traditions ... Accepting Turkey into the European Union will set a dangerous precedent that will spell the end of Europe as we know it today. (EP 2006)

Turkey also became a central topic in the election campaigns in Germany and France, and conservative leaders cultivated the anti-Turkish public opinion in their countries. Prior to the September 2005 German legislative elections, the leaders of the Christian Democratic Movement captured public attention and sympathy by pronouncing their view overtly against Turkish membership in the EU. In August 2005, Angela Merkel (before elections) wrote a letter to the EU's conservative heads of government stating that the negotiations with Turkey should not automatically lead to membership; instead they should be open-ended and lead to a "privileged partnership" (*Guardian*, August 27, 2005). Also in France, politicians who oriented their politics on security issues and took a stand against Turkish membership (like current President Nicolas Sarkozy) gained popularity.

In addition, the prospective Turkish enlargement was pronounced as the main culprit of the failed constitutional referenda in France and the Netherlands, and thus Turkey became a centerpiece of the debates on the EU's democratic deficit. As independent MEP Claeys put it in a 2004 European Parliament debate on Turkey:

> An appeal is being made for including a non-European and Islamic country in the European Union without holding a fundamental discussion on this ... Fundamental decisions are being taken without reference to Europe's citizens. That is the democratic deficit all over. (EP 2004)

Accordingly, prior to the December 2004 decision to start accession negotiations with Turkey, French President Chirac announced that the French people will have the ultimate say through a referendum prior to Turkey's accession. Austria has also announced that it will put the decision of Turkish enlargement to a referendum. Needless to say, these political decisions have increased the uncertainty surrounding Turkey's accession prospects. The newly elected French President Nicholas Sarkozy openly voiced his objection to Turkish full membership and in June 2007 successfully blocked the opening of negotiations on the key chapter of economic and monetary policy.

While Turkey's liminality has persisted beyond 1999, in terms of the continued prevalence of discourses of inherent difference, there has been a significant change in how Turkey's acquired differences are represented and dealt with. The successful record of Turkish political reform post-1999 strengthened the view that a credible EU membership perspective is essential for the continuation of the reform process. Association with Turkey became securing of the inclusive aspects of

European identity, and, as a result, advocates of an inclusive European identity have begun to more consistently support closer relations with Turkey.

Overall, one can say that the structure of the debate on Turkey has shifted. Continuation of the reform process in Turkey became a fundamental rationale for EU–Turkey relations, and alternative policies towards Turkey came to be evaluated with respect to their contribution to this objective. As Andreassen (ELDR) explained in a 2004 debate in the European Parliament:

> There is no doubt that it is precisely the EU's demands that have contributed significantly to the democratic progress that has taken place in Turkey and a signal from the European Parliament that Turkey cannot become a member of the EU, or that Turkey must be given special status would undoubtedly put a stop to this positive development. (EP 2004)

This understanding has opened up the space for chastising opponents of Turkey's full membership on the basis of undermining the reform process in Turkey. Thus, the articulation of an outright opposition to Turkish full membership has been constrained in this fashion. As Posselt (PPE) complains in a 2006 European Parliament debate on Turkey:

> Turkey is not a European country. Its accession would overstretch, overstrain, weaken, perhaps even endanger the EU. Anyone who says so exposes himself to the accusation of refusing to support the process of reform and push the criteria through. (EP 2006)

Similarly, Brok (PPE) argues in the same debate that "it is not permitted to mention facts in case this is taken as criticism or misinterpreted in Turkey" (EP 2006).

There has been a growing awareness in Europe that the continuation of the reform process requires a much more delicate and carefully crafted approach towards Turkey, which takes into account how the signals sent by the European Union are received in Turkey. A monolithic understanding of Turkey has given way to a more pluralistic perception. As Lagendijk from the Greens/European Free Alliance (Vert/ALE) group explains, in Turkey there is "a constant struggle between, on the one hand, reformers – strong in the government and in Parliament – and on the other, the conservatives, strong in the army, the police and the judiciary" (EP 2003a). That is why, according to Lagendijk, it is very important that European Parliament reports on Turkey are "critical and, at the same time, fair" because the European Parliament should "continue to play a role in the reform debate in Turkey by supporting those groups and those people who, day in and day out, are fighting for the same things that we are" (EP 2006). Similarly, De Keyser (PSE) notes that it is necessary to send "clear signals to Turkey regarding human rights, minority rights, women's rights, and the recognition of Cyprus" but in a "constructive spirit" (EP 2006).

A "constructive spirit" entails leaving no ambiguity with regard to full membership prospects of Turkey and refraining from stipulating additional conditions, i.e. moving the goal posts. The discussion that took place in the European Parliament in 2006 on whether the recognition of the Armenian "genocide" should be stipulated as an additional condition for Turkey reflects the weight of such concerns. Despite the widely agreed position that "reconciliation [with the past] is an important principle of European integration," and the 1987 decision of the European Parliament recognizing the Armenian "genocide," MEPs agreed that the European Parliament should act in a way to encourage the internal debate in Turkey on this issue. Reporting on his exchanges with dissident Turkish intellectuals, Ozdemir (Verts/ALE) concluded that "anyone wishing to assist the debate in Turkey should not make recognition of the genocide a precondition for membership of the EU" (EP 2006).

Hence, within the position of modified liminality, the discourse on European identity as inclusive structured the debate on Turkey into the rival camps of "open door" and "arduous path." While formally acknowledging Turkey's eligibility for membership and the ongoing accession process, some argued that Turkey's path to Europe will necessarily be arduous, and pointed to the areas in which Turkey was lagging behind, such as in the implementation of reforms, rights of non-Muslim minorities, extending the Customs Union Agreement to the Republic of Cyprus, and recognition of the Armenian "genocide." Others argued that such an arduous path will discourage Turkey from the path of reform, and issues that are not formally part of Copenhagen criteria should not be stipulated as conditions on the ground of fairness. As Verheugen reminded the European Parliament in 2004:

> The adoption of Community law is what accession negotiations are about; it is not a precondition for them taking place. They cannot now be used to justify our saying that we cannot start negotiating with Turkey because they have not yet done those things about which we are going to negotiate. (EP 2004)

While the proponents of an "arduous path" justify their position as the strict application of conditionality, others dismiss their arguments as hypocritical. The discussion on Turkey's continued deficiencies led a German MEP of Turkish origin, Ceyhun, to break out in protest (PSE):

> I came to this Parliament as a German … but it is as a Turk that I leave it. Many of you have made me into a Turk, for I am ashamed of the speeches that really can only be described as hypocritical … Others may take pride in bravely defending the Christian EU against the Turks … but I am ashamed, such is not my European Union. (EP 2004)

In short, the nature of self/other interaction between the EU and Turkey following the declaration of Turkey's candidacy is simultaneously similar to and different from Turkey's previous liminal position. That is why I have deemed it appropriate to label it as a modified liminal position. The interaction is characterized by the continued prevalence of discourses of inherent difference, which advocate dissociation from Turkey in order to secure European identity. The important difference is that, in light of Turkey's progress in political reform, association with Turkey has become necessary to secure inclusive aspects of European identity. Supporting the reform process in Turkey has become an important focal point around which the EU debates on Turkey revolve.

IV. Conclusion

The interactions of community-building institutions with liminal states are sites where the discursive opportunity for a transformation to a post-modern collectivity exists. This is because, as entities that are partly self and partly other, they undermine and hence provide the opportunity for transcending the categories of self and other. This chapter has discussed the ways in which Turkey has challenged the construction of Europe/Asia and Europe/Islam as mutually exclusive and inherently incompatible identities in the course of (re)negotiating its identity. While this process of re-construction and re-negotiation has modified Turkey's liminal position, and allowed for the EU's closer association with Turkey, it has not undermined or blurred the distinctions between these dichotomous identities.

Many regard the EU's December 2004 decision to begin accession negotiations with Turkey as a "key moment in the early development of a reborn Europe as a more cosmopolitan society and less of a fortress" (cf. Koenig *et al.*, 2006: 150). My analysis of the representations in the EU's interaction with Turkey after 1999 shows important elements of continuity and change. There are significant changes in the EU discourses on Turkey, which now highlight the contribution that Turkey makes to a multi-cultural Europe and stress the importance of supporting the reform process in Turkey. But these new representational practices on Turkey coexist with exclusive conceptions of European identity based on differentiation from Asia and Islam. While Turkey seeks to represent itself as a hybrid, both European and Asian, both Muslim and European, the European representations of Turkey do not reflect a recognition of Turkey as simultaneously other and like. Thus, even though its interaction with Turkey provided Europe the opportunity for transforming itself to a postmodern collectivity, such a transformation is yet to take place.

5
European Union and Regional Order

I. Introduction

How does the way the EU interacts with difference affect the broader regional order in Europe? How, and under what conditions, can the EU contribute to a successful resolution of conflicts at its external borders? This question carries a lot of policy significance nowadays in EU circles, mainly because the continued existence of such disputes, such as Cyprus, reflects badly on the EU's stated missions to export peace and become a foreign policy actor in and of its own right (Richmond 2000). The status of conflicts around the external borders of the EU and the role played by the EU in relation to these conflicts have a lot to say about the nature of the collectivity that the EU is set to become. This chapter shows that the EU's differing institutional/identity relations with various states on its periphery have affected the conflicts on the EU's external borders in different ways. In this chapter, I will discuss how the EU has impacted three conflicts between member and non-member states situated in different institutional/identity relations with respect to the EU: the Polish–German (prior to 2004 enlargement), Moroccan–Spanish, and Greek–Turkish conflicts.

The three sets of bilateral relations analyzed in this chapter and the issues involved are qualitatively different from each other in terms of conflict intensity and the positions of conflict parties. In Polish–German relations, there has been the potential of a border dispute which has not erupted; in Moroccan–Spanish relations, several serious disputes are sought to be contained by conflict parties within a framework of good neighborly relations; and in Greek–Turkish relations (prior to 1999), we have a case of identity conflict, where the disputes are interwoven with perceptions of identity incompatibility. While complicating the analysis, this diversity is not an obstacle to the assessment of the EU's relative impact on these conflicts in terms of conflict escalation and de-escalation.

II. Polish–German relations

The Polish–German border has been one of the most serious frictions in post-World War 2 European politics. After World War 2, the Polish–German border was moved westward to the Oder–Neisse line, giving Poland one-fourth of Germany's pre-war territory. This border change left approximately 9 million Germans behind, the majority of whom were forcefully expelled into allied occupation zones by Soviet and Polish authorities (Elliot 1993). The Cold War hostilities further aggravated the Polish–West German relations and justified Bonn's continued non-recognition of the Polish–East German border. The communist regime in Poland used the threat of German revisionism in the "Recovered Territories" as a means of bolstering their internal legitimacy and exploited the anti-German attitude of the majority of Polish society as determined by their experience of German occupation (Lebioda 2000). In Germany, the expellees organized in order to claim back their lost properties.

While Brandt's Ostpolitik included the recognition of the Oder–Neisse border with the 1970 Warsaw Treaty, this recognition was watered down by the opposition during the ratification process with the inclusion of a qualification that West Germany was speaking only for itself and not for a future reunited Germany, and that if and when the two Germanies were reunited, the question of the Polish–German border would have to be raised again (Elliot 1993). This qualified recognition of the post-war border continued to be a major irritant in Polish–West German relations and the "Oder–Neisse line remained the only post-World War Two border whose legal status remained provisional" (Hyde-Price 2000: 14).

In contrast to what these past trends would lead us to expect, with the end of the Cold War and the reunification of the two Germanies, the Polish–German border dispute did not flare up. Instead, German–Polish relations came to constitute the "hinge of an emerging 'zone of stable peace' in Mitteleuropa" (Hyde-Price 2000: 2). By the summer of 1989, the two states had worked out the basis of an agreement in which Poland would take concrete steps to protect the rights of the German minority in Poland in return for West German financial help. In November 1990, just over a month after the two Germanies voted to reunite, Germany and Poland signed a treaty recognizing the permanent nature of their Oder–Neisse border. The preamble to this treaty used the term 'expulsion' which was unthinkable and equivalent to treason in Poland until that time (Lebioda 2000).The agreement in early 1991 to open their borders resolved the issue of German emigration (Elliot 1993). However, the decisive moment came with the Treaty on Friendship and Neighborly Relations of June 1991. The Treaty committed both parties to the peaceful resolution of disputes and pledged their mutual support for cooperative security structures. It called for wide-ranging cooperation across a range of issues, and institutionalized regular consultations at all levels. It also included a commitment by Germany to support Poland's entry into the EU (Hyde-Price 2000).

While Kohl, motivated by domestic political concerns, disputed the legality and permanence of the Oder–Neisse border for a while, the 1991 Treaty and the depth of institutionalized relations established between Poland and Germany afterwards renders simplistic the explanation that Germany recognized the border only because it was pressured by the 2 plus 4 Agreement. Rather, developments in 1990–1 demonstrated the willingness of both sides to draw on the successful Franco-German model to institutionalize their relations and generate a shared understanding of common interests and concerns. Both German and Polish political elites based their foreign policy strategies on the notion of a "community of interests," a phrase coined by Poland's first non-communist Foreign Minister Krzysztof Skubiszewski upon the conclusion of the 1991 Treaty.

German–Polish relations certainly constitute a success case in terms of the EU facilitating the transformation of conflicts around its external borders. The EU has been the catalyst and the normative/institutional model for the resolution of the potentially destabilizing Oder–Neisse border dispute between Poland and Germany on the external borders of the EU (Hyde-Price 2000). In relation to Poland and other CEES, the EU invoked inclusive aspects of its identity and constructed their differences to be on the basis of acquirable characteristics. Such a construction delegitimized discourses of difference and threat that might possibly have been employed against Poland in Germany to stir up the Oder–Neisse dispute and seek revision of the border. Since 1989, Germany has played the part of the unofficial spokesman of Poland's interests in its efforts to join the European structures. Even the revisionist Union of the Expellees, which was the most powerful domestic pressure group during the 2 plus 4 Agreement negotiations, seeking revision of the border and restitution of their property, has later partly revised its stance in favor of Poland's EU membership (Lebioda 2000).

Had Poland's European credentials been more in doubt, it would have been possible for Germany to adopt a hard line towards Poland, just as it did during the Cold War when their identities were differentiated as capitalist and communist.

The European Union also provided the normative and ideational basis for deepening cooperation. In a June 1997 speech, German Chancellor Helmut Kohl stated:

> We want to create with our eastern neighbor Poland what was possible with ... France. This is all the more important as German–Polish history and the German–Polish border are linked on both sides with bitter experiences ... [We] must draw a decisive lesson ... that there will never again be border problems in Europe ... We must make borders porous, as between Germany and France ... For this reason we want Poland ... to become a part of the European Union. (Feldman 2000: 337)

Also in Poland, the credible carrot of EU membership and the guiding philosophy of a "return to Europe" have been influential in affecting policy change towards Germany. According to Hyde-Price (2000), this vision has united nearly all strands of Poland's post-communist domestic political scene. German support for Poland's EU membership has been greatly appreciated and radically altered perceptions. Germany has been perceived by as many as 59 per cent of respondents as the state which has been most helpful for Poland on the road to EU membership (Stadtmuller 2000: 40). According to Lebioda (2000), the acceptance by the majority of Polish society that Germans should play such a role would have been very difficult to imagine earlier.

The EU membership perspective also facilitated the internalization of "European" standards and principles – human rights and rights of ethnic minorities, democracy, liberalism and tolerance – as requirements of a "European" identity and made possible the change in Poland's policies towards German minorities (Freudenstein 1998). The process of Europeanization, i.e., internalization of European norms and principles, also shifted the general "style" of foreign policymaking towards consensus-seeking and a preference for solving interstate conflicts by diplomatic means. According to Zaborowski (2002), in most of Central and Eastern Europe, "Europeanization has been presented as an alternative to Balkanization, with the latter notion symbolizing conflict and violence."

In addition, the EU has supported cross-border efforts between Poland and Germany, including the Europa University in Viadrina and the

Euregio Neisse linking Germany, Poland and the Czech Republic (Feldman 2000).

III. Moroccan–Spanish relations

Moroccan–Spanish relations are another case of bilateral relations on the external borders of the EU. Even though the two countries regard each other as important partners, according to Gillespie (2000), there is as much friction and suspicion as there is harmony between the two countries. The first important dispute is the status of the small coastal cities of Ceuta and Melilla, which are the remaining territories of Spain in North Africa. While Spain handed the Spanish protectorate of Northern Morocco back to Rabat in 1956, it retained these two coastal cities, on the argument that these cities were Spanish even before the establishment of Morocco. On the other hand, Morocco's claims to the cities, made since the 1950s, rest on geographical proximity, and the claim that they are colonial enclaves (Gillespie 2000).

In fact, this dispute holds the dubious honor of leading to the latest near-war situation on EU borders. On July 11, 2002, a dozen Moroccan soldiers arrived on the Isla de Perejil (Parsley Island), an islet the size of a football field, 200 yards away from the Moroccan mainland for, as the Moroccan Foreign Minister claimed, an operation against illegal immigration and drug smuggling into Europe. While Morocco considered Parsley Island as part of the Spanish protectorate of Northern Morocco handed back to Rabat in 1956, Spain considered Isla de Perejil as part of the remaining Spanish enclave of Ceuta (Jones 2002). Spanish Defense Minister Federico Trillo asserted that Spain was "attacked by force in a very sensitive part of its geography" (*The Times*, July 20, 2002). On July 17, 2002, Spain "retook" Parsley Island, by sending elite troops, transported in attack helicopters and supported by five warships and two submarines. Morocco protested to the United Nations, condemning Spain's "unjustified aggression" and demanding the immediate and unconditional withdrawal of its forces. On July 21, 2002, Spain withdrew its troops and the island returned to its demilitarized status under a US-brokered deal. However, Morocco has continued to complain that Spain is repeatedly breaking the agreement (*The Times*, October 5, 2002).

A second issue concerns the regulation of the access of Spanish fishermen to Moroccan waters, especially the rich waters off the disputed territory of Western Sahara. While Spain has a huge consumer demand and a large fishing industry, Morocco is concerned about the overdepletion of its resources. Illegal fishing by the Spanish has been subjected to high fines, confiscations, and security risks, and Morocco and Spain have negotiated several fishing agreements, which regulated and limited the access of Spanish fishermen (Gillespie 2000). These agreements however, have been tenuous, and of limited term, and frequently revised and revoked at will by the Moroccan authorities. After Spanish membership, the EC/EU has negotiated on this issue with Morocco, which has led to three agreements in 1988, 1992, and 1995. As will be discussed shortly, these agreements were linked to developments in EU–Morocco relations. In 1992 Morocco reacted to the European Parliament's failure to approve a financial aid package by asking for a reduction in catches (Vaquer i Fanes, 2003). In 1995, during the tough negotiations of the EU–Morocco Association Agreement, Morocco displayed an uncompromising stance in the fisheries negotiations and forbade Spanish boats from fishing in her waters. This caused over 600 Spanish boats to remain in port for months until the conflict was settled in November 1995.

Despite Spain's and Morocco's institutional links with the EU, the community formation process in Europe has not had a transformative effect on their disputes. Spain has become a member of the EC in 1986, and Morocco has signed a Cooperation Agreement with the EC in 1976 and an Association Agreement in 1996. The EU has failed to positively influence Moroccan–Spanish relations in the way it has influenced Polish–German relations because it has interacted with Morocco and Spain through different identity relations. As has been described in Chapter 3, the EU has invoked mainly the exclusive aspects of its identity in relation to Morocco, constructed Morocco as absolutely non-European despite its membership application, and dissociated from Morocco in order to validate its identity. This form of a self/other interaction incapacitated the EU from having a positive impact on Moroccan–Spanish relations.

First of all, although the EU could offer Morocco weaker forms of association in the form of an Association Agreement, the EU's compulsory influence on Morocco was weak. In 1995, the EU induced Morocco to make significant concessions in the fisheries issue with the carrot of the Association Agreement. Similarly, in the 1988 agreement, the commercial and financial protocols attached to the 1976 Cooperation Agreement functioned as carrots. However, these proved to be short-lived and were not grounded in a policy change. The fisheries issue was merely used by Morocco as a negotiating card in its relations with the EC/EU (Gillespie 2000, Vaquer i Fanes 2003). When the 1995 agreement terminated in 1999, the Moroccans could not be convinced for a renewal, as the EU could not offer a new carrot in the form of advancing relations. In addition, Morocco used fisheries negotiations to retaliate against hostile acts by the EC. In 1992, it reacted to the European Parliament's failure to approve a financial package by asking for a reduction in catches. The Parliament was concerned about Moroccan human rights abuses and non-compliance with the UN Peace Plan for Western Sahara.

Neither in Spain nor in Morocco could the EU legitimize policy change in the fisheries issue area. In 1995, Spain used its ability to prevent the EU from finalizing the Association Agreement with Morocco as a lever against Morocco. However, the resulting fisheries agreement has been perceived as a national defeat in Morocco, and since 1999 all Moroccan senior officials and politicians have affirmed that there would not be another agreement with the European Union (Vaquer i Fanes 2003: 71). Accordingly, the 2000–1 negotiations between the EU and Morocco broke down. In response to the news, the Spanish Prime Minister declared that: "no one can think ... that this will not have consequences on the relationship between Spain and Morocco and between Morocco and the European Union." This declaration was perceived as a threat in Morocco, and marked the beginning of a period of tense bilateral relations which culminated in the Perejil incident (Vaquer i Fanes 2003: 73).

Following the 2002 reform of the Common Fisheries Policy, a new approach to fisheries agreements that put an equal emphasis on achieving sustainable fisheries beyond EU borders developed. This resulted in a new EU/Morocco Fisheries Partnership Agreement, which was signed in July 2005.

Similarly, during the Perejil incident, the EU could neither convince Moroccans to withdraw – (the President of the European Commission warned the Moroccan Prime Minister that a protracted "occupation" of "territory of the Union" would have "pernicious consequences" for his country's relations with Europe) nor prevent the Spanish military operation (the EU offered mediation and measures at EU level but Spain wanted support, and stood back while the situation was cooled down by the US (Jones 2002)).

Because the EU invoked mainly the exclusive aspects of its identity in relation to Morocco, its constructive influence was actually negative. As pointed out by Pace (2006), the historical memory of Muslim presence in the Iberian peninsula serves to reproduce in Spain the fear of being attacked from the South. The construction of Morocco as inherently different in the EU's community-building discourse legitimized and compounded the construction of Morocco as different and threatening in Spain. This can be clearly seen in how the Perejil incident was represented as a conflict between a European self and a non-European other in the Spanish press, rather than as an incident between any two neighbors. Claiming that "the obvious symbolism of this hostile act" could not be ignored, the Spanish daily *El Mundo* declared: "The King of Morocco has chosen the path of confrontation with one of the great European democracies and this should have a serious cost for him" (Jones 2002). According to *The Times*, the storming of Perejil islet has been "hailed throughout Spain as a famous victory," against "the first invasion of Western Europe since the Second World War" (Jones 2002).

Also, the construction of Morocco as "non-European" helped justify Spain's digressing from EU norms in dealing with the Perejil crisis. While, according to the Spanish daily *El Pais*, "the civilized thing would be to allow the International Court at the Hague to settle the crisis," the construction of the event as the "invasion of European territory by a non-European state" domestically justified the Spanish operation and muted international criticism (Jones 2002).

IV. Greek–Turkish relations

What the comparison of Polish–German and Moroccan–Spanish relations illustrate in terms of the different implications of opposite identity positions, the trajectory of Greek–Turkish relations demonstrates temporally. While previously territorial disputes in the Aegean routinely brought Turkey and Greece to near-war situations, since 1999, the two states have entered into a hopeful period of rapprochement. I argue that the transformation in their bilateral relations has been made possible by their changing identity positions in relation to the EU. As the EU associated more closely with Turkey, the role played by the EU in their rivalry changed from serving as an additional battlefield to being the basis for cooperation.

Until recently, relations between Turkey and Greece constituted an anomaly in the security community of Europe. While many interstate conflicts have been ameliorated or resolved in the context of the community formation process in Europe, the conflicts between Turkey and Greece have been repeatedly reproduced. Turkey and Greece have been allies in NATO since 1952. They have also been associate members of the European Community since 1959 and 1963; Greece became a full member in 1981, and Turkey became a candidate of the European Union in 1999. Despite their joint participation in and/or close association with these institutions, Turkey and Greece have continued to maintain antagonistic relations. The two states came dangerously close to war over Cyprus in 1964 and during Turkey's 1974 military operation, which put approximately one-third of the island under Turkish control. In addition, the two states have been in numerous near war situations in 1976, 1987, and 1996 over the continental shelf, airspace, and small islets in the Aegean.

By grounding the future relations between the EU and Turkey on a membership track and by symbolizing the EU's recognition of Turkey as a "potential European," the Helsinki European Council's decision to grant candidacy status to Turkey entailed a fundamental change in the EU's identity relations towards Turkey. It is true that the EU–Turkey relations, as demonstrated in the previous chapter, retained some degree of controversy and ambiguity. However, the December 1999 decision definitely marked at least *a shift towards* a relationship of closer association with Turkey.

Starting from 1999, Greek–Turkish relations began to benefit from the conflict-diminishing effects of the EU. Though, as I will explain below, domestic developments in Turkey and Greece initiated the change, the EU's decision to offer a membership perspective to Turkey helped to consolidate it, leading to a sustained rapprochement between Turkey and Greece within an EU framework. First, it empowered the moderates and provided the basis for alternative policies in both countries. Secondly, by facilitating EU funding and legitimization, Turkey's EU candidacy has broadened the scope of Greek–Turkish civil society cooperation activities. Finally, the prospect of Turkey's inclusion in Europe has facilitated the emergence of an alternative discourse on Greek–Turkish identities.

Pre-1999 period

Until 1999, the nature of the EU's relations with Turkey incapacitated the EU from having a positive impact on the Greek–Turkish conflicts in several ways. First of all, it helped legitimize the existing foreign policies in both countries vis-à-vis each other. In Greece, the potentially permanent exclusion of the "arch-enemy," Turkey, from the EU institutions furthered the perception of the EU as an alliance against Turkey. Therefore, the EU indirectly helped to empower the hardliners in Greece, who perceived the conflicts with Turkey in zero-sum terms, and who valued the EU as a convenient instrument of leverage against Turkey. In this context, the EU could not serve as the basis for any alternative policy of the moderates, who saw the futility of the ongoing Greek–Turkish conflicts. Similarly, in Turkey, the exclusionary stance of the EU furthered the perception of the EU as hostile towards Turkey and captured by Greece, and therefore disabled the EU's interventions in Greek–Turkish conflicts. Change in Turkish foreign policy towards Greece could not be legitimized either by the prospect of EU membership (which was not perceived as credible) or by reference to EU norms. Secondly, the nature of the EU's relations with Turkey posed institutional constraints on the EU's ability to directly support Greek–Turkish civic initiatives, and helped perpetuate the legitimacy problem of Greek–Turkish civil society activities. Finally, the "Othering" of Turkey by the EU also helped to reproduce Greek and Turkish identities as different from and antagonistic towards each other.

Following Turkey's military operation in Cyprus in 1974, a foreign policy consensus has emerged in Greece that Turkey poses a revisionist threat in the Aegean, Thrace, and Cyprus (Triantaphyllou 2001; for a critical account, Heraclides 2001). Turkey's status as an outsider to the EU served to further the foreign policy consensus. In this context, the EC membership was perceived as and valued for having provided Greece with security and negotiating leverage in its dealings with Turkey; in short, within the logic of alliance (Valinakis 1994; Tsakonas and Tournikiotis 2003). Hence, within the EC, the established Greek strategy of deterrence of Turkey (Platias 2000) found new means of implementation. Greece pursued a policy of conditionality towards Turkey, blocking its relations with the EU until Turkey offered some concessions and/or agreed to the endorsement of the Greek positions by the EU. For example, in 1986, Greece vetoed the resumption of the Association relationship between Turkey and the EC and the release of frozen aid to Turkey (Guvenc 1998/9). When, in 1987, Turkey applied for EC membership, Greece was the only member state that openly opposed referring the application to the Commission for an Opinion (Guvenc 1998/9). In December 1994, the Customs Union Agreement with Turkey was not finalized due to Greece's opposition, and Greece lifted its veto in March 1995 only after the EU pledged to start membership negotiations with Cyprus. Greece also vetoed the release of the EC financial assistance to Turkey under the Fourth Financial Protocol, the EC's Mediterranean Program, and the Matutes Package until March 1995. Following the Imia/Kardak crisis over the status of two tiny islets in the Agean Sea in 1996, Greece blocked the release of EU financial aid to Turkey, which was granted as part of the Customs Union Agreement.

The use of the EU lever as a short-term instrument of pressure against Turkey remained attractive to the Greek elite because it was generally successful (Author Interview #1) and politically less risky and more rewarding than alternative policies (Veremis 2001). The nature of the

EU's relations with Turkey rendered this policy of negative conditionality not only possible, but also successful and legitimate. It enabled Greece to score short-term institutional victories against Turkey, which Greek governments could then use to muster domestic support. In addition, it served to legitimate such policies domestically and at the EU level because they reproduced the understanding of Turkey as an outsider to Europe; hence different and potentially threatening.

On the other hand, the EU's dissociation from Turkey placed the proponents of alternative policies towards Turkey on uncertain and shaky grounds. While Costas Simitis, who assumed the governing Pan-Hellenic Socialist Movement Party (PASOK) leadership in 1996, advocated a fundamental change in Greek foreign policy towards supporting Turkey's European orientation, on many occasions he had to give in to the hardliners, who favored the continuation of the exclusionary policies of negative conditionality (Author Interview #2). This disabling effect on the moderates in Greece can be clearly seen in the period between 1996 and 1999. For example, in 1997, the EU Presidency sought a solution to the continuing Greek veto on the EU financial package offered to Turkey by proposing to establish a committee of wisemen to study the problems between Turkey and Greece. Right after the protocol on the establishment of the Committee was signed, 32 MPs from the governing PASOK addressed an open letter to Simitis stating their opposition to any discussion on the substance of the Greek–Turkish problems and the lifting of the Greek veto on Turkey in the EU. As a result of this pressure, the Greek government diluted the wisemen proposal and the Greek veto on EU funds to Turkey remained.

Mirroring Greece, the prevailing perception among Turkish policy-makers is that Greece is pursuing a revisionist policy against Turkey (Gunduz 2001; for an elaboration of this position, see Bilge 2000). In response to this policy, Turkey pursues a policy centered on military deterrence (Ayman 1998), and not leaving Greece alone in international organizations like the EU (Birand 2000).

Prior to 1999, the perceived ambivalence of the EU to Turkish membership has hindered the potential impact of the EU on Turkish policy in many areas, including Greek–Turkish relations (Diez and Rumelili 2004). The EU's direct interventions in Greek–Turkish relations, through statements and warnings that the Cyprus problem and Greek–Turkish disputes would adversely affect EU–Turkey relations were negatively interpreted as broader reflections of a European reluctance to admit Turkey into Europe (Ugur 1999). The EU's exclusionary stance towards Turkey also fuelled a dominant conviction in Turkish political culture that "Europe" is conspiring to weaken and dismember Turkey, aptly called the "Sevres syndrome" after the "Sevres Treaty," which conceded large parts of the Ottoman Empire to European powers after the First World War (Kirisci and Carkoglu 2003). This conviction has naturally hindered the EU's impact on sensitive, sovereignty-related issues such as territorial disputes with Greece. In a particularly telling episode in February 2002, the Representative of the EU Commission to Turkey, Karen Fogg, was made the personal target of accusations that the EU is undermining Turkish interests in Cyprus and sponsoring secessionist activity in the Kurdish-dominated south-eastern Turkey.

Second, and more indirectly, by enabling Greece to pursue the above-described policies of negative conditionality, the EU's dissociation helped create and sustain the understanding in Turkey that the EU is captured by the hostile Greece (Aksu 2001). In other words, the EU was perceived as just another platform through which Greece pursues its revisionist agenda with respect to Turkey. Under these perceptual conditions, alternative policies could not be legitimized by reference to the EU, because then their critics would automatically frame them as concessions to Greece.

The developments leading to and in the immediate aftermath of Turkey's Customs Union Agreement with the EU constitute a clear example. When, initially, the Agreement could not be finalized due to the opposition of Greece, the EU decided to resolve the problem of the Greek veto through a linkage strategy. In March 1995, Greece was induced to lift its veto on the Customs Union with Turkey in return for the EU's pledge that accession negotiations with Cyprus would begin six months after the conclusion of the intergovernmental conference. While the majority of the Turkish elite regarded this linkage as fundamentally a Greek tactic to force Turkey to concede in Cyprus, some perceived no problem in Cyprus joining the EU before Turkey if a solution is reached on the island priorly (Author Interview #3).

When the Turkish media released the details of the deal, it became the focal point of opposition. The alternative argument that the membership of a reunited Cyprus could even be to Turkey's benefit was effectively silenced. In order to counter the criticisms on Cyprus sell-off and to regain domestic legitimacy, the Turkish government made some communications, which in turn fueled the perception of threat in Greece and Cyprus. For example, in June 1995, the Turkish parliament issued a perennial resolution that it would view the extension of Greek territorial sea to 12 n.m.s as a casus belli.[13] On December 28, 1995, Turkey and the Turkish Republic of Northern Cyprus started an institutional mechanism to achieve partial integration. This conflict escalation process shortly culminated in the Imia/Kardak crisis that brought the two states to the brink of war in January 1996.

In this perceptual environment, the EU's various interventions in Greek–Turkish disputes had become reference points in legitimizing the continuation of non-compromising positions with respect to Greece. For example, in a follow-up debate on the Luxembourg European Council decisions in the TGNA, MPs from various political parties were united in characterizing the EU as "an organization that implements Greek policy," and "strongly condemning the EU's tendency to see itself as [an impartial] party in Greek-Turkish disputes," warning of the "dangerous consequences of this imprudent tendency" (TGNA 1998). It is interesting how Bulent Akarcali explained why the EU could not be a conflict resolution mechanism for the disputes between Turkey and Greece:

> After the EU tells Turkey to unilaterally resolve its disputes with Greece, why would Greece cooperate with us? … Continuing its disputes with Turkey is to Greece's advantage … Like Germany and Poland … Turkey could have resolved its border disputes in the Aegean within the EU context. If there is friendship, that is the right thing to do. But if friendship has been unilaterally destroyed, then it is up to us to decide what is worth it and what is not. (TGNA 1998)

The EU's exclusionary approach towards Turkey also did not aid the development of transnational links between Turkey and Greece. Civil cooperation between Greece and Turkey remained weak because the civil society in both countries was underdeveloped and the Greek–Turkish activities particularly lacked legitimacy because of the ongoing conflicts (Rumelili 2005). Groups – among businessmen, journalists, artists, and activists – dedicated to the intensification of transnational relations remained as small, isolated minorities in both societies, and their activities were often subjected to criticism and, in a few instances, to physical attack. Although, following the 1996 Imia/Kardak crisis, civil society efforts intensified, they remained vulnerable to crises at the governmental level and were easily disrupted. For example, in reaction to Ocalan's capture on his way out of the Greek embassy in Kenya, Turkish businessmen unilaterally cancelled the scheduled meeting of the Turkish–Greek Business Council and "even the most pro-Greek business personalities felt the need to make anti-Greek statements" (Ozel, 2004: 167).

Its exclusionary approach also posed limitations to the EU's ability to financially support the development of civil society in Turkey and direct funds to Greek–Turkish initiatives. Turkey became eligible for most forms of EU funding only after it signed an Accession Partnership with the EU in 2002. For example, while the Greek–Turkish civil society activity peaked following the 1999 earthquakes, the European Commission was able to initiate its Greek–Turkish Civic Dialogue Program only in 2002. In 1999, the then Representative of the European Commission in Ankara had actually put forward such a proposal, but was not able to obtain funding from Brussels (Author Interview #4).

Finally, the EU's dissociation from Turkey also helped to reproduce Greek and Turkish identities as different from and antagonistic towards each other. The European/non-European distinction that the EU discourse respectively superimposed on Greek and Turkish identities reinforced and legitimized the perceptions of threat and conflict (Rumelili 2003). In order to validate its identity as a part of Europe, Greece sought to sharply distinguish itself from the non-European Turkey, by underscoring Turkey's differences from Greece and, in turn, from Europe. Similarly, in Turkey, the traditional rival Greece functioned as the expedient scapegoat as Turkey sought to validate its European identity in the context of European discourses that constructed it as an "outsider." Exclusion from Europe accentuated Turkey's identity insecurity, and this has led to the reproduction of discourses that constructed Europe, and in particular Greece, as threatening.

An analysis of the Greek media, parliamentary debates, and other relevant texts prior to 1999 reveals a prevalent construction of Turkey as inherently aggressive and provocative. For example, in a debate in the Greek Parliament on November 6, 1997, Karamanlis explained as the leader of the main opposition party New Democracy that "Turkey has a very clear policy … in breach of international law, aggressive, provocative, dangerous, consistent, and timeless. It advances its own objectives … chooses the time … " (Hellenic Parliament 1997: 1250). Another major characteristic of the discourse on Turkey is the depiction of Turkey as monolithic and unable to change. During the same debate, Karamanlis also added that "there is a systematic policy from the other side which everyone pursues" (Hellenic Parliament 1997: 1250) and Tsovolas, leader of the opposition party Democratic and Social Movement (DIKKI) noted that the "Turkish political system and the Turkish economy do not allow for a different type of relations … This system can never become democratic" (Hellenic Parliament 1997: 1269).

In this period, the constructive influence of the EU discourse manifested itself in the representations of Turkey also as inherently non-European and unable to Europeanize (Rumelili 2003). It was argued, for example, in the Greek daily *Ta Nea* that "Turkey's Europeanness stems from geo-political and geo-strategic factors ... In actuality, Turks are closer to Asia by civilization, thinking, language, and instinct" (Dountas 1995). A Turkey constructed as such can only be disciplined through the compulsory influence of the EU. The political debates in Greece prior to 1999 thus revolved around the question of whether Greece could convince other EU member states to direct this compulsory influence in a concerted way or whether it should resort to the veto. There was little if any discussion of the possible enabling influence of the EU on Turkey (i.e. Hellenic Parliament 1999a).

Prior to 1999, the question of how to relate to Turkey within the EU context was further complicated by the ambivalent approach towards Europe and the EU in the Greek discourse. According to Herzfeld (1987: 7), this stems from Greece's "paradoxical status in the Eurocentric ideology." Ascribed the identity of the living ancestors of the European civilization, Greece has had to continuously live out the perceived imbalance between its mythical past and its present backwardness in relation to the contemporary states of Europe (Herzfeld 1987: 19). Prior to 1999, the representations of the EU in Greek discourse, on the one hand, positively identified with the EU as the centre of civilization that includes Greece and excludes Turkey. However, on occasions where the EU was perceived as favoring Turkey against Greece, positive identification quickly gave way to the construction of the EU as imperialist and hostile. For example, the Athens daily *Niki* characterized the EU's conclusion of the Customs Union Agreement with Turkey as an "unethical policy:" "The Europeans, who bear responsibility for the Turkish barbarism against the Greeks and Armenians at the turn of the century, have returned back to their imperialist roots" (*Niki* newspaper, December 12, 1995).

In Turkey, prior to the improvement in relations with Greece, the prevalent representation of Greece was as a "neighbor" and an 'ally' (in name only) that "has made a habit of hostility towards Turkey" (TGNA 1996b), and "lives off" (TGNA, 1996a) its problems with Turkey. The Greek policy of using the EU as a lever against Turkey has been made sense of in terms of the dominant metaphor on Greece as "the spoiled kid of Europe," which implies immaturity, undeservedness, and abuse of position. Therefore, Greece was identified at best as a "fake-European" (Rumelili 2003). Thus, as in Greece, Europe served as the basic denominator of identity, reflecting the EU's constructive influence.

Also in Turkey, as in Greece, these constructions of Greece and the EU were rooted in an ambivalent identification with Europe and the West in general. There is a fundamental tension in Turkish discourse, emanating from the simultaneous construction of Europe as an aspiration and as a threat (Rumelili 2004). The construction of the EU as a threat flourishes on the memories of the dismemberment of Ottoman Empire at the hands of European powers (i.e. Sevres syndrome), while the desire to validate Turkey's identity as modern and European constitutes the EU as an aspiration. The deteriorating state of Turkey's relations with Greece and the EU prior to 1999 has legitimized and reproduced the constructions of the EU as a threat and the related historical analogies. For example, during a debate in the Turkish Parliament on April 20, 1996, in opposing the referral of the Greek–Turkish disputes to the ICJ, Dincer made an analogy with how Mousul was "taken away ... by international institutions ... even though Turkey was right" (TGNA, 1996a). Within this historically inspired discourse, many representations of Greece and the EU assumed as natural that the EU would support [Christian] Greece in relation to [Muslim] Turkey. Kislali argued in the Turkish daily *Cumhuriyet*: "We have to accept that whether due to efforts of the Greek lobby in the US, or stemming from a close culture like in the EU, the West favors the Greek side" (Kislali 1999).

Post-1999 period

Starting with the Simitis leadership of PASOK in 1996, there were indications of a change in Greek foreign policy towards supporting Turkey's European orientation. However, the intra-party divisions did not allow for the consistent implementation of this new policy. In this context, the Ocalan crisis in February 1999 paved the way for the removal of three hardliner ministers from the Greek cabinet and the placement of the moderate George Papandreou in the foreign ministerial post. Soon after, the twin earthquakes that devastated Izmit and Athens respectively in August and September 1999 created a mood of popular empathy in both countries that allowed the leaders "to claim a popular mandate for changing policies historically supported by a large majority on both sides" (Gundogdu 2001). Thereby, Greece was able to make a historic departure away from the previous policy of negative conditionality, and not use its veto against the EU's decision to grant Turkey candidacy status in December 1999.

These precipitating developments should not, however, draw our attention away from the essential role played by the EU in structuring the foreign policy change in Greece. In Greece, Turkey's EU membership perspective has been a crucial element of the logic upon which the alternative policy of supporting Turkey's Europeanization has been formulated and advocated: for Greece to eliminate the Turkish threat, Turkey needs to Europeanize. For Turkey to Europeanize, the EU must be both willing and able to start Turkey's membership process. This logic therefore legitimizes, and renders rational, that Greece should work towards bringing its main rival into the European Union. However, the logic is doomed to fail if the EU insists on dissociating itself from Turkey: the exclusion of Turkey from the EU would make it much more difficult – if not impossible – for Turkey to Europeanize. As one of my interviewees surmised in October 2004, "if Turkey is not given a date [to start accession negotiations] in December, Greece's Turkey policy would lose its foundation" (Author interview #1).

The EU's inclusive approach towards Turkey has constrained the hardliners in Greece by rendering the policy of negative conditionality less possible, successful, and legitimate. The more the EU commits to Turkey's membership, the more Greece loses its power within the Union to block Turkey's path, and it can exercise a veto only at great cost to its reputation (Author Interview #5). This awareness was highly visible among Greek policymakers in the lead-up to the December 2004 European Council (Bourdaras 2004).

Turkey's EU membership perspective not only provided the backbone for the new Greek policy on Turkey, but also facilitated the emergence of a broad domestic coalition necessary to maintain this policy. Differences in policy approach towards Turkey are accommodated within a broad consensus on supporting Turkey's European orientation. While the main opposition party New Democracy had criticized the government in 1999 for failing to tie the candidacy carrot to certain pre-conditions (Hellenic Parliament 1999b), it has later admitted that the strategy was right and continued it since taking government in 2004 (Author Interview #12). Most Greek analysts believe that the Helsinki strategy is built on the "right assumptions" (Author Interview #13). Whereas the hardliners want Turkey to remain on the membership track because they believe they will thereby be able to extract more concessions from Turkey, the moderates support Turkish membership because they believe it will socialize Turkey into changing its foreign policy along EU norms. This domestic coalition has proven flexible enough to survive potentially serious episodes in bilateral relations, such as the outbreak of the airspace "violations" issue during April–May 2003. Following the 2004 elections that brought Karamanlis to power, policy differentiation has been contained within the overall framework of EU–Turkey relations, with Papandreou

criticizing the Karamanlis government for failing to tie EU–Turkey relations to a strict timetable and conditions on Greek–Turkish relations.

The EU's December 1999 decision to grant candidacy status to Turkey
has triggered a process of reform and transformation in Turkey in all
areas of politics, including foreign policy. In the 1990s, Turkey perceived
nearly all of its neighbors as security threats, and pursued policies of
deterrence. The AKP government, on the other hand, has adopted
"zero-problems with neighbors" as the guiding maxim of its foreign policy (Author Interview #6). The policy change towards relations with
Greece manifested itself in many ways: Turkey has first tacitly, and then
more explicitly, accepted a linkage between Turkey's EU membership
process and the resolution of Greek–Turkish disputes; agreed to the
adjudication of the Aegean disputes in the Hague if bilateral negotiations were to fail; actively maintained the détente with Greece through
various confidence-building measures and cooperation agreements; and
supported the Annan Plan for the re-unification of Cyprus. On the other
hand, despite some encouraging statements by the government, the
casus belli on the expansion of territorial waters by Greece has been
recently reasserted by the Turkish military (*Radikal*, April 14, 2005).

This foreign policy change in Turkey was facilitated by the prospect of
EU membership and the concomitant positive identification with the EU.
The EU began to function both as a legitimate reference point and as an
attractive carrot, enabling the moderates to justify policy change, to convince the skeptics and to silence their opponents. The prospect of co-
membership in the EU with Greece offered to Turkish policymakers a
perspective for an alternative future when the border disputes with Greece
would lose their meaning. As one of my interviewees recounts: "Once
Turkey is in the EU, the problems with Greece will be resolved. We give
the example of France and Germany. Many issues are resolved within the
EU in the long-term" (Author Interview #7). Thus, the perception of
the EU as a successful security community is well established among the
Turkish elite, and serves to legitimize the joint efforts to gain membership
in the EU and to resolve the outstanding disputes with Greece. The skeptics are in turn convinced to support Greek–Turkish cooperation because
maintaining good relations with Greece is essential to Turkey's EU membership bid. One of my interviewees put this in crude give-and-take terms,
"we are pursuing good relations with Greece because we want to be in the
EU" (Author Interview #8). For another, it is a matter of realism:

> It is a fact that without Greece's positive stance – I am not saying if it
> does not just use its veto – it will not be possible for Turkey to enter

the EU. We have to assess this realistically, and we're doing so, Greece is one of the countries that have to be on our side. (Author Interview #7)

Civil society cooperation between the two countries had received a boost following the deadly earthquakes that Izmit and Athens suffered in September 1999. Its December 1999 decision to grant Turkey membership candidacy enabled the EU to help consolidate this process in two ways.[14] First of all, the institutional status of candidacy made Turkey eligible for many additional forms of EU funding, and thus allowed the EU to directly support the development of civil society in Turkey, and assist Greek–Turkish civil initiatives. The Civil Society Development Program was introduced in 2002, with a budget of 8 million euros for two years to promote Greek–Turkish dialogue at the grass roots level, and to enhance the capacity of NGOs in Turkey. In February 2004, the European Commission introduced a 35 million euro package to support cross-border cooperation between Greece and Turkey for 2004–6. The availability of EU funding has been important especially for Turkish NGOs, which are more dependent on foreign funding than their counterparts in Greece (Belge, 2004). The EU has specifically supported local and grassroots organizations, which would have difficulty accessing other forms of funding, and encouraged the formation of new partnerships between Greek and Turkish organizations (Author Interview #9).

Secondly, and perhaps more importantly, Turkey's EU membership has provided a common denominator or reference point for activists in Turkey and Greece to gather around (Author Interviews #10 and #11). Especially the Turkish activists perceive themselves and are also perceived by others as working not only for Greek–Turkish cooperation but also for [Turkey's membership in] the EU. The VEN Volunteers Association, for example, states this very explicitly in its mission statement:

It became apparent that the common denominator of our vision was to contribute to Turkey's process of European Union membership and this vision directed us to re-orient ourselves. The active members all agreed that the most important advantage for Turkey in the EU membership process would be the establishment of strong and healthy relations between Turkey and Greece. (Tarikahya, 2004)

Finally, the EU's inclusive approach towards Turkey encouraged the formation of a new discourse on Greek–Turkish identities that dwells on a common European future. Keridis (2001:14) argues that the now dominant perception of Turkey in Greece "is not a monolith but a complicated and rapidly changing reality with a variety of constituencies." As a result of this changed perception, negative representations in the media, such as barbaric, primitive, etc., that used to be totalized onto Turkey are now reserved only for certain groups within Turkey. This pluralistic perception of Turkey has also triggered the realization of common identities and interests that cut across national lines: "People who are pro-Europe in Greece are probably more like people who are pro-Europe in Turkey than they are with their compatriots who might subscribe to some outlandish beliefs or conspiracy theories" (Konstandaras, 2002).

The de-escalation of Greek–Turkish conflicts within the EU context in the post-1999 period was made possible by and, in turn, brought out three fundamental changes in the Greek discourses on Turkey and the EU. The first was the shift from monolithic to more pluralist perceptions and representations of Turkey, while still employing the European/non-European distinction. Zoulas argues in the Greek daily *Kathimerini*: "Greece's Foreign Minister is deeply convinced that there are two Turkeys. One is the Turkey of Prime Minister Recep Tayyip Erdogan: *pro-European*, moderate, and flexible. The other is that of Turkish Chief of Staff Gen. Hilmi Ozkok: typically *eastern*, intransigent and aggressive" (Zoulas 2003).

Secondly, the representation of Turkey as pluralistic and able to change has made possible its construction as susceptible to the EU's enabling influence. This representation has become prevalent in Greece to such an extent that almost everything about Turkey has been made sense of within the discourse of "Europeanization." To justify the policy change towards Turkey, Prime Minister Simitis argued in Greek Parliament on December 15, 1999 that "[W]e have opened the door to Turkey because we believe that the Europeanization of Turkey would favor everyone" (Hellenic Parliament 1999b: 2364). Similarly, the political turmoil in Turkey and even conflict-enhancing behavior towards Greece are represented as a 'Europeanization crisis' (Ioakimidis 2002).

Thirdly, the policy change towards Turkey has been grounded in a more positive identification with Europe and the EU. Reflecting a complete identification, the Greek Foreign Ministry spokesman Koumoutsakos reportedly said during the December 2004 Brussels European Council that "whatever is European is also Greek and whatever is Greek is also European" (Bourdaras 2004). Similarly, the Greek daily *Kathimerini* commended the Greek Prime Minister for attempting "to behave like a European leader, and not a Balkan leader" during his visit to the US in

January 2002 (*Kathimerini* newspaper, January 18, 2002). Greek policy-makers have repeatedly justified their policy change towards Turkey by reference to European norms. In fact, the Greek Foreign Minister Papandreou explained the policy change in December 2002 as: "Our experience in Europe has taught us that the stability of our neighbor gives us strength" (Papandreou 2002).

The improvement in Greek–Turkish relations after 1999 has brought out and, in turn, was made possible by two significant changes in the Turkish discourses on Greece and the EU. The first is the ensuing positive identification with the EU, such that the constructions of the EU as an aspiration gained prevalence over the constructions of the EU as a threat. Turkey's new identity position as an EU candidate also facilitated the gradual internalization of EU norms and procedures on the resolution of border disputes as requirements of European identity and a neutral basis to build a cooperative relationship with Greece. Turenc argued in the Turkish daily *Hurriyet*:

> [S]eeing the benefits of sharing common values and interests will bring the two countries closer to each other with every passing day. No one can believe that Turkey and Greece, who have come together in the same family, will remain foes from now on. (Turenc 1999)

The second important discursive change is the shift towards the construction of Greece as a "full, mature, and rational" European state, and in a lot of ways as a "model" for Turkey. Kohen argued in the Turkish daily *Milliyet* that "it is also difficult not to admire Greece's current position within the Union ... just a few years ago certain EU circles harshly criticized its weak economy and uncooperative attitude ... Let's admit that the pragmatic, progressive policies of the Simitis administration have played an important role in Greece's successful rise within the EU ranks" (Kohen 2003). Coupled with the unwavering Greek support for Turkey's EU membership, this construction of Greek identity has facilitated the perception of Greek behavior towards Turkey in the EU context in less hostile and conspiratorial terms.

V. Conclusion

The conclusions of this chapter validate the main argument of the book; that community-building is a double-sided process, the cultivation of a sense of collective identity among states within a community inevitably entails the production of difference with states outside of the community.

As a result, the security implications of community-building are also double-sided. While collective identity may promote sustained peace and cooperation among states within the community, the production of difference from outsider states may help aggravate conflicts between insider and outsider states.

This chapter analyzed three sets of bilateral relations that are situated in different institutional/identity relations with respect to the EU. The cases of Polish–German relations and Greek–Turkish relations in the post-1999 period demonstrate the EU has been able to positively affect conflicts involving outsider states with whom it has strong relations of association. As a result of EU involvement, the sources of dispute in Polish–German relations were resolved, and Greek–Turkish relations de-escalated into issue conflicts. Relations of association and the construction of the outsider state as a potential part of self facilitated various forms of EU influence on these conflicts. The carrot of EU membership induced both Poland and Turkey to undertake policy changes. The eventual possibility of co-membership in the same security community empowered moderate domestic actors in Poland and Germany and in Greece and Turkey, who would like to use the EU as a means of reconciliation. Relations of association enabled the EU to fund and support transgovernmental and transnational links. The construction of the outsider state as a potential part of self weakened the conflict enhancing, oppositional discourses of self versus other.

However, the EU's impact on conflicts involving outsider states, which the EU has dissociated from and produced strong discourses of difference in relation to, has been negative or non-existent at best. The cases of Moroccan–Spanish relations and Greek–Turkish relations in the pre-1999 period demonstrate how the EU can perpetuate and aggravate conflicts between insider and outsider states. Production of difference and Othering securitized the existing conflicts. Both in Spain and in Greece, those actors who approach the EU as a means of power against Morocco and Turkey respectively were empowered. The conflict enhancing self versus other identity distinctions were reinforced.

6
Identity/Difference and the ASEAN

I. Introduction

Southeast Asia stands out as the region in the non-Western world that most closely approximates a community. In a region with great political, economic, and cultural diversity, the Association of Southeast Nations (ASEAN), initially established in 1967 among Indonesia, Malaysia, Singapore, the Philippines, and Thailand, has fostered a collective Southeast Asian identity around the norms of non-interference, mutual respect for sovereignty and consensus-building. As a result, in Southeast Asia, the likelihood of war has been significantly reduced among a diverse group of states with histories of conflict.

There is an ongoing debate in the literature as to whether ASEAN qualifies as a "security community." Like the condition of Europe during and prior to World War 2, the likelihood of war in Southeast Asia was very high in the 1960s, before the establishment of ASEAN. To indicate the threat of internal strife, inter-state conflict, and Cold War-induced proxy wars in the region, it was frequently portrayed as a "region of revolt," the "Balkans of the East," or a "region of dominoes" (Acharya, 2001: 4). Given the high likelihood of inter-state conflict prior to the establishment of the organization, the very fact that the original ASEAN members have not fought a war against each other since 1967 attests to its success (Kivimaki 2001). However, Denoon and Colbert (1998) and Narine (1998) argue that the continued existence of intra-ASEAN territorial disputes – the Philippines continues to dispute Malaysia's sovereignty over Sabah, and Malaysia's relations with Thailand are also strained due to border disputes – disqualifies Southeast Asia from being a security community. Acharya (1998; 2001), on the other hand, claims that the distinguishing feature of a security community is its ability to manage conflicts and not the absence of conflict, and that ASEAN has fared very well in this regard.

From another perspective, Southeast Asia does not qualify as a security community because it is not underpinned by a liberal collective identity. According to Adler (1992: 293), "members of pluralistic security communities hold dependable expectations of peaceful change not merely because they share just any kind of values, but because they share liberal democratic values." Most states in Southeast Asia are (or have been) homes to repressive regimes, and, in creating a sense of collective identity among these states, ASEAN does not uphold liberal norms. If anything, through the norm of non-interference in member states' internal affairs, ASEAN legitimizes and ensures the continued existence of authoritarian regimes, as in the case of Myanmar. Kivimaki (2001) and Acharya (2001), however, argue that norms against killing one's own kind can evolve and be sustained among states that share non-liberal identities, and that an "intersubjective consensus about the common interests, norms, and identity has contributed to the interstate peace among illiberal non-democracies of Southeast Asia" (Kivimaki 2001: 5).

This book adopts the position that regardless of whether Southeast Asia currently qualifies or has succeeded in becoming a security community, ASEAN is a community-building institution, which promotes a discourse of collective identity. As an alternative example of a regional community-building institution, how does ASEAN interact with difference and with what implications for regional order? Mirroring the analysis of the EU undertaken in the previous three chapters in a condensed form, this chapter analyzes how ASEAN interacts with difference, how the collective identity promoted by ASEAN is negotiated with outsider states, and how the way ASEAN interacts with difference affects the broader regional order in Southeast Asia and beyond.

II. ASEAN and difference

Unlike in the case of the EU, there is not a developed literature with distinct arguments on how ASEAN relates to its "outside," its mode of differentiation. In this section, I identify and analyze ASEAN's mode of differentiation using the analytical categories I developed in Chapter 2 and applied to the case of the EU. This enables me to both evaluate the general applicability of my categories and comparatively analyze the community-building practices of EU and ASEAN. Just like in Europe, the formation of a Southeast Asian collective identity has entailed the production of a sense of difference with states outside of the collectivity.

The main and significant difference is that, while the European collective identity promoted by the EU is a hybrid in terms of embodying both inclusive and exclusive aspects, the Southeast Asian collective identity promoted by ASEAN is predominantly exclusive.

Two factors contribute to the exclusiveness of Southeast Asian collective identity. The first is the shared beliefs about the certainty of regional boundaries. The 1967 Bangkok Declaration that founded the ASEAN stated that "the Association is open for participation to all States in the South-East Asian Region subscribing to the aforementioned aims, principles and purposes." Even though the Declaration did not explicitly define Southeast Asia's geographical limits, there was considerable certainty among ASEAN member states about where the region's ultimate boundaries lay. ASEAN's vision of One Southeast Asia is to build a regional community encompassing all ten states of Southeast Asia.

The shared beliefs about the certainty of regional boundaries cannot be explained by an essentialist logic. It is not that the boundaries of community in Southeast Asia are strictly determined and dictated by geography. Quite to the contrary, the differences between the mainland states like Thailand and island states like Indonesia can easily lead us to question the geographical logic behind their grouping together within the same region. In addition, how can one justify geographically that Papua New Guinea is not part of the ASEAN region, even though it occupies the eastern half of an island the western half of which is part of the Indonesian archipelago? Southeast Asia is not somehow geographically more natural and clearly demarcated a region than Europe. What differentiates Southeast Asia from Europe, and also what makes their comparison rather interesting, is that the states in Southeast Asia share a belief about the ultimate boundaries of their community, while states in Europe do not, at least with respect to Europe's Eastern boundary.

The shared beliefs about the certainty of the region's boundaries are reflected in the intentional building of institutional relations with regional states, even when the possibility of their membership seemed distant. Burma (now Myanmar) and Cambodia were initially asked to join, but declined on the basis that ASEAN's perceived pro-US sympathies were incompatible with their declared neutrality (Henderson, 1999). During the late 1960s and early 1970s, Cambodia, Laos and South Vietnam attended some of the ASEAN Ministerial Meetings as observers. The Treaty of Amity and Cooperation – Bali Treaty of 1976 – was opened to accession by states outside of Southeast Asia, pending the consent of all states in Southeast Asia. In this document, the definition of Southeast Asia explicitly included Cambodia, Laos, Burma, and Vietnam even though they were not members of ASEAN then (Amer 1999). The goal of One Southeast Asia was deemed accomplished with the membership of Vietnam in 1995, Laos and Burma in 1997, and Cambodia in 1998. As Severino, the Secretary-General of ASEAN stated at the time: "Southeast Asia has fulfilled the destiny set for it by geography" (Severino, 2000a).

The shared beliefs about the certainty of regional boundaries among ASEAN members have not obviated the need to produce a sense of difference from outside states in order to maintain the boundary and the sense of collective identity. But, differently from Europe, these beliefs have not left any room for ambiguity on the part of ASEAN members regarding who is in and who is out. ASEAN has produced a sense of inherent difference from outside states and precluded the possibility of their becoming eventual members of the community. While, as will be discussed later, it has entered into overlapping institutional arrangements with states in Northeast Asia, South Asia, and the Pacific, it has maintained the distinctiveness of the Southeast Asian community in all these endeavors.

This does not mean that the states on ASEAN's periphery do not have a potentially liminal character. The shared beliefs about the certainty of regional boundaries have not made these boundaries free of contention, as evident when states outside these boundaries have either applied for or implied interest in membership. In other words, the external definition of the region has not necessarily coincided with the internal definition, necessitating the re-inscription of the boundary through the production of difference in relation to these potentially liminal states.

When ASEAN refused Sri Lanka's desire to join the grouping[15] and dismissed India, China, or Australia from ever acquiring membership status, it was similarly re-inscribing the boundaries of the Southeast Asian community through the production of inherent difference. Also, in 1996, Papua New Guinea proposed that it should be made a "permanent associate member" of ASEAN. Although Papua New Guinea had observer status since 1976 and had acceded to the Treaty of Amity and Cooperation in 1987, these arrangements were not intended to lead Papua New Guinea into ASEAN membership. Thus, its request for permanent associate membership received a lukewarm reception (Henderson 1999: 82). Among ASEAN's interactions with these outside states, its interaction with Australia took on a liminal character because, as will be discussed later on in this chapter, Australia repeatedly and vocally resisted the reinscription of this boundary in the 1980s and early 1990s.

The second factor that has contributed to the exclusiveness of Southeast Asian collective identity has been the fact that community norms and principles, such as non-interference and consensual decision-making, have not had a universalizing aspiration. Instead, ASEAN has underlined the cultural specificity of the community norms and values, and their appropriateness for Southeast Asia's political and historical circumstances. While arguing that "non-interference policy is not ASEAN's exclusive preserve, but the conceptual bulwark of the international system" (Severino 2000b), it has legitimized its strict adherence to these principles through the collective regional memory of colonization. The region's historical narrative stresses how the political, economic, and cultural ties among the peoples of Southeast Asia were severed through colonial designs, but then rebuilt through ASEAN (Severino 2000a). National sovereignty and the principle of non-interference are seen as essential to "protect the small and the weak from domination by the powerful" (Severino 2000b). In addition, the community's procedural norms of consensual decision-making and settling differences through consultation have been presented as a uniquely "ASEAN way" to cooperation. Setting formal institutions and dispute settlement procedures are dismissed as "Western" ways that presume the pre-existence of an adversarial relationship between states. The ASEAN community has explicitly distinguished itself from Europe, stating that, unlike the European Union, "it does not mean to transform itself into a political union under any form of central supranational authority" nor has it "assigned itself the mission of converting its members to a uniform political set-up." [16]

In the case of European collective identity, the universalizing aspirations of democracy and capitalism have entailed the production of acquired difference from outside states. Because such inclusive identities are sustained by others who aspire to become like self, defining the European collective identity's content as democratic and capitalist necessitated the recognition of the possibility that others may become like self one day. In contrast, the defining of the Southeast Asian identity around the principles of sovereignty, non-interference, and consensual decision-making has not entailed the production of acquired difference, but instead has reinforced ASEAN's sense of inherent difference from outside states. In the context of universalizing and hegemonic Western norms, the sustenance of ASEAN's norms rests on their recognition by others as culturally specific to and appropriate for Southeast Asia. In other words, ASEAN's norms are sustained by others who recognize them as equally legitimate and appropriate, but do not necessitate others who aspire to them. To promote this recognition, ASEAN needs to underscore its inherent differences from others.

After the Asian economic crisis, the norm of non-interference has become increasingly questioned, with internal critics arguing that, had ASEAN not been so tightly bound by it, it could have issued timely warnings to Thailand about its worsening condition. ASEAN took a first step in this direction by establishing a regional financial and macroeconomic surveillance process, known as the ASEAN Surveillance Process. While Acharya argues that this indicates a trend towards the increasing "intrusiveness" of ASEAN regionalism, he also notes that ASEAN proved resistant to the inclusion of political issues (such as Myanmar's human rights record) or to the institutionalization of the Surveillance Process into a Surveillance Mechanism (Acharya 2002: 29).

In short, community norms and principles, such as consensual decision-making, do not have a universalizing aspiration or inclusive orientation; they are presented as unique to ASEAN. Thus, in contrast to Europe, where the hybrid identity criteria have been productive of inherent and acquired differences, in Southeast Asia we encounter a single conception of difference because what could possibly be acquired differences are presented as manifestations of inherent differences. In the absence of conflicting orientations towards difference, the Southeast Asian community has produced a clear demarcation of self from other. While the former have been incorporated as members with no conditions attached, ASEAN has interacted with the latter solely as dialogue and trade partners.

Myanmar

ASEAN has interacted with Myanmar (previously Burma) as part of self. In terms of the three dimensional framework of self/other interaction, this means that ASEAN constructs Myanmar to be inherently similar and Myanmar recognizes the construction of its identity, and thus association with Myanmar is securing of the ASEAN collective identity. Myanmar has always been viewed by ASEAN states as an inherent part of their region, and their interaction has, from the beginning, been governed by ASEAN norms. It is important to note that this interaction is different from the EU's interaction with the CEES after the end of the Cold War because there is no interim status of candidacy. While the EU, through the institution of candidacy, has constructed a hierarchy of superior/inferior between itself and the CEES. Myanmar has, from the beginning, been perceived and acted toward as an equal. While the interaction of the EU with the CEES has been characterized by a sense of acquired difference, ASEAN's clear demarcation of self from other has ensured that there is no sense of constitutive difference between Myanmar and ASEAN.

That ASEAN perceived and acted toward Myanmar as a part of self is very apparent in their institutional relationship. Right after the establishment of ASEAN, Burma was invited to become a member of the organization, an offer which Burma declined because of its isolationist stance. Though Burma was officially not a member, it was explicitly included in the definition of Southeast Asia in the 1976 Bali Treaty. That meant that states outside of Southeast Asia that wanted to accede to the Bali Treaty had to get the consent of all states within Southeast Asia – including Burma – regardless of whether those states were members of ASEAN. After the end of the Cold War, the inclusion of Myanmar within ASEAN was seen as an essential component of the realization of ASEAN's vision of One Southeast Asia. That ASEAN made Myanmar a member in 1997 in spite of vocal opposition from Europe, the United States, and the international community is a clear indicator of the fact that ASEAN viewed Myanmar as an essential part of its collective self.

Persistent political repression in Myanmar is the basis for the international community's objection to its membership in ASEAN. In September 1988, after a wave of nationwide pro-democracy demonstrations, a military coup brought a junta to power. The junta established the State Law and Order Restoration Council (SLORC) and in 1990 organized the first parliamentary polls in three decades. However, when the elections were won by an opposing coalition, the National League for Democracy led by Aung San Suu Kyi, the SLORC refused to convene the parliament and transfer power. Aung San Suu Kyi was put under house arrest roughly from 1989 to present, and the military junta has not yet relinquished power to a civilian government. These developments in Myanmar drew a great deal of negative publicity and international criticism, and led to the isolation of Myanmar in various international forums as well as the suspension of Western and Japanese aid. In the Western view, association with Myanmar had to be avoided because it would encourage and support the military regime.

Under these circumstances, the norm of non-interference formed the basis of ASEAN's engagement with Myanmar and its determination to admit Myanmar into ASEAN. Western condemnation of the SLORC's violation of the democratic process was viewed by ASEAN as outside interference in the internal affairs of a regional country. In ASEAN's view, political repression in Myanmar could not be used to justify the exclusion of Myanmar since such a move would constitute interference in internal affairs. ASEAN put forth the concept of "constructive engagement" to explain its response to the Myanmar situation. As explained by an Indonesian foreign policy official, this meant that ASEAN is telling the Myanmar regime to change "very quietly, in a Southeast Asian manner, without any fanfare, without any public statements" which would "embarrass and isolate them" *(Straits Times*, August 26, 1992, cited in Acharya 2001: 110). The symbolic incentive to realize the One Southeast Asia concept by ASEAN's thirtieth anniversary in 1997 also contributed to the speedy admission of Myanmar. In addition, the US decision to impose sanctions against Myanmar made it impossible for ASEAN to delay its admission since that would imply caving in to US pressure and thereby would compromise its goal of regional autonomy.

In short, ASEAN's interaction with Myanmar exemplifies how an international community founded on an exclusive identity interacts with an outside state that is constructed as inherently similar, as part of self. In contrast to the EU's interaction with the CEES, there is no production of acquired difference. Neither did ASEAN pose a list of conditions that Myanmar needed to fulfill, nor was there a probationary period of candidacy during which Myanmar's capabilities and willingness were assessed.

The liminal: Australia

A dramatic change in Australia's foreign policy orientation in the 1980s and 1990s challenged this clear demarcation of identity/difference that ASEAN promoted. States in Southeast Asia had traditionally interacted with Australia as an "absolute other," and this conception of difference was shared and thereby reinforced by Australia. To Southeast Asian states, Australia was a white community in alliance with great power interests in the region. Australia's difference had been constitutive of Southeast Asian collective identity; the community had represented Australia to be Western, arrogant, imperialist, and disrespectful of sovereignty. Similarly, until the mid-1960s, Australian identity had revolved around being a white, British community. White Australia policy restricted immigration to those of the white race. The region was something that Australians and their governments looked across and sailed past to Britain. If the region mattered at all, it was as a source of anxiety in the Cold War context (G. Smith *et al.*, 1996).

In the 1980s and 1990s, the Hawke and Keating governments self-consciously sought to change the identity and image of Australia from being a distant outpost of the British empire to a member of the Asia–Pacific region in economic, diplomatic, and security terms. The most visible manifestation of this policy has been the launching of the Asia Pacific Economic Cooperation (APEC) in 1989 under Australian initiative. In addition, Australian governments have engaged in various symbolic efforts to forge a deeper integration between Australian and Asian cultural identities. Examples of these efforts include the making of maps whose projections place Australia in the center of the East Asian hemisphere, and statements that the Australian icon of mateship might be understood as an Asian value, or that an Asia–Pacific community means a big family as in Chinese (Wiseman 1998; G. Smith *et al.* 1996; Higgott and Nossal 1998).

Australia's efforts at redefining its identity have placed it in a liminal position with respect to the Southeast Asian community. While Australia's efforts have intensified the institutional relations between ASEAN and Australia, they have also increased the necessity to (re)articulate the differences that separate Australia from Southeast Asia. Institutionally, Australia participates in a series of consultative meetings with ASEAN, which include the ASEAN Regional Forum (ARF), ASEAN–Australia Forum, the Post Ministerial Conferences (PMC) 9+1 and 9+10. However, coupled with these are institutional contexts that Australia does not or is not allowed to participate in. In addition to the fact that Australia is not a member of ASEAN (Australia has not sought membership), Australia is not included in the Asia–Europe (ASEM) meetings despite its overt request to be, the proposals for an ASEAN Free Trade Area (AFTA), and the East Asian Economic Caucus (EAEC).

In the course of their relations with Australia, ASEAN states have continued with their exclusive conception of the Southeast Asian region, and view APEC and cooperation with Australia as institutional cooperation between two distinct regions. Despite Australia's efforts at redefining its identity as a member of the region, ASEAN has explicitly dismissed the possibility of Australian membership in ASEAN. In the eyes of at least several Southeast Asian states, Australia cannot cooperate in the ASEAN way because it lacks "Asian"ness. As Malaysia's former President Mahathir Mohamad stated bluntly, "calling Australia an Asian country has no meaning whatsoever" (Higgott and Nossal 1998: 283). Australia's attempts at redefining its identity have challenged the Southeast Asian collective identity by threatening to blur the community's firm boundaries between self and other. Hence, there has been a greater necessity to (re)inscribe the boundary in relation to Australia. The interaction of Australia with ASEAN has become a site where "Asianness" and the "Southeast Asian collective identity" are challenged and simultaneously reproduced and (re)articulated.

Beyond membership

In its external relations, ASEAN has entered into various forms of flexible and overlapping institutional arrangements with outsider states. The earliest example is the Post-Ministerial Conferences, which provide a forum for consultation with non-ASEAN "dialogue partners" following ASEAN's Ministerial meetings. Currently, the ASEAN dialogue system includes Australia, Canada, the European Union, Japan, New Zealand, the United States, China, South Korea, Russia, India, and the UN Development Program. ASEAN states are founding members of APEC, a regional grouping initiated by Australia and Japan in 1989 to bring together states on both sides of the Pacific. ASEAN initially opposed APEC on the grounds that a new regional forum was not necessary; economic cooperation between ASEAN and its dialogue partners could be facilitated through an expanded ASEAN Post-Ministerial Conference (PMC). ASEAN participation in APEC was realized only through formal assurances that cooperation would be based on independence, mutual respect, and equality, and that it would only complement ASEAN's regional activities and role in the Pacific: Initially, APEC's membership comprised the ASEAN-6 and the United States, Canada, Australia, New Zealand, Japan, and South Korea; later, China, Taiwan, Hong Kong, Mexico, Papua New Guinea, Chile, Peru, Russia, and Vietnam became members.

In 1994, ASEAN states and dialogue partners created the ASEAN Regional Forum in order to discuss political and security issues of common interest and to contribute to the confidence-building and preventative diplomacy efforts in the Asia–Pacific region. In addition to the current ASEAN members and dialogue partners, the Forum now also includes Mongolia, and Papua New Guinea and North Korea as observers. ASEAN remains at the core of both APEC and the ARF, and their modus operandi remains entrenched in the ASEAN way. The ARF remains formally an extension of ASEAN, and not only does APEC adhere to ASEAN ways of doing business, but APEC summits are always held in a strict two-year rotation of an ASEAN country and a non-ASEAN country (A. Smith, 2004).

Institutionalized cooperation with China, Japan, and South Korea has been developed since 1997 in the form of the ASEAN Plus Three Process. The Process revitalized the ideas about East Asian economic cooperation, passionately advocated by the former Malaysian President Mahathir in the early 1990s. Mahathir's East Asian Economic Caucus (EAEC) similarly included Japan and China but not Australia, Canada, New Zealand and the US, thus in effect excluding countries with population majorities of European origin. Australia and the US opposed the idea on the grounds that it would "divide the region into two opposing camps." The EAEC never fully materialized because, in order not to alienate the United States, Japan placed a condition that both Australia and New Zealand must be allowed to join. In November 2001, ASEAN and China announced their intention to forge a Free Trade Agreement to be completed in 2010, which was followed by the Chiang Mai initiative that established a currency swap arrangement and the 2002 Framework Agreement on ASEAN–China Economic Cooperation (Smith, A. 2004). ASEAN has also agreed to an FTA with India by 2012. During ASEAN's Bali Summit in October 2003, China and India have also acceded to the ASEAN's Treaty of Amity and Cooperation.

In 2004, ASEAN leaders agreed to create a new forum – the East Asian Summit (EAS) – which would include India, Australia, and New Zealand in addition to the ASEAN Plus Three (China, Japan, and South Korea). In order to participate in the Summit, Australia and New Zealand acceded to the Treaty of Amity and Cooperation, which was stipulated as a condition. The EAS held its first meeting in December 2005.

III. Negotiating "Asia": ASEAN–Australia relations

The institutional relationships between ASEAN and Australia are embedded in an identity interaction in which Australia occupies a liminal position. By challenging the demarcation between self and other, liminals make the community identity more insecure, and hence they are perceived and represented as threatening. But also, as sites that challenge the demarcation between self and other, they provide the discursive opportunity for the possible transcendence of the categories of "self" and "other" through the recognition that self and other can coexist as they do in the liminal. Hence, like EU–Turkey relations, ASEAN–Australia relations constitute a site where the collective identities of "Asia" "Asianness" are negotiated.

It may be argued that Australia's liminal position is pre-given. Much like Turkey, Australia is often understood and represented as occupying a unique place in the contemporary discourse on identities in international relations. A society of white European descent, that is loyal to the British crown and governed by liberal norms, Australia is constituted as a "misfit" in its part of the world inhabited by Asian post-colonial societies and mostly semi-authoritarian regimes. Also, in a world where the Western and European identities constitute the high parlance, Australia, as a state that is traditionally accepted as Western and

European but which is now striving to be recognized as Asian, seems an odd case. That is why, according to Huntington (1996: 132), if Turkey is a "torn" country, Australia is a "torn country in reverse." In this section, I reiterate a point that I have made with regard to the case of Turkey, that the constitution of Australia as "torn" stems from a discourse that constructs the identities of "European" and "Asian" as incompatible and mutually exclusive. Moreover, Australia's "oddity" and "reverse" condition, as different from the case of Turkey, stems from the discursive construction of the "European" identity as superior, such that, while it is "normal" to seek a "European" identity, it becomes "odd" and "peculiar" for Australia to be seeking an "Asian" identity.

That liminality is not an objective condition that is inherent in a state's identity and cultural characteristics, but one which is historically and socially produced, is also demonstrated in the case of Australia. Established as a settler colony, Australia's identity has been based on its superiority to and social distance from the states in Asia and Southeast Asia. A corresponding sense of difference and social distance from Australia was reproduced by ASEAN through its anti-colonial identity. The mutual recognition of difference has sustained cooperative relations between Australia and ASEAN. Australia has consistently supported ASEAN for its contribution to regional stability. This support was based on a shared understanding that Pacific and Asian regions were distinct, and therefore Australia would not be in an organization for the Asian region. This shared understanding was reflected, for example, in the cultural agreement signed between Australia and Indonesia in 1968 that expressed "the need for widening the mutual understanding and respect of the diverse peoples and nations of the Asian and Pacific regions, recognizing that history and geographical propinquity have presented Australia and Indonesia, as countries of widely different cultural background, with unique opportunities for learning from each other" (Catley and Dugis, 1998).

The shared understanding and mutual recognition of difference unraveled as changes in the regional political economy encouraged a process of identity rethinking in Australia and Southeast Asia. Australia's sense of superiority to and social distance from Southeast Asia became harder to maintain in the 1980s as Australia found itself outpaced by Southeast Asian states in economic and industrial development. Perceiving the situation as the coming of the "much heralded Pacific century" (Evans 1989), Australian policymakers presented involvement in regional initiatives as the answer to Australia's economic problems. These efforts were legitimized and supported through an identity discourse which delegitimized Australia's previous approach to the region as anachronistic and racist, and represented Australia as predominantly an Asian and an Asia–Pacific state. In a rapid profusion of the "Asia rhetoric," it became commonplace for policymakers to talk of the "historic shift to Asia" and of "Australians finding their true place in Asia" (Milner, 1997). As Australian Minister for Foreign Affairs and Trade, Gareth Evans, put it at the time: "It is simply no longer possible for Australia to see itself first and foremost as a transplanted European nation, a cultural misfit trapped by geography" (Evans, 1990).

Similarly, among the states in Southeast Asia, the pace of development encouraged a sense of self-confidence that they projected outward through articulations of Asian (cultural) superiority instead of the defensive anti-colonial identity. For much of the 1990s, an "Asian way debate" raged among East Asian political leaders and academics (Funabashi 1993; Mahbubani 1995). The proponents argued that, despite the ethnic, cultural, and religious diversity, a specific set of "Asian values" – Confucianism, collectivism, and importance of family – exists that makes the region uniquely different from the "West," in terms of economics, politics, and civilization (Bessho 1999). Hence, the divergent cultures and values between East Asia and the West make it inappropriate for the West to meddle in the internal affairs of the region's states in its pursuit of "universal" values. Much of the symbolic interaction between Australia and the ASEAN states in the 1990s took place within the parameters of the Asian way debate.

Australia was put in a liminal position as the Asian way debate constituted Asia and Europe as mutually exclusive identities while Australia resisted the construction of its identity as European and hence inherently different from Asia. One strategy employed by Australian policymakers is to place and thereby subsume the Asian region in a broader Asia–Pacific region, and thereby attempt to redefine the relevant region for community-building. As Gareth Evans argued:

> It has to be acknowledged that geographically, in any strict technical sense, Australia is not and cannot be a part of Asia: we are not in Asia but alongside it. What we are unequivocally part of is the Asia–Pacific region. (Evans 1992)

A simultaneously pursued representational strategy has been to claim that "Asia" is nothing more than a European construct. Gareth Evans has, on multiple occasions, noted the irony of the fact that Australia is excluded from regional initiatives in Southeast Asia on the basis that it is not Asian, i.e. on the basis of a "European" construct.

> There was, before the Europeans, no word for 'Asia' and no 'Asian' consciousness – perhaps not surprisingly given the presence of six or more important and distinct cultural traditions, and living languages. That diversity means that, while we in Australia are manifestly not an Asian people, we are culturally and demographically more or less equidistant from all its elements ... We no longer need to be the odd man out in Asia – even if we are destined to be the oddest man in. (Evans 1991)

While the representational strategies discussed above sought to deconstruct Asia as an exclusive identity, Australia has also sought to frame "Asianness" or the "Asian Way" as an inclusive identity that can be acquired by others. This entailed, according to Evans, making "some adjustments of style" in relating to Asian countries without giving up on Australian values and culture. According to Evans, this is a necessity that stems from Australia's "otherness."

> Our 'otherness' is not a constraint on our freedom of action, but does affect how we should exercise it. We should be conscious that in some contexts public and formal initiatives will be appropriate, but that in others the emphasis should be on informal and incremental activity. (Evans, 1989b)

The issue of Australia's ability to behave in an "Asian" fashion has manifested itself most prominently with regard to human rights concerns, where the Asian governments are most sensitive about outside interference. The Australian government's attempts to behave in an "'Asian'" fashion have often been met with fierce domestic opposition that Australia was sacrificing its liberal identity and values by appeasing the Asian states. Hence, the government's Asian engagement has been constructed by critics as compromising and diluting Australian identity as liberal and democratic.

That Australia's interaction with ASEAN is characterized by perceptions and representations of identity threat was very apparent during a 1993 row between Australian Prime Minister Keating and Malaysian President Mahathir. While the economic liberalization of the 1980s generated a shared interest among ASEAN states and Australia in broader economic groupings, as a result of their conflicting notions of collective identity, Australia and ASEAN did not always agree on their geographical scope.

The competition between Malaysia and Australia to promote the rival economic groupings of EAEC and APEC led to a nasty row in November 1993. The episode clearly demonstrates how Australia's liminal position in relation to ASEAN aggravated the necessity on both sides to articulate their differences and construct the other as threatening to their identity. Mahathir said that he would not attend the November 1993 APEC summit, because he claimed that the decision to hold the summit was dictated by the US and not democratically decided by all APEC members. Disappointed, Australian Prime Minister Keating referred to Malaysia in a press conference as "recalcitrant." Regarding this statement as an insult, Malaysian officials and businesses announced various actions against Australia, ceasing all broadcasts of Australian films on state-owned radio and television, canceling investment trips to Australia, and freezing joint-venture projects with Australian firms (*The Straits Times*, December 10, 1993).

Keating sent a letter to Mahathir that explained that his remark was not intended to be offensive and expressed regret if offense was taken. In reaction to the incident, Mahathir remarked that Australia considers itself an Asian nation but does not seem to behave like an Asian nation: "It is difficult to love them ... they have less manners and do not behave like Asians" (Makabenta, 1993). Other commentators in Malaysia also characterized Keating's response as typically Western: "Frankness and speaking one's mind may be a virtue for the West but in the East, such actions come across as downright rude" (Hassan, 1993).

The incident underlined the necessity to reinscribe the boundary between Asia and the West, and between acceptable and unacceptable Asian behavior. That is why the reaction to Australia took the form of clearly marking Australia as Western and inherently different from Asia, and also essentially incapable of becoming and behaving like an Asian. Also in Australia, Keating responded by saying that his country should not bow its head to Asian neighbors while it pushes into the Asian region. Closer links with Asia, Keating said, did not mean Australians had to lose pride in their own culture or their democratic traditions. In Australia, the use of the word "recalcitrant" was framed and understood as free speech, a manifestation of Australian identity as a democratic society. Once interpreted in this fashion, the widespread resentment the expression caused in Malaysia was in turn explained by the fact that Malaysia is an autocratic society which does not allow the exercise of free speech.

Similar representational practices characterized the tensions that arose over Australian non-participation in the ASEAN Free Trade Area (AFTA) and the Asia Europe Meetings (ASEM). In arguing that Australia cannot attend the first Asia–Europe Meeting (ASEM) in 1996 Mahathir said he cannot accept Australia being called part of East Asia and argued that Australia joining the ASEM would be like Arabs joining the European Union (BBC Summary of World Broadcasts, March 3, 1996). Commenting on Australia's exclusion, Stephen Fitzgerald, the director of the Asia–Australia Institute, argued that "to be denied participation in the critical political councils of the coalition of states which dominates us economically is comparable to a colonial status for Australia" (Fitzgerald 1997: 2).

After 1996, the conservative Howard government downplayed engagement with Asia, and underscored Australia's distinct identity and values and strong ties with the United States and Europe. Yet, the decision to sign the Treaty of Amity and Cooperation with ASEAN in order to be eligible to participate in the EAS in 2005 can be taken as a strong signal of renewed Australian commitment to the region (Jain 2007). Participation in the EAS has not altered Australia's liminal identity position with respect to Southeast Asia. While Richardson (2005) argues that EAS marks the beginning of a more open and inclusive regionalism in Asia, it is necessary to note that ASEAN remains in the driving seat of this external relations initiative. The prominence of ASEAN is evident in the fact that EAS meetings will be held annually alongside the ASEAN summit in Southeast Asian countries only (Malik 2006). The insistence of Chinese Premier Wen that the EAS should be led only by East Asian countries, and the following comments by the Malaysian President Badawi attest to the persisting exclusive definition of Asian and Southeast Asian identities:

> You are talking about a community of East Asians; I do not know how the Australians could regard themselves as East Asians. We are not talking about being a member of the community, we are talking about common interests. (cited in Sunday Morning Herald, December 15, 2005)

IV. ASEAN and regional order

Despite the lack of an explicit conditionality mechanism, ASEAN has contributed to the management of some conflicts beyond its boundaries. The first is the Chinese claim to exclusive sovereignty over the South China Sea as a "lost" Chinese territory, which conflicted with the Malaysian claim to the Spratlys islands and the Philippine claim zone of

Kalayaan. In February 1992, China passed a controversial territorial law, which effectively converted South China Sea area to Chinese internal waters and imposed a series of limitations on navigation. In July 1992, ASEAN issued the Declaration on the South China Sea, which indicated ASEAN's desire to negotiate a code of conduct with the Chinese over the issue. Tensions further escalated in the region after February 1995, when China occupied the Mischief or Panganiban Reef in the Philippine claim area. This occupation further unified the ASEAN states – both claimant and non-claimant – around the issue (Buszynski 2003). While initially resisting multilateral involvement in the issue, China eventually signed a declaration on conduct for the South China Sea with ASEAN in November 2002. This marked the first time that China accepted a multilateral agreement over the issue. According to Buszynski (2003), China was led to this change of strategy by the realization that it was pushing the ASEAN states militarily closer to the US and by the desire to maintain economic links with the ASEAN countries.

A second security issue in its near-abroad to which ASEAN has made a positive contribution is nuclear armament. At the ASEAN Summit in Bangkok on December 15, 1995, the leaders of all the ten Southeast Asian countries (the non-members at the time included) signed the Treaty on the Southeast Asia Nuclear Weapon-Free Zone (SEANWFZ). The treaty expressed ASEAN's determination to contribute towards general and complete nuclear disarmament and to protect the region from environmental pollution and the hazards posed by radio-active waste and other toxic materials. Although India refuses to sign the Comprehensive Test Ban Treaty, Prime Minister Vajpayee has recently indicated that India as a nuclear weapons state is willing to respect the nuclear-free status of Southeast Asia. This could possibly take the form of India becoming a party to the SEANWFZ (Yahya 2003: 101). Similarly, while acceding to the Treaty of Amity and Cooperation, China has pledged to continue to abide by ASEAN's SEANWFZ.

The EAS constitutes the first instance where ASEAN used conditionality in its external relations as a contribution to broader regional order. In 2005, ASEAN leaders set three criteria for non-East Asian states to attend the EAS: substantive relations with ASEAN, dialogue-partner status, and accession to the TAC. The TAC requires signatories to settle disputes peacefully and refrain from interfering in each other's internal affairs (Richardson 2005). Having acceded to the TAC in 2003, India had met all these conditions, but New Zealand and Australia signed the TAC in order to participate in the EAS. Australia was initially concerned over the TAC's possible effects on US-Australia relations and resistant to the notion of non-interference. But the perceived benefits of participation in the EAS prevailed in Australian policymakers' calculations. As Australian Foreign Minister Downer put it:

> We see the East Asian Summit as the birth of a growing East Asian community, so it makes good sense for the region for Australia to be involved and if the price is signing the Treaty of Amity and Cooperation, we'll do that ... (Richardson 2005: 352)

Australian-Indonesian relations

In contrast, ASEAN has not been able to positively influence the bilateral relations between Australia and Indonesia, which have historically been volatile and prone to quick escalation of tensions. Even though Australia and Indonesia have had no experience of military conflict, the dominant security discourse in each country portrays the other as the primary threat to national security. In Australia, defense reports focus on threats from and through Indonesia. Sections of the Indonesian elite believe that Australia is conspiring to subvert Indonesia from within.

These tensions and volatility between Australia and Indonesia have been reproduced, as conflicts based on actual territorial disputes between Indonesia and Malaysia, Philippines and Malaysia, and Thailand and Malaysia have been successfully managed by ASEAN. The reproduction of tensions between Australia and Indonesia on the periphery of ASEAN has become even more puzzling in the 1980s and 1990s, as Australia actively sought deeper engagement in the region. The existing constructivist literature would lead us to expect that, as institutional relations between Australia and ASEAN intensify, through the diffusion of ASEAN's conflict management norms to Australia, the relations between Australia and Indonesia would progressively improve. Instead, the perceptions of difference and threat between Australia and Indonesia escalated to new heights during the 1999 East Timor intervention.

The East Timor intervention occurred ten years into the dramatic change in Australia's foreign policy towards the region, which was coupled with a discourse of Australia's regional belonging and ability to behave like an Asian state. Plus, the events followed and were in fact precipitated by a dramatic change in the Indonesian position on East Timor, which was coupled with a new discourse on Indonesia's relationship to the West, including Australia. In this discursive and institutional context, it made sense to expect that Australia and Indonesia would interact differently over East Timor. Therefore, explanations of how relations between Australia and Indonesia deteriorated during the East

Timor intervention should take into account the implications of Australia's liminal position.

A quick review of the history of relations between Australia and Indonesia clearly indicates their volatility and proclivity towards quick escalation of tensions.[17] Between 1945 and1949, Australian–Indonesian relations were remarkably good, as Australia supported the Indonesian struggle of independence against the Dutch in the UN. Between 1950 and 1965, however, relations soured as Indonesia developed a strong nationalist and anti-imperialist orientation under Sukarno. Indonesia's policy of confrontation and support for communist-leaning rebels in Borneo further exacerbated the perceptions of threat. In 1964, Australian troops were deployed in Malaysia against the Indonesians. In April 1965, Sukarno warned Australia: "do not think that the Pacific Ocean will remain pacific forever."

The relations improved when Suharto took office in 1965 after a failed leftist coup. With Suharto, Indonesia became a loyal ally of the West, and began a policy of capitalist economic development, relying on Western and Australian aid. It also ended its policy of confrontation against Malaysia. It was in this period that ASEAN was first established between Indonesia, Malaysia, Singapore, Thailand, and Philippines, as a non-communist solidarity organization. In July 1968, Australia and Indonesia signed a cultural agreement which expressed "the need for widening the mutual understanding and respect of the diverse peoples and nations of the Asian and Pacific regions, recognizing that history and geographical propinquity have presented Australia and Indonesia, as countries of widely different cultural background, with unique opportunities for learning from each other" (Catley and Dugis, 1998). Thus, while the regime change in Indonesia established a basis for cooperation between Australia and Indonesia, this cooperation was predicated on the mutual recognition of difference and belonging to separate regions.

After 1965, the primary source of conflict between Australia and Indonesia was East Timor. In December 1975, Indonesia took control of the neighboring Portuguese colony of East Timor. Official Indonesian accounts emphasize that Portugal mismanaged the decolonization process by allowing the situation in the territory to deteriorate to the point of civil war. Under these circumstances, Indonesian accounts argue that the East Timorese practiced their "inherent right to decolonize themselves" by choosing "independence through integration with Indonesia."[18] Not recognizing the legality of the integration, the UN Security Council demanded the immediate withdrawal of Indonesia.

After the Indonesian takeover, East Timor began to function as a test of Australia's commitment to regional engagement and seeking closer relations with Indonesia (Cotton 1999). ASEAN held onto its non-interference principle and continued to regard East Timor as Indonesia's domestic affair (Dupont, 2000). The Australian public has consistently supported independence for East Timor; however, Australian governments have followed an inconsistent policy, fluctuating between recognition and opposition. The Australian Foreign Minister at the time of East Timor's incorporation, Whitlam, is reported to have given a green light to Indonesia. The following Fraser government at first voted against Indonesia at the UN on the issue of East Timor (1976), but later gave de facto recognition (1978).

As the Keating government made "regional enmeshment" its top foreign policy priority, it undertook significant efforts to improve relations with Indonesia. In 1988, the Australian Foreign Minister Evans expressed hope for "the day when the interests of Australia and Indonesia are so varied and so important that we no longer talk of the relationship as though it were a patient of precarious health, sometimes sick, sometimes healthy, but always needing the worried supervision of diplomatic doctors" (Evans 1988). However, despite some improvements, the bilateral relations remained in "precarious health." With the Timor Gap Treaty signed in 1989, Australia and Indonesia agreed to establish a 40-year cooperation regime in a disputed area of the Timor Sea, where many believe rich oil and natural gas fields lie. However, by 1991, the relations faced a crisis when Australia threatened to reverse its recognition policy on East Timor in response to the Dili Massacre, when Indonesian troops shot demonstrators at a peaceful East Timorese rally. Afterwards, Keating's decision to make his first official visit to Indonesia normalized the relations. Relations tensed up again in 1995 over the appointment of Mantiri, a general who had served in East Timor, as the Indonesian ambassador to Australia. Indonesia refused to reconsider his appointment, and threatened to leave the Canberra post vacant for an indefinite period of time. On December 18th, 1995, Australia and Indonesia signed the Agreement on Maintaining Security, which embodied a regular consultation process on matters of mutual and regional security and the consideration of joint measures to deter any "adverse challenges" to those interests. During the 1999 East Timor intervention, Indonesia announced that it no longer recognized the Agreement.

ASEAN's interaction with Australia has not paved the way for stable cooperative relations between Australia and Indonesia. To the contrary, relations remained in "precarious health" because, as a result of the positioning of Australia in a liminal position with respect to the community formation process in Southeast Asia, Australia's cooperation and engagement efforts in the region simultaneously became threatening to the identities of Indonesia and ASEAN. Just as the policy of "regional enmeshment" brought Australia closer to ASEAN, it aggravated the need to maintain a sense of difference between Australia and ASEAN. Only through an understanding of the politics of liminality that characterize Australia–Indonesia relations can we make sense of how the Australian–Indonesian relations quickly deteriorated during the 1999 East Timor conflict.

As I indicated before, what is further puzzling is that the relations deteriorated in spite of a radical change in the Indonesian position on East Timor. The collapse of the Suharto regime in Indonesia initiated the period of Reformasi that entailed a wholesale reassessment of the policies and institutions of the Suharto era, including the question of East Timor. In June 1998, the new Indonesian President Habibie offered East Timor special status with wide autonomy. Speaking before the House of People's Representatives, Habibie (1999) argued that this historic change in Indonesia's position "would enable us to present ourselves in the world intercourse as a more civilized and honorable nation."

Habibie's decision was welcomed and supported by the Australian Foreign Minister Downer, who suggested that after a substantial period of autonomy the East Timorese should be allowed self-determination. Portugal made the same demand during the tripartite negotiations held at the UN. On January 27, 1999, Indonesian Foreign Minister Alatas announced that in case the autonomy offer was rejected by the East Timorese, they would be allowed to separate from Indonesia in a peaceful manner. On May 5, 1999, Indonesia and Portugal agreed on a UN-sponsored popular consultation to ascertain whether the majority of the people of East Timor would accept autonomy within Indonesia or reject it in favor of separation from Indonesia. The UN mission in East Timor (UNAMET) was established and under its supervision on August 30, 1999, the Timorese voted 78.5% to 21.5% in favor of independence.

Though disappointed, Indonesian officials still emphasized how the results validate Indonesia's new identity as a democratic and civilized state. After the pro-independence vote, pro-integration militia launched a campaign of violence against the pro-independence forces. The inability, or allegedly the unwillingness, of the Indonesian government to suppress the violence invited accusations from Australia and the rest of the international community that the Indonesian armed forces were deliberately supporting the pro-integration militias. Speaking before the UN Special Commission on Human Rights on the Situation in East Timor on September 23, 1999, Indonesian authorities claimed that the Indonesian security apparatus found themselves "overwhelmed by the veracity of violent reactions from pro-integrationist groups," and that human rights violations "tend to be overblown and misrepresented by the media and NGOs." The Indonesian Minister for Foreign Affairs, Ali Alatas, also urged the international community not to "sacrifice the principle of sovereignty and sovereign equality," and ruin "the process of reconciliation" among the East Timorese groups, while dealing with the human rights problems (Alatas 1999).

The campaign of violence and its international condemnation gave rise to strong criticism of ASEAN's non-interventionist stance in some ASEAN countries. In Thailand and the Philippines, commentators urged that ASEAN, which has long been part of the problem through its inaction, now "must be part of the solution," even if it entails taking action against Indonesia. A columnist in the *Business World* argued that "ASEAN must call an emergency meeting of its foreign ministers to condemn the Indonesian government's abetting the massacre and offer police and troops from its member countries – with the exception of Indonesia to serve as the core of the UN peace-keeping mission. This must be made even without the Indonesian government's approval ... " (Bello, 1999). Nelson Navarro writing for the *Manila Standard* contended that "the first litmus test [for ASEAN] will have to be the peaceful settlement of the separatist problems in East Timor and Aceh" (Navarro 1999). Other commentators argued that the UN and the world community must do more and that Indonesia must request international help.[19]

Even after the militias' campaign of violence started in East Timor, there were indications that Indonesia and Australia would deal with the situation in East Timor in a non-confrontational manner, without letting it undermine the relations between the two states. Australia's Prime Minister Howard voiced his expectation that the settlement of the East Timor issue would improve Australian–Indonesian relations. The reluctance of the US to commit troops to East Timor, at least to some commentators, demonstrated the need for Australia to cultivate a regional commitment through ASEAN to enforce human rights in the region (Australian Financial Review, September 10, 1999). To end the bloodbath in East Timor, many officials and commentators in ASEAN states advocated the formation of an ASEAN peacekeeping force, a response which would have been in line with the ASEAN norm of regional autonomy, even though it would violate the norm of non-interference.

On September 12th, 1999, after substantial international pressure (US cut military aid and the IMF ceased its funding), Indonesia agreed to accept international assistance in quelling the violence. After agreeing to international assistance, Indonesia also repeatedly voiced its preference for a peace-keeping force predominantly composed of troops from ASEAN states. It is interesting that, despite Australia's long-term involvement in ASEAN-led regional organizations, and even though there was considerable ASEAN participation in the peacekeeping force,[20] relations between Australia and Indonesia quickly deteriorated when Australia assumed leadership of the International Force East Timor (INTERFET). Australia's involvement was constructed as foreign and Western interference; it was suspected of ulterior motives. Upon the arrival of Australian troops, Indonesia tore apart the 1995 security agreement with Australia.

Australia's liminal position with respect to ASEAN precluded an alternative interpretation of Australian involvement, which would entail the construction of Australia as a friendly regional state intervening in a regional problem. During the INTERFET mission, commentaries in major Indonesian newspapers represented Australia as deeply antagonistic, and as working to dismember the Indonesian state (Milner, 2000). Arguing that Australia's leadership of INTERFET "reflects a failure [on the part of the UN] to take into account Indonesian sensitivities," *Kompas* surmised that "who knows whether, with such an approach, the West wants to apply a 'Balkanization policy' in Southeast Asia" (September 16, 1999). The beliefs that Australia regarded Indonesia as a major military threat and that it had "a long-standing ambition for a foothold on East Timor" were offered as further evidence for Australia's hostile intentions (*Bisnis Indonesia*, September 20, 1999). The magnitude of military presence was another source of worry. *Pos Kota* cautioned that "this formidable force may be prepared to hit Indonesia solely on the basis that Indonesia has not cooperated with INTERFET" (September 20, 1999).

What strikes the attention in all these articulations of threat from Australia is that they are based on a construction of Australia's identity as Western and non-Asian. The construction of "Western" and "Southeast Asian" identities as mutually exclusive by the community-building discourse of ASEAN allows for the representation of Australia as inherently different from Southeast Asia. What makes Australia particularly threatening is that it is an inherently "Western" state within Southeast Asia, which enables it to act as the instrument of a broader hostile policy towards Southeast Asia by the West. Australia is simultaneously too far and too near, which makes it both dangerously alike and precariously different. In the texts, symbolic efforts to underscore and absolutize Australia's difference employ notions of inherent difference, such as race and religion. In Indonesia, reports of the intervention presented pictures of white Australians pointing guns at the heads of small dark-skinned men, which helped aggravate the perception of threat from Australia. Some commentators in Muslim papers in Indonesia have been quick to portray Australians as acting on behalf of Christian groups against Islamic Indonesians (Milner 2000).

Representations of Indonesia in Australia reinforced and gave further legitimacy to these articulations of difference and threat. Even though taking joint action with ASEAN had opened up the possibility of reconciling the policy of regional enmeshment with the identity of Australia as the defender of human rights, Australia perceived that its identity as a liberal democratic state was severely compromised with the developments in East Timor. In an effort to sustain its identity, Australia sought to reproduce its sense of difference from and to re-assert its superiority to the region, to Indonesia in particular. In an interview with *Bulletin*, Howard was quoted as favoring the idea of Australia as the "deputy sheriff" to the US in the region (September 28, 1999). Howard denied having ever used the term "deputy sheriff," but only a week after the interview's publication. By that time, the statement had received a great deal of negative publicity in Indonesia and other ASEAN states.

While Howard's remarks provoked a lot of criticism in Australia, the representations of Australia employed in the text below demonstrate the degree of resonance that Howard's statement achieved. Hogue (2000) underscores that Australian leadership of the region has a long history in Australian thinking, "which, when it did not see Asia as a threat, saw it as a backward region which it was [its] Christian duty to uplift and develop."

In a space of a few weeks, Australia's role and responsibilities in the region have been transformed. We have taken on the role of the regional policeman and peacemaker ... Rightly we have embraced our responsibilities but we must be in no doubt that our commitment is for as long as it takes and as much as it costs ... We are in East Timor for the long haul. (*Australian*, September 21, 1999)

However, to Southeast Asian and Indonesian audiences, these notions of benevolent superiority resonate too strongly with colonial notions of "white man's burden." Therefore, this rediscovered notion of Australian identity lent further credibility to the constructions in Southeast Asia of Australia as arrogant, meddling, and white imperialist. Hence, in a mutually reinforcing pattern, Australian discourses that construct a sense of difference with Indonesia lend credibility to Indonesian discourses that construct Australia as different, and vice versa. Arguing that Howard's statement is a manifestation of the "emerging spirit of white imperialism in Asia," *Berita Buana* argued that it represents the "failure of the West (especially Caucasians) to understand Asia's character and culture" (September 27, 1999).

The discourse of conspiracy also infiltrated the official Indonesian perceptions of Australian intentions. In a speech to the Australian National Press Club in February 2000, Indonesia's ambassador to Australia, Arizal Effendi, accused Australia of the "jingoism of using humanitarian pretexts to justify unilateral armed intervention into the internal affairs of a developing country" (Dupont 2000: 164). The Malaysian President Mahathir, known for his usual scathing criticisms of Western countries, also reproduced the discourse of conspiracy in relation to the East Timor developments. He argued that the crisis in East Timor was of the West's own making, because President Habibie had been pressured to allow a premature and in some ways unnecessary act of self-determination just as Indonesia was struggling with a difficult transition to liberal democracy. He also accused the West of hypocrisy for rejecting Indonesia's occupation of East Timor while turning a blind eye to similar transgressions by other countries. He claimed that with the East Timor intervention the West wanted once again to breakup Indonesia, and that Australia would be the main beneficiary of such a breakup (Dupont 2000: 165).

The initial support in other ASEAN states for INTERFET also waned, as they began to share Mahathir's concern that humanitarian intervention could be used to undermine and eventually subvert ASEAN's norm of non-intervention (Dupont 2000). In Thailand, for example, this concern was reflected in the intensified criticism of the government for having participated in the INTERFET peacekeeping force. *Thai Rath* claimed that "a closer look will reveal that [Thailand] is being exploited politically by the US, the UN, and Australia" (September 21, 1999). Commentators claimed that "East Timor is overshadowed by subversive influences of Western imperialists and the United States" (*Ban Muang*, September 16, 1999) and that as an issue it is "a by-product of the bygone Western colonialism and therefore must be the responsibility of the West" (*Thai Rath*, September 21, 1999). Matichon warned that a weaker Indonesia is to the benefit of Australia, and that the Australians were keen to support Christians against Muslims. Another paper argued that Australia was driven by economic motives to intervene in East

Timor and expected to control the economy of the new state. Even in Singapore, where Australia's actions received a real measure of praise, commentators emphasized the need for Australia to adopt a quieter Asian style of diplomacy (Milner 2000).

The East Timor experience also led the Secretary-General of ASEAN, Severino, to argue that:

> the international community must also develop the capacity to discern whether humanitarian intervention is not being used merely for national policy purposes ... The welfare of people, particularly in Southeast Asia today, is better served through economic interaction and integration ... than through blatant intervention and ostentatious gestures. (Severino 2000b)

In short, during the East Timor intervention, Australian–Indonesian relations quickly deteriorated because the representation of Australia as inherently different from and threatening to Asia gave legitimacy and credibility to threat perceptions. Had Australia been situated as unequivocally a part of the Southeast Asian collective identity, Australian involvement would not have generated these threat perceptions, because it would have been represented and interpreted as involvement by a friendly regional state.

Since Australia's intervention in East Timor, the relationship between Australia and Indonesia has been a difficult one (McDougall 2001). Bilateral relations have begun to improve especially following the generous Australian contribution to the victims of December 2004 earthquake and tsunami in Indonesia. In April 2005, Australia and Indonesia issued a Joint Declaration on Comprehensive Partnership. Yet, Indonesia has not been enthusiastic about the Australian proposal to conclude a new bilateral security agreement in place of the one abrogated by Indonesia in the wake of East Timor crisis (Jain 2007).

V. Conclusion

Even though the collective identity espoused by ASEAN is non-liberal and hence differs greatly from the EU, we see that similar patterns govern the interactions of these community-building institutions with outside states. Both community-building institutions produce difference from states on their peripheries, and in some cases this sense of difference is coupled with perceptions and representations of identity threat. Yet, ASEAN promotes a predominantly exclusive collective identity, and as a result the content of its interactions with outside states is different. As an exclusive community, ASEAN clearly distinguishes self from other, and is characterized by fixed boundaries. The case of Myanmar illustrates how exclusive communities interact with states constituted as part of self. Despite pressures from the international community, Myanmar was directly admitted into ASEAN membership, without any attempts to use the membership as a carrot to induce political change in Myanmar. Fixed boundaries do not prevent the perception of certain outside states as an identity threat, however. This chapter demonstrated how the efforts by Australian policymakers to contest the exclusive definition of Southeast Asian collective identity in the 1980s and 1990s produced forceful representations of Australia as an identity threat.

Hence, Australia's relations with ASEAN constituted an analogous case to Turkey's relations with the EU. Both countries were situated in liminal positions and perceived and represented as identity threats as a result of their non-recognition of community identity. Just as Turkey negotiated the European collective identity, Australia contested the construction of Southeast Asian or Asian collective identity. These contestations produced a greater necessity to articulate the differences of Turkey and Australia and construct these differences as threatening. Yet, while Turkey has been successful to some extent in negotiating and modifying its liminal identity position, Australian policymakers since the 1990s have simply lost interest in their Asia policy.

As an exclusive community, ASEAN cannot be characterized as a postmodern collectivity. So, even though, with its hard boundaries and pan-nationalist identity, ASEAN arguably replicates the nation-state at a higher level of aggregation, its effects on the broader regional order are not entirely negative. In fact, as a result of the fixity of its boundaries, ASEAN faces fewer complications in its external relations compared with the EU. In contrast to the EU, ASEAN's external relations are not under the shadow of enlargement, and thus ASEAN is able to enter into various flexible institutional arrangements as a community. These flexible arrangements have enabled ASEAN to contribute to the management of some conflicts beyond its boundaries.

Production of difference and Othering have securitized conflicts between member and non-member countries in the two cases. This chapter analyzed how, during the East Timor crisis, the conflicts between Australia and Indonesia escalated into an identity conflict. In this case, ASEAN's constructive influence on Australian–Indonesian relations was very pronounced and negative. The dominant representation of Australia as inherently different from and threatening to Asia gave legitimacy and credibility to threat perceptions.

7
Conclusion

Following the end of the Cold War, regional organizations once again came to be represented as attractive remedies for regional problems and as the building blocks of global peace. With the growing interest in the concept of identity, the international relations discipline likewise embraced regions and regional organizations as cases of community-building and collective identity formation. Revisiting the Deutschian thesis, it was argued that these regions represent and can evolve into security communities, where states neither expect nor prepare for war against each other. As such, it was expected that these regional communities would become the building blocks of a qualitatively different form of global order, where peace is secured not through a power balance, but through shared norms and identities. Policymakers in regional organizations and member states, similarly, cultivated a sense of regional consciousness through constructions of shared regional experiences, history, and identity.

This book argued that something very fundamental has been ignored in this set of expectations. It is the very basic premise of the constitution of identity in relation to difference. Building on this premise, this book argued that the implications of regional community-building for regional and global order are more complex and contingent, and possibly double-sided. The construction of regional communities is made possible through the production of outsider states as different. And if a sense of collective identity generates dependable expectations of peaceful change within the community, then, by virtue of the same logic, production of difference may generate conflict beyond the community.

Perhaps one reason that policymakers and analysts have not been sufficiently attentive to the double-sided nature (i.e. construction of identity/production of difference) of community formation is because they have been misled by theses that posit a conflictual relationship between self and other as an ontological assumption, such as Huntington's Clash of Civilizations thesis and the applications of Social Identity Theory to the field of international relations. Adopting a constructivist approach to identity formation, this book argued that, while identity depends on difference, this does not necessarily lead to conflict between self and other. In other words, the construction of a sense of collective identity at the regional level entails the production of outsider states as different, but that does not necessitate that the regional community's relations with outsider states will be necessarily conflictual.

There has been a tendency among some constructivist scholars to downplay the dependence of identity on difference in the cases of international communities. I argued that downplaying the role of difference distracts us away from the constructivist ontology into assumptions about fixed and pre-given identities. What we should instead be critical of is the relationship between difference and conflict. Through a critical engagement with the literature, I argued that self/other relations are constituted along several dimensions which mediate between relations of difference and conflict. As a result, what is constructed as different is not necessarily perceived and represented as a threat to identity; the nature of the collective identity, the social distance between self and other, and the response of the other all interact to produce a variety of self/other relations. Thus, my expectations before commencing on the analysis of actual regional communities were that their identity discourses would be producing outsider states as different from the community, but that their relations with those outsiders would not be necessarily characterized by threat perceptions and conflict.

I selected EU and ASEAN for analysis by virtue of their being discussed in the literature as security communities, one in the Western and the other in the non-Western world. I also realized that, within the framework of self/other interaction, they constituted comparable cases in terms of the nature of their collective identities: while the EU promoted a partly inclusive/partly exclusive collective identity combining universalist norms of democracy and free markets with a bounded notion of Europeanness, the ASEAN endorsed a predominantly exclusive collective identity based on shared beliefs about regional norms and boundaries. I comparatively analyzed the interactions of these organizations with various outsider states on the basis of the nature of the collective identity invoked by the community, the social distance, and the response of the other to the construction of its identity.

In line with my expectations, I found that these interactions are characterized by considerable diversity and variability. In the EU's interaction with the CEES (prior to 2004 enlargement), the EU invoked inclusive aspects of its identity, associated with the CEES, which in turn recognized the construction of their identities as different. In the case of Morocco, the EU invoked exclusive aspects of its identity, constructed Morocco to be inherently different, and dissociated itself from Morocco. Morocco was not able to effectively resist the construction of its identity as different. As an exclusive community, ASEAN constructed Myanmar to be an inherent part of self, and directly admitted it to membership. In the EU and ASEAN, I found two cases where the self/other interaction was characterized by forceful representations of difference and frequent articulations of threat: these were the cases of Turkey and Australia respectively. In both cases, the constitutive dimensions of self/other interaction were not in congruity with each other. The EU constructed Turkey to be different on the basis of both inherent and acquired characteristics, oscillated between association with and dissociation from Turkey, and Turkey resisted the construction of its identity as different. Similarly, the ASEAN constructed Australia to be inherently different, yet Australia resisted this construction as it sought to situate itself as a state in the Asia–Pacific. As a result, both the EU–Turkey and ASEAN–Australia interactions, as different from the other cases, were characterized by Othering, the representation of the other as a threat to identity.

In addition to this diversity in the forms of self/other interaction, there is potential variability as well. To show this variability, I focused on the case of EU–Turkey interaction. While Turkey was constructed as an identity threat, the EU declared Turkey to be a candidate for membership in 1999 and started accession negotiations with Turkey in 2005. I discussed the ways in which Turkey negotiated the construction of its identity in order to make such strong relations of association possible.

How do these diverse and variable relations of self/other interaction produce implications for regional and global order? In order to understand the implications for regional order, I focused on bilateral relations between member and non-member states on the borders of the community because as states that are constituted as self and other by community-building, I assumed that their relations would be the most affected. In Europe, I comparatively analyzed Polish–German relations, Moroccan–Spanish relations, and Greek–Turkish relations. My analysis showed that the effects of community-building on such conflicts are mediated by the nature of self/other interaction with conflict parties. In the case of Polish–German relations, the EU's invocation of an inclusive identity in relation to Poland and the EU membership perspective aided the resolution of outstanding border disputes after the end of the Cold War. In the case of Moroccan–Spanish relations, on the other hand, the impact of the EU was mainly negative. The construction of Morocco as inherently different from Europe and the EU's dissociation from Morocco did not aid the resolution of the disputes between Morocco and Spain, and instead aggravated the threat perceptions.

The EU's impact on Greek–Turkish relations, on the other hand, reflected the temporal variation in the nature of the self/other interaction between EU and Turkey. When the EU dissociated from Turkey, the impact of the EU was negative; the EU, in fact, was exploited as an additional battlefield between Greece and Turkey in their ongoing conflicts. However, following the declaration of Turkey's EU candidacy in 1999, the impact of the EU on Greek–Turkish relations turned positive and consolidated the rapprochement process between the two countries. Similarly, in Southeast Asia, Australian–Indonesian relations were adversely affected by the construction of Australia as different from and threatening to Southeast Asian collective identity.

The experiences of two regional community-building institutions analyzed in this book suggest that their identity relations with outsider states are very much shaped by the nature of their collective identities. Although they represent alternative forms of collective identity, neither has been able to avoid the discrimination and exclusion of (certain) outsiders. Thus, we can conclude that neither has advanced to a post-territorial logic. However, both institutions have been careful to adopt policies that can possibly mitigate the potentially adverse implications of such exclusion. In the case of the EU, this has taken the form of cross-border cooperation programs and institutionalized cooperation with outsider states. The ASEAN has also adopted various forms of flexible and overlapping cooperation arrangements with outsider states.

What do the findings of this book entail in terms of the realization of alternative scenarios for global order? Are contemporary patterns of community-formation pointing towards a systemic cultural transformation or are they basically reproducing the logic of anarchy? What do my findings tell us about how to build communities in international relations and what kinds of communities to build?

My findings do not predict the realization of either systemic scenario, but show that their realization is contingent. Granting the dependence of identity on difference, the scenario of systemic cultural transformation would materialize if and when community-building blurred self/other distinctions, and constructed the differences of the other as non-threatening. According to my analysis, communities built around inclusive identities that accept the possibility that the other may become like self are a necessary but not a sufficient condition. Only if those constituted as "others" also aspire to community identity may such community-building patterns lead to a systemic cultural transformation. Thus, by itself, the prevalence of community-building processes around universalizing identities, such as liberal and democratic, cannot guarantee a peaceful global order. Perhaps this is the most powerful lesson that should have been drawn from the events of 9/11 and the ensuing War on Terror. After the end of the Cold War, this shock was largely unexpected in the West because visions had been clouded by the belief that community-building around liberal norms can progressively rid the world of difference, and, in turn, by the failure to recognize the complicity of the West in the production of difference.

Yet, contemporary patterns of community-building mostly revolve around regional institutions and identities and as such necessarily have an exclusive component. In other words, patterns of regional community-building cannot be purely inclusive; they can either be partly inclusive/partly exclusive (i.e. the EU) or predominantly exclusive (i.e. the ASEAN). Within this set of possibilities, partly inclusive/partly exclusive regional communities can also transcend self/other distinctions and be the building blocks of a systemic transformation through their interaction with liminal states. Constituted as partly self and partly other, liminal states hold the discursive opportunity for their recognition as simultaneously other and like. If community-building discourses come to reflect and be at home with this ambiguity, then they may pave the way for a systemic cultural transformation. In this book, I devoted a great deal of attention to the case of EU–Turkey relations because I argued that, through its interaction with Turkey, the EU may possibly transcend the self/other distinctions that revolve around the Europe/Asia and Europe/Islam dichotomies. However, my analysis showed that, despite an ongoing process of identity negotiation between the EU and Turkey, the community-building discourses of the EU have not been able to transcend these dichotomies.

Patterns of regional community-building around exclusive identities cannot blur self/other distinctions, yet they do not need to be conflict-producing. If the distinctness of their identities and the strict self/other distinctions they promote are recognized by others, then they would not be paving the way for a systemic cultural transformation, but they would not be reproducing the logic of anarchy either. Their implications for global order would fall in between these two alternative scenarios.

ASEAN constitutes a good example of such a community, because, despite the lack of a conditionality mechanism, ASEAN has been able to manage some conflicts beyond its boundaries through building flexible and overlapping institutional relations with outsider states.

The question of what kinds of communities to build in international relations depends on the normative criteria that we are advocating. For this book, the normative criterion was the avoidance of war between states at the regional and global level. In terms of this normative criterion, the conclusions of this book are ambivalent. This is because the potential for production of conflict beyond the community exists for inclusive as well as exclusive collective identities. Communities built around inclusive identities need others that aspire to the community, and, in cases where this is not the case, such community formation processes can lead to conflicts. Communities built around exclusive identities need to maintain a clear sense of difference from outside, and, in cases where their distinctness is not recognized, such community formation processes can also lead to conflicts. If, however, alternatively, the normative criterion adopted had been the diffusion of liberal norms, or equitable relations between self and other, then the answer to the question of what kinds of community to build would have been different.

Finally a caveat is in order. The conclusions of this book derive from the analysis of two regional communities, and the analysis of other community-building processes, perhaps less institutionalized and more global ones such as the community of democratic states, may necessitate a further qualification of arguments.

Notes

1 Introduction

1. On the importance of representation and "talk" in the constitution of collective identity, see Wendt (1999: 347).
2. Constructivists successfully remedied some of the weaknesses of the Deutschian literature. For example, the Deutschian literature had been unnecessarily preoccupied with the problem of finding an objective empirical basis by which to delineate regions relevant for community (Russett 1967). With the concept of an imagined/cognitive region, constructivists underscored that regions are socially constructed, not necessarily based on contiguous space (Adler and Barnett 1998: 33), and susceptible to redefinition through changing patterns of identification among states. A second drawback of the Deutschian literature was the contradiction between its behavioralist epistemology and intersubjective ontology, which represented itself in efforts to ascertain "we-feeling" through quantitative measures of transactions (ibid.: 8). Acknowledging that collective identity is primarily a cognitive and discursive phenomenon, constructivists have studied community formation mostly through representations of self and other.
3. For further discussion on the depiction of states as persons, see Neumann (2004) and Wendt (2004).

2 Self/Other Interaction in International Relations (IR)

4. IR constructivism also draws upon feminist theory, historical institutionalism, sociological institutionalism, and structuration theory (Wendt 1999: 1). But specifically on the relationship between self and other, the influences of symbolic interactionism and poststructuralism are more prominent.
5. Several studies have pointed to the importance of social recognition of state identities to underscore the influence of international norms. For example, while all states may claim to be democracies, the recognition of the international community distinguishes true democracies from others. See Gurowitz (1999).
6. For a similar critique of Todorov, see Grovogui (2001).
7. It is theoretically possible that any state may become Islamic, if a large majority of its population become Muslims (through conversion or immigration) and the state's identity reflects this demographic change. It is also possible that any state may become European in the geographical sense, if it acquires territory in Europe and/or the geographical definition of Europe somehow changes radically. "European" and "Islamic" are exclusive identities by virtue of the fact that these are not deemed very realistic possibilities.

3   Identity/Difference and the EU

8. "The Treaty of Rome was concluded by six continental states ... Whether it is a question of their industrial or agricultural production, their foreign trade, their customs and commercial ties, or their living and working conditions, they have more similarities than differences. ... England is insular, maritime, connected by its trade, its sales and its food supplies, to very different and often distant countries. It follows an essentially industrial and commercial activity, with very little agriculture. Across the whole of its experience, it has very conspicuous, very special, customs and traditions. In short, the nature, structure, and the attitudes, which are appropriate to England, differ from those of the continentals" (De Gaulle, Press Conference in the Elysee Palace, January 14, 1963, http://aei.pitt.edu/5777/01/003749_1.pdf).
9. After the velvet divorce, Czech Republic and Slovakia took divergent paths. In Slovakia, the prime minister Vladimir Meciar resorted to authoritarian tactics to maintain his power and dispose of his rival President Michal Kovac (Meszaros 1999).
10. For accounts of Turkey's relations with the European Union, see Muftuler-Bac (1997, 1999); Onis (1995, 2000); Buzan and Diez (1999); Wood (1999), Yesilada (2002).
11. "Some in the West are trying to 'exclude' the Soviet Union from Europe ... Such ploys, however, cannot change geographic and historic realities ... We are Europeans. Old Russia was united with Europe by Christianity ... The history of Russia is an organic part of the great European history" (Mikhail Gorbachev, cited in Neumann 1999: 163).

4   Negotiating "Europe": EU and Turkey

12. By arguing that "torn" is an ascribed condition, I am not presupposing that there is a homogeneous Turkish discourse of identity vis-à-vis Europe. Because identities are always unstable and contested, in every society there are competing discourses of national and state identity. But these competing discourses on identity, by themselves, do not make a society "torn."

5   European Union and Regional Order

13. This resolution was issued right after the Greek Parliament ratified the 1985 Law of the Sea Treaty, which grants states the right to extend their territorial waters up to 12 n.m.s. Turkey has lobbied to make the Aegean Sea an exception in the Treaty, but has failed.
14. This discussion draws on Rumelili (2005).

6   Identity/Difference and the ASEAN

15. Henderson (1999:14) states that Indonesia and Malaysia initially strongly supported Sri Lanka's application.
16. http://www.aseansec.org/11516.htm

17. This review draws on Catley and Dugis (1998).
18. Indonesian Ministry for Foreign Affairs website (www.deplu.gov.id).
19. See *Bangkok Post (Thailand)*, September 8, 1999 and *Nation (Thailand)*, September 6, 1999.
20. Of the 9900 strong force, 5500 were from Australia, and approximately 2500 were from ASEAN states. While the Force Commander was an Australian, the Deputy Commander was a Thai (Dupont 2000: 166).

References

Abizadeh, A. (2005) "Does Collective Identity Presuppose an Other? On the Alleged Incoherence of Global Solidarity," *American Political Science Review*, 99:1, pp. 45–60.

Acharya, A. (1998) "Collective Identity and Conflict Management in Southeast Asia" in Adler, E. and Barnett, M. (eds) *Security Communities*, Cambridge: Cambridge University Press, pp. 198–227.

Acharya, A. (2001) Constructing a Security Community in Southeast Asia: ASEAN and the Problem of Regional Order, London and New York: Routledge.

Acharya, A. (2002) "Regionalism and the Emerging World Order: Sovereignty, Autonomy, Identity" in Breslin, S., Hughes, C.W., Phillips, N., and Rosamond, B. (eds) *New Regionalisms in the Global Political Economy*, London: Routledge, pp. 20–32.

Adler, E. (1992) "Europe's New Security Order: A Pluralistic Security Community" in Crawford, B. (ed.) *The Future of European Security*, Berkeley: University of California Press, pp. 287–326.

Adler, E. (1998) "Seeds of Peaceful Change: the OSCE's Security Community-Building Model" in Adler E. and Barnett M. (eds) Security Communities, Cambridge: Cambridge University Press, pp. 119–160.

Adler, E. and Barnett, M. (eds) (1998) *Security Communities*, Cambridge: Cambridge University Press.

Aksu, F. (2001) "Turkish-Greek Relations," *Turkish Review of Balkan Studies*, 6, pp. 167–201.

Akyol, T. (2004) "Tam Ip Kopuyordu ki [The Rope was almost Broken]," *Milliyet (Istanbul)*, December 18.

Alatas, A. (1999) *54th Session of the UN General Assembly*, New York, September 23.

Amer, R. (1999) "Conflict Management and Constructive Engagement in ASEAN's Expansion," *Third World Quarterly*, 20:5, pp. 1031–48.

Anderson, M. (1998) "European Frontiers at the End of the Twentieth Century" in Anderson, M. and Bort, E. (eds) *The Frontiers of Europe*, London: Pinter, pp. 1–10.

Ayman, S.G. (1998) "Turkiye'nin Ege Politikasinda Muzakere ve Caydiricilik [Negotiation and Deterrence in Turkey's Aegean Policy]" in Ozcan, G. and Kut, S. (eds) *En Uzun On Yil [The Longest Decade]*, Istanbul: Boyut, pp. 285–325.

Ayoob, M. (1999) "From Regional System to Regional Society: Exploring Key Variables in the Construction of Regional Order," *Australian Journal of International Affairs*, 53:3, pp. 247–60.

Banerjee, S. (1998) "Narratives and Interaction: A Constitutive Theory of Interaction and the Case of the All-India Muslim League," *European Journal of International Relations*, 4:2, pp. 178–203.

Belge, M. (2004) "Observations on Civil Society" in Belge, T. (ed.) *Voices for the Future: Civic Dialogue Between Turks and Greeks*, Istanbul: Bilgi University Press, pp. 27–32.

Bello, W. (1999) "Time for ASEAN to Be Part of the Solution," *Business World (Philippines)*, September 9.

Bessho, K. (1999) "Identities and Security in East Asia," *Adelphi Paper 325, International Institute for Strategic Studies*, Oxford: Oxford University Press.

Bially Mattern, J. (2000) "Taking Identity Seriously," *Cooperation and Conflict*, 35:3, pp. 299–308.

Bilge, A.S. (2000) *Buyuk Dus, Turk-Yunan Siyasi Iliskileri [Megali Idea: Turkish-Greek Political Relations]*, Ankara: 21. Yuzyil Yayinlari.

Birand, M.A. (2000) *Turkiye'nin Avrupa Macerasi 1959–1999 [Turkey's European Venture 1959–1999]*, Istanbul: Dogan Kitapcilik.

Blumer, H. (1969) *Symbolic Interactionism: Perspective and Method*, Englewood Cliffs, NJ: Prentice Hall.

Bourdaras, G. (2004) "Greece will Shun Veto but may Raise the Bar Higher for Ankara," *Kathimerini (Athens, English ed.)*, November 29.

Breslin, S. and Higgott, R. (2000) "Studying Regions: Learning from the Old, Constructing the New," *New Political Economy*, 5:3, pp. 333–52.

Breslin, S., Higgott, R., and Rosamond, B. (2002) "Regions in Comparative Perspective" in Breslin, S., Hughes, C. W., Phillips, N., and Rosamond, B. (eds) *New Regionalisms in the Global Political Economy*, London: Routledge, pp. 1–19.

Buszynski, L. (2003) "ASEAN, the Declaration on Conduct, and the South China Sea," *Contemporary Southeast Asia*, 25:3, pp. 343–62.

Buzan, B. and Diez, T. (1999) "The European Union and Turkey," *Survival*, 41:1, pp. 41–57.

Buzan, B. and Waever, O. (2003) *Regions and Powers: The Structure of International Security*, Cambridge: Cambridge University Press.

Buzan, B., Waever, O. and DeWilde, J. (1998) *Security: A New Framework for Analysis*, Boulder, CO: Lynne Rienner.

Campbell, D. (1992) *Writing Security*, Minneapolis: University of Minnesota Press.

Campbell, D. (1998) *National Deconstruction: Violence, Identity, and Justice in Bosnia*, Minneapolis: University of Minnesota Press.

Catley, B. and Dugis, V. (1998) *Australian-Indonesian Relations since 1945*, London: Ashgate.

Casanova, J. (2006) "The Long, Difficult, and Tortuous Journey of Turkey into Europe and the Dilemmas of European Civilization," *Constellations*, 13:2, pp. 234–47.

Cederman, L. (2001a) "Political Boundaries and Identity Trade-Offs" in Cederman, L. (ed.) *Constructing Europe's Identity: The External Dimension*, Boulder, CO: Lynne Rienner, pp. 1–34.

Cederman, L. (2001b) "Exclusion Versus Dilution: Real or Imagined Trade-Off?" in Cederman, L. (ed.) *Constructing Europe's Identity: The External Dimension*, Boulder, CO: Lynne Rienner, pp. 233–256.

Cem, I. (1994) "Is This How This Love Affair Was Going to End?" *Sabah (Istanbul)*, December 18.

Cem, I. (1997) "We Won't Be the Ones to Lose," *Milliyet (Istanbul)*, December 10.

Cem, I (2000) "Turkey and Europe: Looking to the Future from a Historical Perspective" *Perceptions: Journal of International Affairs*, 5:2, pp. 1–4

Checkel, J. (1999) "Norms, Institutions, and National Identity in Contemporary Europe," *International Studies Quarterly*, 43:1, pp. 83–114.

Christiansen, T., Petito, F. and Tonra, B. (2000) "Fuzzy Politics around Fuzzy Borders: The European Union's 'Near Abroad'", *Cooperation and Conflict*, 35:4, pp. 389–415.

Cichowski, R.A. (2000) "Western Dreams, Eastern Realities: Support for the European Union in Central and Eastern Europe," *Comparative Political Studies*, 33:10, pp. 1243–78.

Ciller, T. (1995) "Turkey's European Vocation," *Washington Post*, March 5.

Connolly, W.E. (1991) *Identity/Difference: Democratic Negotiations of Political Paradox*, Ithaca, NY: Cornell University Press.

Cotton J. (ed.) (1999) *East Timor and Australia*, Canberra: Australian Defense Studies Center.

Cox, M. (2005) "Beyond the West: Terrors in Transatlantia," *European Journal of International Relations*, 11:2, pp. 203–33.

Cronin, B. (1999a) "From Balance to Community: Transnational Identity and Political Integration," *Security Studies*, 8:2/3, pp. 270–301.

Cronin, B. (1999b) *Community Under Anarchy*, New York: Columbia University Press.

Dagi, I. (2005) "Transformation of Islamic Political Identity in Turkey: Rethinking the West and Westernization," *Turkish Studies*, 6:1, pp. 21–37.

Darby, P. and Paolini, A.J. (1994) "Bridging International Relations and Postcolonialism," *Alternatives*, 19:3, pp. 371–97.

Delanty, G. (1995) *Inventing Europe: Idea, Identity, Reality*, New York: St. Martin's Press.

Denoon, D.B.H. and Colbert, E. (1998) "Challenges for the Association of Southeast Asian Nations," *Pacific Affairs*, 71:4, pp. 505–23.

Deutsch, K., Burrell, S., Kann, R., Lee, M., Lichterman, M., Lindgren, R., Loewenheim, F. and Van Wagenen, R. (1957) *Political Community and the North Atlantic Area: International Organization in the Light of Historical Experience*, Princeton: Princeton University Press.

Diez, T. (1999) "Speaking "Europe": The Politics of Integration Discourse," *Journal of European Public Policy*, 6:4, pp. 598–613.

Diez, T. (2001) "Europe as a Discursive Battleground: Discourse Analysis and European Integration Studies," *Cooperation and Conflict*, 36:1, pp. 5–38.

Diez, T. (2004) "Europe's Others and the Return of Geopolitics," *Cambridge Review of International Affairs*, 17:2, pp. 319–35.

Diez, T. and Rumelili, B. (2004) "Open the Door: Turkey and the European Union," *The World Today*, Aug/Sept., pp. 18–19.

Diez, T., Stetter, S. and Albert, M. (2006) "The European Union and Border Conflicts: The Transformative Power of Integration," *International Organization*, 60, pp. 563–93.

Dinan, D. (1999) *Ever Closer Union: An Introduction to European Integration* (2nd edn), Boulder, CO: Lynne Rienner.

Doty, R. (1996) *Imperial Encounters*, Minneapolis: University of Minnesota Press.

Dountas, M. (1995) "Turkey: in Europe or in Asia?" *Ta Nea (Athens)*, March 1.

Dupont, A. (2000) "ASEAN's Response to the East Timor Crisis," *Australian Journal of International Affairs*, 54:2, pp. 163–70.

Elliott, T.L. (1993) "Poland, Germany, and the End of the Cold War," *East European Quarterly*, 27:4, pp. 535–50.

Erdogan, R.T. (2005) "The Turkish Model on the Axis of Democracy, Islam and Political Secularism," Speech at the Sun Valley Conference, July 6.

Etzioni, A. (1965) *Political Unification: A Comparative Study of Leaders and Forces*, New York: Holt, Rinehart and Winston.

European Commission (1987) *Opinion on Turkey's Membership Application*, December 18 (Bull. 12-1989, point 2.2.37.).

European Commission (2004) *Regular Report on Turkey's Progress Towards Accession*, {COM (2004) 656 final}.

European Commission (2005) *Negotiating Framework*, Luxembourg, October 3.

European Commission (2006) *Turkey 2006 Progress Report*, {COM (2006) 649 final}.

European Council (1993) *Presidency Conclusions*, European Council in Copenhagen, June 21–22.

European Council (1997) *Presidency Conclusions*, European Council in Luxembourg, December 12–13.

European Parliament (1987) *Debate on Protocol to EEC–Turkey Association Agreement*, December 15.

European Parliament (1994) *Resolution on the Trial of Turkish MPs of Kurdish Origin*, December 15.

European Parliament (1995) *Debate on EC–Turkey Relations–Human Rights in Turkey*, December 13.

European Parliament (1996a) *Debate on Agreement with Morocco–Human Rights in Morocco and Western Sahara*, June 5.

European Parliament (1996b) *Topical and Urgent Debate on Turkey*, September 16.

European Parliament (1996c) *Resolution on the Situation in Turkey*, January 18.

European Parliament (1996d) *Debate on Customs Union with Turkey*, July 17.

European Parliament (1997a) *Debate on Enlargement – Agenda 2000*, December 3.

European Parliament (1997b) *Debate on European Council in Luxembourg – Six Months of the Luxembourg Presidency*, December 17.

European Parliament (1998) *Debate on Assistance to the Applicant Countries in Central and Eastern Europe – Accession Partnerships*, March 11.

European Parliament (1999a) *Debate on the State of Relations between Turkey and the EU*, October 6.

European Parliament (1999b) *Debate on Preparation of European Council of 10–11 December 1999*, December 1.

European Parliament (2003a) *Debate on Turkey's Application for EU Membership*, June 4.

European Parliament (2003b) *Report on Turkey's Application for Membership of the European Union*, May 20 (Final A5-0160/2003).

European Parliament (2004) *Debate on Progress Towards Accession by Turkey*, April 1.

European Parliament (2006) *Debate on Turkey's Progress Towards Accession*, September 26.

Evans, G. (1988) "Australia's Relations with Indonesia," address to the Australia Indonesia Business Cooperation Committee, Bali, October 24.

Evans, G. (1989a) "Australia in Asia: The Integration of Foreign and Economic Policies," Seminar on Australia and the Northeast Asian Ascendancy, Sydney, November 22.

Evans, G. (1989b) "Australia's Regional Security," Ministerial Statement on Australia's Regional Security, The Senate, December 6.

Evans, G. (1990) "Australia's Asian Future," Institute for Contemporary Asian Studies, Monash University, July 19.

Evans, G. (1991) "Managing Australia's Asian Future," Third Asia Lecture, Asia–Australia Institute, University of New South Wales, Sydney, October 3.

Evans, G. (1992) "Australia in Asia," Foreign Correspondents Club of Thailand, Bangkok, September 9.

Fawcett, L. (1995) "Regionalism in Historical Perspective" in Fawcett, L. and Hurrell, A. (eds) *Regionalism in World Politics*, Oxford: Oxford University Press, pp. 9–36.

Fawcett, L. and Hurrell, A. (1995) "Introduction" in Fawcett, L. and Hurrell, A. (eds) *Regionalism in World Politics*, Oxford: Oxford University Press, pp. 1–6.

Feldman, L.G. (2000) "The principle and Practice of "Reconciliation" in German Foreign Policy: Relations with France, Israel, Poland, and the Czech Republic," *International Affairs*, 75:2, pp. 333–56.

Fine, G.A. (1993) "The Sad Demise, Mysterious Disappearance, and Glorious Triumph of Symbolic Interactionism," *Annual Review of Sociology*, 19, pp. 61–87.

Finnemore, M. (1993) "International Organizations as Teachers of Norms: The United Nations Educational and Social Cooperation Organization and Science Policy," *International Organization*, 47:3, pp. 565–97.

Finnemore, M. and Sikkink, K. (1998) "International Norm Dynamics and Political Change," *International Organization*, 52:4, pp. 887–917.

FitzGerald, S. (1997) *Is Australia an Asian Country? Can Australia Survive in an East Asian Future?*, St. Leonards: Allen and Unwin.

Foucher, M. (1998) "The Geopolitics of European Frontiers" in Anderson, M. and Bort, E. (eds) *The Frontiers of Europe*, London: Pinter, pp. 235–50.

Freudenstein, R. (1998) "Poland, Germany, and the EU," *International Affairs*, 74:1, pp. 41–54.

Funabashi, Y. (1993) "The Asianization of Asia," *Foreign Affairs*, 72: 5, pp. 75–85.

Gillespie, R. (2000) *Spain and the Mediterranean: Developing a European Policy towards the South*, New York: St. Martin's Press.

Gilpin, R. (1975) *U.S. Power and the Multinational Corporation: The Political Economy of Foreign Direct Investment*, New York: Basic Books.

Glaser, B. and Strauss, A. (1967) *The Discovery of Grounded Theory: Strategies for Qualitative Research*, Hawthorne, NY: Aldine Publishing Co.

Goffman, E. (1959) *Presentation of Self in Everyday Life*, Garden City, NY: Doubleday Anchor Books.

Gole, N. (2006) "Europe's Encounter with Islam: What Future?", *Constellations*, 13:2, pp. 248–62.

Gregory, D. (1989) "Foreword" in Der Derian, J. and Shapiro, M.J. (eds) *International/ Intertextual Relations*, Lexington, MA: Lexington Books, pp. xiii–xxi.

Grovogui, S.N. (2001) "A Postcolonial Turn: Criticism, Truth, and Transcendence," paper presented at the International Studies Association Meeting, Chicago, IL, Feb. 20–24.

Gundogdu, A. (2001) "Identities in Question: Greek-Turkish Relations in a Period of Transformation?", *Middle East Review of International Affairs*, 5:1, pp. 106–17.

Gunduz, A. (2001) "Greek-Turkish Disputes: How to Resolve Them?" in Keridis, D. and Triantaphyllou, D. (eds) *Greek-Turkish Relations in the Era of Globalization*, Everett, MA: Brassey's, pp. 81–101.

Gurowitz, A. (1999) "Mobilizing International Norms: Domestic Actors, Immigrants, and the Japanese State," *World Politics*, 51(April), pp. 413–45.

Guvenc, S. (1998/9) "Turkey's Changing Perception of Greece's Membership in the European Union: 1981–1998," *Turkish Review of Balkan Studies*, pp. 103–130.

Haas, E. (1958) *The Uniting of Europe*, Berkeley, CA: Stanford University Press.

Haas, E. (1964) *Beyond the Nation-State: Functionalism and International Organization*, Berkeley, CA: Stanford University Press.

Habermas, J. (1995) "Citizenship and National Identity: Some Reflections on the Future of Europe," *Praxis International*, 12:1, pp. 1–15.

Habibie, B. J. (1999) Address Before the House of the People's Representatives on the Occasion of the 54th Independence Day, August 16.

Haddadi, S. (2003) "The EMP and Morocco: Diverging Political Agendas?", *Mediterranean Politics*, 8:2/3, pp. 73–89.

Hall, R.B. (2001) "Applying the 'Self/Other' Nexus in International Relations," *International Studies Review*, 3:1, pp. 101–11.

Hansen, L. (2006) *Security as Practice: Discourse Analysis and the Bosnian War*, London: Routledge.

Harle, V. (ed.) (1990) *European Values in International Relations*, London: Pinter Publishers.

Hassan, K. (1993) "Keating Must Respond in an Asian Way –analysts," *The Straits Times*, December 5.

Hellenic Parliament (1997) *Minutes*, November 6.

Hellenic Parliament (1999a) *Minutes*, January 29.

Hellenic Parliament (1999b) *Minutes*, December 15.

Henderson, J. (1999) *Reassessing ASEAN*, Adelphi Paper 238, Oxford University Press.

Henrikson, A. K. (1995) "The Growth of Regional Organizations and the Role of the United Nations" in Fawcett, L. and Hurrell, A. (eds) *Regionalism in World Politics*, Oxford: Oxford University Press, pp. 122–168.

Heraclides, A. (2001) *Yunanistan ve 'Dogudan Gelen Tehlike' [Greece and 'the Threat from the East']*. Trans. Vasilyadis, M. and Millas, H. Istanbul: Iletisim.

Herzfeld, M. (1987) *Anthropology Through the Looking Glass: Critical Ethnography in the Margins of Europe*, Cambridge: Cambridge University Press.

Hettne, B. (2000) "The New Regionalism: A Prologue" in Hettne, B., Inotai, A., and Sunkel, O. (eds) *The New Regionalism and the Future of Security and Development*, London: MacMillan, pp. xviii–xxxii.

Hettne, B. and Soderbaum, F. (2000) "Theorising the Rise of Regionness," *New Political Economy*, 5:3, pp. 457–73.

Higgott, R.A. and Nossal, K.R. (1998) "Australia and the Search for a Security Community in the 1990s" in Adler, E. and Barnett, M. (ed.) *Security Communities*, Cambridge: Cambridge University Press, pp. 265–94.

Hinkle, S. and Brown, R. (1990) "Intergroup Comparisons and Social Identity" in Abrams, D. and Hogg, M. (eds) *Social Identity Theory: Constructive and Critical Advances*, New York: Springer-Verlag, pp: 48–70.

Hogg, M. and Abrams, D. (1988) *Social Identifications: A Social Psychology of Intergroup Relations and Group Processes*, New York: Routledge.

Hogue, C. (2000) "Perspectives on Australian Foreign Policy, 1999," *Australian Journal of International Affairs*, 54:2, pp. 141–50.

Huntington, S. (1996) *The Clash of Civilizations and the Remaking of World Order*, New York: Touchstone.

Hurd, E.S. (2006) "Negotiating Europe: The Politics of Religion and the Prospects for Turkish Accession," *Review of International Studies*, 32:3, pp. 401–18.

Huysmans, J. (2001) "European Identity and Migration Policies" in Cederman, L. (ed.) *Constructing Europe's Identity: The External Dimension*, Boulder, CO: Lynne Rienner, pp. 189–211.

Hyde-Price, A. (2000) "Building a Stable Peace in *MittelEuropa*: The German-Polish Hinge," University of Birmingham Institute for German Studies Discussion Paper (2000/18).

Inayatullah, N. and Blaney, D. (2004) *International Relations and the Problem of Difference*, London: Routledge.

Ioakimidis, P.C. (2002) "Turkey in a Europeanisation Crisis," *Ta Nea (Athens)*, August 16.

Jain, P. (2007) "Australia's Attitude Toward Asian Values and Regional Community Building" Politics & Policy, 35:1, pp. 26–41.

Jacob, P. and Toscano, J. (eds) (1964) *The Integration of Political Communities*, Philadelphia and New York: J.B. Lippincott.

Jepperson, R., Wendt, A. and Katzenstein, P. (1996) "Norms, Identity, and Culture in National Security" in Katzenstein, P. (ed.) *The Culture of National Security*, New York: Columbia University Press, pp. 33–75.

Jones, L. (2002) "Rabat has chosen the path of confrontation, says Spain's El Mundo," *Washington Report on Middle Eastern Affairs*, 21:7 (Sept/Oct), pp. 48–50.

Junemann, A. (1998) "Europe's Interrelations With North Africa In The New Framework Of Euro-Mediterranean Partnership – A Provisional Assessment of the 'Barcelona Concept'" in *The European Union in a Changing World* (a selection of conference papers from 3rd ECSA-World Conference, Brussels, 09/19-20/ 1996), Office for Official Publications of the European Communities.

Kahl, C.H. (1999) "Constructing a Separate Peace: Constructivism, Collective Liberal Identity, and Democratic Peace," *Security Studies*, 8:2/3, pp. 94–144.

Keohane, R. (1984) *After Hegemony: Cooperation and Discord in the World Political Economy*, Princeton: Princeton University Press.

Keridis, D. (2001) "Domestic Developments and Foreign Policy" in Keridis, D. and Triantaphyllou, D. (eds) *Greek-Turkish Relations in the Era of Globalization*, Everett, MA: Brassey's, pp. 2–18.

Kirisci, K. and Carkoglu, A. (2003) "Perceptions of Greeks and Greek-Turkish Rapprochement by the Turkish Public" in Rubin, B. and Carkoglu, A. (eds) *Greek-Turkish Relations in an Era of Détente*, London: Frank Cass, pp. 117–53.

Kislali, A.T. (1999) "The Importance of Cyprus," *Cumhuriyet (Istanbul)*, July 14.

Kivimaki, T. (2001) "The Long Peace of ASEAN," *Journal of Peace Research*, 38:1, pp. 5–25.

Koenig, T., Mihelj, S., Downey, J., and Gencel Bek, M. (2006) "Media Framings of the Issue of Turkish Accession to the EU: A European or National Process?", *Innovation*, 19:2, pp. 149–69.

Kohen, S. (2003) "Greece, the EU's New Term President," *Milliyet (Istanbul)*, January 2.

Konstandaras, N. (2002) "The Turkish Touchstone," *Kathimerini (English edn)*, November 30.

Krasner, S. (ed.) (1983) *International Regimes*, Ithaca: Cornell University Press.

Lake, D. and Morgan, P. (eds) (1997) *Regional Orders: Building Security in a New World*, University Park, Pennsylvania: The Pennsylvania State University Press.

Lebioda, T. (2000) "Poland, die Vertriebenen, and the Road to Integration with the European Union" in Cordell, K. (ed.) *Poland and the European Union*, London: Routledge, pp. 165–81.

Le Gloannec, A. (2006) "Is Turkey Euro-compatible? French and German Debates about Non-Criteria," *Constellations*, 13:2, pp. 263–74.

Leifer, M. (1987) *ASEAN's Search for Regional Order*, Singapore: Faculty of Arts and Social Sciences, National University of Singapore.

Lindberg, L. and Scheingold, S. (eds) (1971) *Regional Integration: Theory and Research*, Cambridge, MA: Harvard University Press.

Litfin, K. (1994) *Ozone Discourses: Science and Politics in Global Environmental Cooperation*, New York: Columbia University Press.

McDougall, D. (2001) "Australia and Asia-Pacific Security Regionalism: From Hawke and Keating to Howard," *Contemporary Southeast Asia*, 23:1, pp. 81–101.

Mahbubani, K. (1995) "The Pacific Way," *Foreign Affairs*, 74:1, pp. 101–11.

Makabenta, L. (1993) "Australia-Malaysia: Fragile Ties Suffer Another Setback," *Inter Press Service*, November 27.

Malik, M. (2006) "The East Asia Summit" *Australian Journal of International Affairs*, 60:2, pp. 207–11.

Manners, I. (2002) "Normative Power Europe: A Contradiction in Terms," *Journal of Common Market Studies*, 40:2, pp. 235–58.

Mansfield, E.D. and Milner, H.V. (1999) "The New Wave of Regionalism," *International Organization*, 53:3, pp. 589–627.

Mead, G.H. (1934) *Mind, Self, and Society*, Chicago: University of Chicago Press.

Mearscheimer, J. (1994/5) "The False Promise of International Institutions," *International Security*, 19, pp. 5–49.

Menendez, A.J. (2005) "A Christian or a Laic Europe? Christian Values and European Identity," *Ratio Juris*, 18:2, pp. 179–205.

Mercer, J. (1995) "Anarchy and Identity," *International Organization*, 49:2, pp. 229–52.

Meszaros, A. (1999) "Divergent Neighbors: The Czech Republic and Slovakia Since Independence," *Harvard International Review*, 21:2, pp. 30–3.

Milliken, J. (1999a) "The Study of Discourse in International Relations: A Critique of Research and Methods," *European Journal of International Relations*, 5:2, pp. 225–54.

Milliken, J. (1999b) "Intervention and Identity: Reconstructing the West in Korea" in Weldes, J., Laffey, M., Gusterson, H. and Duvall, R. (eds) *Cultures of Insecurity: States, Communities, and the Production of Danger*, Minneapolis: University of Minnesota Press, pp. 91–117.

Milner, A. (1997) "The Rhetoric of Asia" in Cotton, J. and Ravenhill, J. (eds) *Seeking Asian Engagement: Australia in World Affairs, 1991–95*, Melbourne: Oxford University Press Australia, pp. 32–45.

Milner, A. (2000) "What is Left of Engagement with Asia?", *Australian Journal of International Affairs*, 54:2, pp. 177–84.

Morgan, P.M. (1997) "Regional Security Complexes and Regional Orders" in Lake, D.A. and Morgan, P.M. (eds) *Regional Orders: Building Security in a New World*, University Park, Pennsylvania: The Pennsylvania State University Press, pp. 20–44.

Muftuler-Bac, M. (1997) *Turkey's Relations with a Changing Europe*, Manchester: Manchester University Press.

Muftuler-Bac, M. (1999) "The Never-Ending Story: Turkey and the European Union" in Kedourie, S. (ed.) *Turkey Before and After Ataturk*, London: Frank Cass Publishers, pp. 240–258.

Muftuler-Bac, M. (2005) "Turkey's Political Reforms and the Impact of the European Union," *South European Society and Politics*, 10:1, pp. 17–31.

Muppidi, H. (1999) "Postcoloniality and the Production of International Insecurity: The Persistent Puzzle of US-Indian Relations" in Weldes, J., Laffey, M., Gusterson, H., and. Duvall, R (eds) *Cultures of Insecurity*, Minneapolis: University of Minnesota Press, pp. 119–146.

Narine, S. (1998) "ASEAN and the Management of Regional Security," *Pacific Affairs*, 71:2, pp. 195–214.

Nathan, L. (2006) "Domestic Instability and Security Communities," *European Journal of International Relations*, 12:2, pp. 275–99.

Navarro, N. (1999) "Indonesia: A Test for ASEAN," *Manila Standard (Philippines)*, August 2.

Neumann, I.B. (1994) "A Region-Building Approach to Northern Europe," *Review of International Studies*, 20, pp. 53–74.

Neumann, I.B. (1996) "Self and Other in International Relations," *European Journal of International Relations*, 2:2, pp. 139–74.

Neumann, I.B. (1998) "European Identity, EU Expansion, and the Integration/ Exclusion Nexus," *Alternatives*, 23:3, pp. 397–416.

Neumann, I.B. (1999) *Uses of the Other: The East in European Identity Formation*, Minneapolis: University of Minnesota Press.

Neumann, I.B. (2004) "The Narrative Self of the State," *Review of International Studies*, 30:2, pp. 289–316.

Neumann, I.B. and Welsh, J.M. (1991) "The Other in European Self-Definition: An Addendum to the Literature on International Society," *Review of International Studies*, 17:4, pp. 327–48.

Norton, A. (1988) *Reflections on Political Identity*, Baltimore: The Johns Hopkins University Press.

Nye, J. (ed.) (1968) *International Regionalism: Readings*, Boston: Little, Brown and Company.

Nye, J. (1971) *Peace in Parts: Integration and Conflict in Regional Organization*, Boston: Little, Brown and Company.

Onis, Z. (1995) "Turkey in the Post-Cold War Era: In Search of Identity," *Middle East Journal*, 49:1, pp. 48–68.

Onis, Z. (2000) "Luxembourg, Helsinki and Beyond: Turkey-EU Relations," *Government and Opposition*, 35:4, pp. 463–83.

Ozel, S. (2004) "Turkish-Greek Dialogue of the Business Communities" in Belge, T. (ed.) *Voices for the Future: Civic Dialogue Between Turks and Greeks*, Istanbul: Bilgi University Press, pp. 163–168.

Paasi, A. (1996) *Territories, Boundaries, and Consciousness: The Changing Geographies of the Finnish-Russian Border*, New York: Wiley.

Pace, M. (2004) "The Euro-Mediterranean Partnership and Common Mediterranean Strategy? European Union Policy from a Discursive Perspective," *Geopolitics*, 9:2, pp. 292–309.

Pace, M. (2006) *The Politics of Regional Identity: Meddling with the Mediterranean*, London: Routledge.

Papandreou, G. (2002) "Why is the Old Enemy Greece Now Supporting Turkey?", *Wall Street Journal Europe*, December 11.

Parry, B. (1995) "Problems in Current Theories of Colonial Discourse," in Ashcroft, B., Griffiths, G., and Tiffin, H. (eds) *The Post-colonial Studies Reader*, London, New York: Routledge, pp. 36– 44.

Phillips, D. (2004) "Turkey's Dreams of Accession," *Foreign Affairs*, September/ October.

Platias, A. G. (2000) "Greek Deterrence Strategy" in Chircop, A., Gerolymatos, A., and Iatrides, J.O. (eds) *The Aegean Sea After the Cold War*, London: MacMillan, pp. 61–86.

Pouliot, V. (2006) "The Alive and Well Transatlantic Security Community: A Theoretical Reply to Michael Cox," *European Journal of International Relations*, 12:1, pp. 119–27.

Puchala, D. (1981) "Integration Theory and the Study of International Relations" in Meritt, R. and Russett, B. (eds) *From National Development to Global Community: Essays in Honor of Karl W. Deutsch*, pp. London: George Allen & Unwin, 145–64.

Richardson, M. (2005) "Australia-Southeast Asia Relations and the East Asia Summit" *Australian Journal of International Affairs* 59: 3, pp. 351–65.

Richmond, O.P. (2000) "Emerging Concepts of Security in the European Order: Implications for 'Zones of Conflict' at the Fringes of the EU," *European Security*, 9:1, pp. 41–67.

Ringmar, E. (1996a) "On the Ontological Status of the State," *European Journal of International Relations*, 2:4, pp. 439–66.

Ringmar, E. (1996b) *Identity, Interest, and Action: A Cultural Explanation of Sweden's Intervention in the Thirty Years War*, Cambridge: Cambridge University Press.

Risse, T. (2000) "Let's Argue! Communicative Action in World Politics," *International Organization*, 54 (Winter), pp. 1–39.

Risse-Kappen, T. (1996) "Collective Identity in a Democratic Community: The Case of NATO" in Katzenstein, P. (ed.) *The Culture of National Security: Norms and Identity in World Politics*, New York: Columbia University Press, pp. 357–99.

Robins, K. (1996) "Interrupting Identities: Turkey/Europe," in Hall, S. and Gay, P.D. (eds) *Questions of Cultural Identity*, London: Sage Publications, pp. 61–86.

Ruggie, J.G. (1993) "Territoriality and Beyond: Problematizing Modernity in International Relations," *International Organization*, 47:1, pp. 139–74.

Rumelili, B. (2003) "Liminality and Perpetuation of Conflicts: Turkish-Greek Relations in the Context of Community-Building by the EU," *European Journal of International Relations*, 9:2, pp. 213–48.

Rumelili, B. (2004) "Constructing Identity and Relating to Difference: Understanding the EU's Mode of Differentiation," *Review of International Studies*, 30, pp. 27–47.

Rumelili, B. (2005) "Civil Society and the Europeanization of Greek-Turkish Cooperation," *South European Society and Politics*, 10:1, pp. 43–54.

Russett, B. (1967) *International Regions and the International System*, Chicago: Rand McNally.

Santer, J. (1998) "Shaping Europe's Future," International Bertelsman Forum, Berlin, July 3.

Schimmelfennig, F. (2000) "International Socialization in the New Europe: Rational Action in an Institutional Environment," *European Journal of International Relations*, 6:1, pp. 109–39.

Schimmelfennig, F. (2001a) "Liberal Identity and Postnationalist Inclusion: The Eastern Enlargement of the European Union" in Cederman, L. (ed.) *Constructing Europe's Identity: The External Dimension*, Boulder, CO: Lynne Rienner, pp. 165–86.

Schimmelfennig, F. (2001b) "The Community Trap: Liberal Norms, Rhetorical Action, and the Eastern Enlargement of the European Union," *International Organization*, 55:1, pp. 47–80.

Severino, R.C. (2000a) "Diversity and Convergence in Southeast Asia," Keynote address, 9th annual conference of the Harvard project for Asian and international Relations, Beijing, August 28.

Severino, R.C. (2000b) "Sovereignty, Intervention and the ASEAN Way," ASEAN Scholars' Roundtable, Singapore, July 3.

Shore, C. (2000) *Building Europe: The Cultural Politics of European Integration*, London and New York: Routledge.

Shore, C. and Black, A. (1994) "Citizens' Europe and the Construction of European Identity" in Goddard, V.A., Llobera, J.R., and Shore, C. (eds) *The Anthropology of Europe: Identity and Boundaries in Conflict*, Oxford: Berg, pp. 275–298.

Sjursen, H. (2002) "Why Expand? The Question of Legitimacy and Justification in the EU's Enlargement Policy," *Journal of Common Market Studies*, 40:3, pp. 491–513.

Smith, A. L. (2004) "ASEAN's Ninth Summit: Solidifying Regional Cohesion, Advancing External Linkages," *Contemporary Southeast Asia*, 26:3, pp. 416–33.

Smith, G., Cox, D. and Burchill, S. (1996) *Australia and the World*, Oxford: Oxford University Press.

Smith, K.E. (2004) *The Making of EU Foreign Policy: The Case of Eastern Europe*, Houndmills, Basingstoke, Hampshire: MacMillan.

Smith, K.E. (2005) "The Outsiders: The European Neighborhood Policy," *International Affairs*, 81:4, pp. 757–73.

Solana, J. (2000) Speech at Fernandez Ordonez Seminar, Madrid, January 14.

Stadtmuller, E. (2000) "Polish Perceptions of the European Union in the 1990s," in Cordell, K. (ed.) *Poland and the European Union*, London: Routledge, pp. 24–44.

Stryker, S. (1987) "The Vitalization of Symbolic Interactionism," *Social Psychology Quarterly*, 50:1, pp. 83–94.

Tajfel, H. and Turner, J.C. (1986) "The Social Identity Theory of Intergroup Behavior" in Worchel, S. and Austin, W.G. (eds) *Psychology of Intergroup Relations (2nd edn)*, Chicago: Nelson-Hall, pp. 7–24.

Tarikahya, N. (2004) "Turkish Greek Culture and Art Festivals for Promoting Dialogue" in Belge, T. (ed.) *Voices for the Future: Civic Dialogue Between Turks and Greeks*, Istanbul: Bilgi University Press, pp. 155–62.

Tetlock, P. and Belkin, A. (1996) "Counterfactual Thought Experiments in World Politics" in Tetlock, P. and Belkin, A. (eds) *Counterfactual Thought Experiments in World Politics*, Princeton, NJ: Princeton University Press, pp. 3–38.

Todorov, T. (1984) *The Conquest of America: The Question of the Other*, trans. Howard, R., New York: Harper and Row.

Triantaphyllou, D. (2001) "Further Turmoil Ahead?" in Keridis, D. and Triantaphyllou, D. (eds) *Greek-Turkish Relations in the Era of Globalization*, Everett, MA: Brassey's, pp. 56–79.

Tsakonas, P. and Tournikiotis, A. (2003) "Greece's Elusive Quest for Security Providers," *Security Dialogue*, 34:3, pp. 301–14.

Turenc, T. (1999) "Northern Cyprus will Stay Where It is," *Hurriyet (Istanbul)*, December 15.

Turkish Grand National Assembly (1996a) *Minutes of 20th Period, 1st Legislative Session, 41st Meeting*, April 20. http://www.tbmm.gov.tr

Turkish Grand National Assembly (1996b) *Minutes of 20th Period, 2nd Legislative Session, 1st Meeting*, October 1. http://www.tbmm.gov.tr

Turkish Grand National Assembly (1997) *Minutes of 20th Period, 2nd Legislative Year, 127th Meeting*, July 29. http://www.tbmm.gov.tr

Turkish Grand National Assembly (1998) *Minutes of 20th Period, 3rd Legislative Session, 38th Meeting*, January 6. http://www.tbmm.gov.tr

Turner, V. ([1969] 1995), *The Ritual Process: Structure and Anti-Structure*, New York: Aldine De Gruyter.

Ugur, M. (1999) *The European Union and Turkey: An Anchor/Credibility Dilemma*, Aldershot: Ashgate.

Vaquer i Fanes, J. (2003) "The Domestic Dimension of EU External Policies: The Case of EU-Morocco 2000–01 Fisheries Negotiations," *Mediterranean Politics*, 8:1, pp. 59–82.

Valinakis, Y. G. (1994) "Security Policy" in Kazakos, P. and Ioakimidis, P.C. (eds) *Greece and EC Membership Evaluated*, London: Pinter, pp. 199–214.

Vayrynen, R. (2003) "Regionalism: Old and New," *International Studies Review*, 5, pp. 25–51.

Veremis, T. (2001) "The Protracted Crisis" in Keridis, D. and Triantaphyllou, D. (eds) *Greek-Turkish Relations in the Era of Globalization*, Everett, MA: Brassey's, pp. 42–55.

Waever, O. (1990) "Three Competing Europes: German, French, and Russian," *International Affairs*, 66:3, pp. 477–93.

Waever, O. (1998) "Insecurity, Security, and Asecurity in the West European Non-war Community" in Adler, E. and Barnett, M. (eds) *Security Communities*, Cambridge: Cambridge University Press, pp. 69–118.

Wallace, W. (1990) *The Transformation of Western Europe*, London: Royal Institute of International Affairs.

Weldes, J., Laffey, M., Gusterson, H., and Duvall, R. (eds) (1999) *Cultures of Insecurity*, Minneapolis: University of Minnesota Press.

Wendt, A. (1994) "Collective Identity Formation and the International State," *American Political Science Review*, 88:2, pp. 384–96.

Wendt, A. (1998) "On Constitution and Causation in International Relations," *Review of International Studies*, 24 (special issue), pp. 101–17.

Wendt, A. (1999) *Social Theory of International Politics*, Cambridge: Cambridge University Press.

Wendt, A. (2004) "The State as Person," *Review of International Studies*, 30:2, pp. 289–316.

Wilcox, F.O. (1965) "Regionalism and the United Nations," *International Organization*, 19:3, pp. 789–811.

Williams, M.C. (2001) "The Discipline of Democratic Peace: Kant, Liberalism and the Social Construction of Security Communities," *European Journal of International Relations*, 7:4, pp. 525–53.

Wiseman, J. (1998) *Global Nation? Australia and the Politics of Globalization*, Cambridge: Cambridge University Press.

Wood, P.C. (1999) "Europe and Turkey: A Relationship under Fire," *Mediterranean Quarterly*, 10:1, pp. 95–115.

Yahya, F. (2003) "India and Southeast Asia: Revisited," *Contemporary Southeast Asia* 25:1, pp. 79–103.
Yesilada, B.A. (2002) "Turkey's Candidacy for EU Membership," *Middle East Journal*, 56:1, pp. 94–111.
Zaborowski, M. (2002) "Europeanization as a Consensus-Building Project: The Case of Polish-German Relations," Europeanization and Foreign Policy Workshop, London School of Economics, June 5.
Zielonka, J. (2002) "Introduction: Boundary Making by the European Union" in Zielonka, J. (ed.) *Europe Unbound: Enlarging and Reshaping the Boundaries of the European Union*, London: Routledge, pp. 1–16.
Zoulas, S. (2003) "Two Turkeys," *Kathimerini (Athens, English edn)*, May 28.

Author interviews

1. Greek journalist, Istanbul, February 18, 2004.
2. Chief Foreign Policy Advisor to George Papandreou on Greek–Turkish and Turkey–EU relations, Athens, February 21, 2005.
3. Former Turkish Minister for Foreign Affairs, Istanbul, February 9, 2004.
4. Project Coordinator, Civil Society Development Program, Representation of the European Commission to Ankara, Athens, March 11, 2004.
5. Head of Policy Planning Unit at the Greek Foreign Ministry, Athens, February 22, 2005.
6. Chief Foreign Policy Advisor to Recep Tayyip Erdogan, Ankara, November 17, 2003.
7. Turkish Foreign Ministry Directorate General for Bilateral Relations with Greece, Ankara, March 3, 2004.
8. Turkey's Former Ambassador to Greece, Ankara, March 4, 2004.
9. Project Coordinator, Civil Society Development Program, Representation of the European Commission to Ankara, Ankara, November 18, 2003.
10. Activist, WINPEACE, Athens, March 12, 2004.
11. Project Coordinator, Turkish-Greek Civic Dialogue Project, Ankara, March 2, 2004.
12. Professor, University of Aegean, Athens, February 25, 2005.
13. Hellenic Foundation for European and Foreign Policy, Athens, February 25, 2005.

Index